What Are Campaigns For?

What Are Campaigns For?

The Role of Persuasion in Electoral Law and Politics

JAMES A. GARDNER

OXFORD
UNIVERSITY PRESS

OXFORD
UNIVERSITY PRESS

Oxford University Press, Inc., publishes works that further Oxford University's objective of excellence in research, scholarship, and education.

Oxford New York
Auckland Cape Town Dar es Salaam Hong Kong Karachi Kuala Lumpur
Madrid Melbourne Mexico City Nairobi New Delhi Shanghai Taipei Toronto

With offices in
Argentina Austria Brazil Chile Czech Republic France Greece Guatemala
Hungary Italy Japan Poland Portugal Singapore South Korea Switzerland Thailand
Turkey Ukraine Vietnam

Published by Oxford University Press, Inc.
198 Madison Avenue, New York, New York 10016

Library of Congress Cataloging-in-Publication Data

Gardner, James A., 1959-
What are campaigns for? : the role of persuasion in electoral law and politics / James A. Gardner.
p. cm.
Includes bibliographical references and index.
ISBN 978-0-19-539261-6 (hardback : alk. paper)
1. Political campaigns—United States. 2. Election law—United States. I. Title.
JK2281.G37 2009
324.70973—dc22

2009001738

---

1 2 3 4 5 6 7 8 9

Printed in the United States of America on acid-free paper

Note to Readers
This publication is designed to provide accurate and authoritative information in regard to the subject matter covered. It is based upon sources believed to be accurate and reliable and is intended to be current as of the time it was written. It is sold with the understanding that the publisher is not engaged in rendering legal, accounting, or other professional services. If legal advice or other expert assistance is required, the services of a competent professional person should be sought. Also, to confirm that the information has not been affected or changed by recent developments, traditional legal research techniques should be used, including checking primary sources where appropriate.

(Based on the Declaration of Principles jointly adopted by a Committee of the American Bar Association and a Committee of Publishers and Associations.)

For Lise

Contents

Preface

THIS BOOK REPRESENTS THE CULMINATION of a long personal journey during which my beliefs about the purposes and desirable characteristics of election campaigns changed dramatically. Like most Americans, I have found electoral politics a constant source of disappointment. Candidates, it has long seemed to me, have been reluctant to speak their minds, to address challenging problems boldly, and to risk their political fortunes on a clear vision capable of inspiring a public hungry for thoughtful and intelligent leadership. As a result, our electoral politics has frequently struck me as inadequate, undignified, and beneath not only our aspirations but also our capacity as a democratic people seeking to shape our own collective destiny in the world.

As a lawyer and legal academic, my point of entry into the field of election campaigns has been the law and, more specifically, the constitutional doctrines that structure our democratic institutions. Upon examining these legal regimes with some care, I came at first to the conclusion that they thwart our ability to produce the kind of campaigns to which we evidently aspire. I consequently began this project with the intention of analyzing and critiquing our legal institutions and then suggesting legal reforms that might be capable, if not of curing the relevant problems, at least of creating conditions in which our electoral politics could better flourish and more closely approach our ideals. As I looked more deeply into the subject, however, I began to doubt my premises. Our beliefs about campaigns are comparatively recent, and from a historical point of view highly contingent. A half-century of social science research continues to affirm the existence of severe and crippling obstacles to the achievement of the kind of campaigns for which most of us wish. Even the most sophisticated theoretical work now being done on democracy relegates campaigns to a much less exalted place in the democratic arena than conventional wisdom would suggest.

As a result, I eventually came around to the view I now hold and have laid out in this book. Campaigns may be ugly and undignified, and they are without question important events in the life of a democratic polity, but—to my mind ironically and paradoxically—they simply are not as critical to the success of democratic self-rule as most of us have come to believe. And if campaigns are somewhat less significant than we have thought, it is harder to work up the same degree of disappointment if they fail to attain the standards to which we seek to hold them. At the same time, I have come to believe strongly that the real threats to democracy are not the flaws we can so easily observe in our campaigns but the ones that lie outside the electoral arena and that we cannot so readily detect.

People who love and respect democracy often have a tendency mistakenly to conflate the political with the electoral. This project has taught me memorably that such a tendency represents a profound and highly dangerous mistake. In a democracy, the electoral comprises but a small fraction of the political, and if we are concerned to assure the health of our democracy, it is to the political, in the broadest sense, that we must attend.

My journey in thinking about and writing this book has been much aided by the help of numerous friends and colleagues who discussed the subject with me and read portions of the manuscript. I owe special thanks in this regard to Jim Campbell, Guy Charles, Ken Ehrenberg, Luis Fuentes-Rohwer, Lise Gelernter, Rick Hasen, Sam Issacharoff, Fred Konefsky, Ethan Leib, Jay Mootz, Jack Schlegel, and Richard Winger. I also thank the Baldy Center for Law and Social Policy and its director, Lynn Mather, for arranging a workshop on a very early version of the manuscript.

An earlier version of material contained primarily in Chapter 2 appeared originally as *Deliberation or Tabulation? The Self-Undermining Constitutional Architecture of Election Campaigns*, BUFF. L. REV, Vol. 54(2007): 1413–82.

JAG
Buffalo, New York
November 14, 2008

Introduction

The Campaign Critique

IT IS AN ARTICLE OF CONTEMPORARY common faith that American election campaigns are of poor quality. A glance at the editorial and opinion pages of the nation's leading newspapers makes this clear. Our campaigns, it is said, are "degraded"; our politicians will "do or say or justify just about anything to win office."[1] The candidates "barely touch fundamental issues America must face," and fail to "treat us as if we could face serious problems seriously."[2] Campaigns are run by "[p]olitical consultants" who "dredge up or invent some factoid" or "package a few quotes," and "politicians build a campaign around it."[3] Should a candidate "start making sense on the issues, an adviser's obsession with pithy soundbites and saleable photo opportunities cuts short any reckless move toward intelligent discourse."[4] As the campaign progresses, it "becomes increasingly about itself"[5] rather than about issues of any significance.

Such criticisms are familiar; we have heard it a thousand times before: our campaigns are insufficiently thoughtful, rational, and deliberative; they are too thin and superficial; they focus insufficiently on issues and excessively on personality or image. Indeed, this kind of public criticism of the quality of campaigns—I shall call it the Campaign Critique—has itself become as regular a feature of the campaign season as lawn signs and thirty-second television spots. But the very familiarity of the Critique obscures perhaps its most important feature: the standard against which critics judge

---

1. Greenfield, "Winning Respect."
2. Darman, "If We Were Serious."
3. Kinsley, "Electio ad Absurdum."
4. Editorial, "Bush and Dukakis Owe Us Answers."
5. Kinsley, "Electio ad Absurdum."

contemporary election campaigns, and find them wanting. Clearly, a campaign devoid of intelligent discourse, meaningful persuasion, or the development of public enlightenment on important political issues poses a problem for democracy only if it is the function of campaigns to provide these public goods. The ubiquity of the Campaign Critique—and its apparently wide acceptance—suggests a prevailing public view that campaigns ought to serve as forums for some kind of meaningful public deliberation on important political issues and that present public unhappiness with election campaigns seems to result from a judgment that they are not in some sense sufficiently deliberative to satisfy our aspirations for meaningful democratic self-governance.

This all sounds perfectly plausible, but it leaves some important questions unanswered. Where did this standard of sober, deliberative rationality come from? What justifies it? Why do we embrace it? If we constantly fall short of it, is it the right standard? My aim in this book is to bring these questions squarely into the foreground and to confront them directly, for purposes of law and policy. To do so, I shall draw on several quite distinct bodies of knowledge, including political history, law, empirical social science, and democratic theory. I shall have more to say shortly about the approach and organization of the book. First, however, I want to lay some groundwork by examining the Campaign Critique a bit more closely.

The Concept of Campaign Quality

A theme that runs consistently throughout this book concerns the distinction between poor quality and high quality campaigns. As we shall soon see, this distinction gets expressed in many different ways, often varying with the disciplinary background of the critic. For historians of American political history, for example, who tend for obvious reasons to invoke the terminology of the times they study, the distinction is often described as one separating campaigns based on *party* or *personality* from campaigns based on *issues*. For courts and legal academics, heavily influenced by constitutional concerns about freedom of political speech, the distinction is usually described in terms of whether and to what extent campaign speech is aimed at the *persuasion* of citizens and voters. Campaigns are deemed to be high quality to the extent that persuasive speech is exchanged vigorously and protected legally.

Political scientists use a variety of terms to describe campaigns. One common distinction concerns whether public political opinion is *endogenous* or *exogenous* to political campaigns. Public political opinion is endogenous to campaigns when it is actually formed during the campaign—when, that is, citizens settle on political beliefs and positions during and in response to the campaign in ways that determine how they will cast their votes. Public political opinion is exogenous to campaigns, in contrast, when citizens have formed their opinions prior to the campaign, and carry those opinions into the campaign, where they remain essentially fixed. When political opinion is campaign-exogenous, voters have for the most part already made up their minds before the campaign starts, and there is little likelihood that anything they see or hear during the campaign will change their opinions.

Political scientists also frequently distinguish among the purposes that campaign activity is meant to serve. Along this dimension, campaign activity might be meant to *persuade* voters of particular views or positions on their merits. Somewhat less ambitiously, campaign activity might be meant merely to *inform* voters of various facts that parties, candidates, or activists think voters ought to know before making up their minds.[6] Least ambitiously, though by no means unimportantly, campaign speech and other activity might be intended merely to *mobilize* voters—to motivate them to pay enough attention and devote enough energy to the election to turn out and cast a vote. Obviously, political actors calculate their campaign activity to mobilize their own supporters rather than supporters of their opponents, although occasionally they may take actions aimed at *demobilizing* opponents' supporters—deflating and demoralizing them so that they fail to turn out to vote or to provide an opponent with other forms of support.

Political philosophers and democratic theorists also distinguish frequently between different kinds and qualities of campaign politics. One common approach distinguishes between campaigns that are *deliberative* and those that are *aggregative* or, to use a term that I prefer, *tabulative*. In tabulative campaigns, political activity centers around the identification and pursuit of self-interest. A politics of self-interest has no great need for persuasion since politics on this view is conceived mainly as a pluralist contest for power among many groups, each seeking to advance its own self-interest. Deliberative campaigns, in contrast, center around the giving of reasons for political beliefs as a way of persuading others and moving toward political consensus. Here, persuasion of others is conceived to lie near the heart

6. Of course, one suspects in the campaign context that no act of providing information is ever entirely unaccompanied by a hope that it will tend to induce some specific reaction.

of democratic politics. Sometimes these two types of campaigns, or the political activity that characterizes them, are called by other, similar terms—*thin* and *thick*, or *shallow* and *deep*.

Finally, it is clear that the general public also accepts a similar distinction between campaigns that are good or bad, high quality or low, thick or thin. This can be inferred from the simple fact that one of the standard rhetorical moves in the repertoire of the democratic politician has long been to claim that he or she is speaking or campaigning in a thick or deliberative way while his or her opponent is speaking or campaigning in a thin or shallow way. I'm talking about the issues, a candidate might say, while you are talking about personalities. I speak to the people deeply, while you speak superficially. I'm about substance, you're about image. Clearly, politicians would not bother to say these things if they did not have a reasonable, time-tested hope of reaping some strategic advantage.

This striking degree of consensus across so many different fields and political points of view suggests in the strongest possible way that the phenomenon being described is real—that there is a genuine, stable distinction between high and low campaigns, and that observers from many perspectives can not only tell the difference between them, but can in all likelihood agree whether any particular campaign is good or bad, or at least better or worse. Yet there is an apparent paradox here, for each of the categorical distinctions just reviewed tends to collapse when pressed.

Consider the concept of political "persuasion," which figures prominently later in this book. In his recent study of political rhetoric, Bryan Garsten offers a serviceable definition of political persuasion: "To truly persuade people is to induce them to change their own beliefs and desires in light of what has been said."[7] Suppose it is claimed, in the spirit of the prevailing Campaign Critique, that some campaign was inferior because of a complete absence of attempts to persuade. I take it that what people who make such a claim mean by it is that candidates, parties, and other political actors did not bother to try to change anyone's mind on the merits of any of the issues facing the electorate. Perhaps the candidates campaigned using glib slogans and sound bites that offered no justifications for the positions they expressed. Such speech is of course generally capable of appealing only to those who already agree with it; certainly, by offering voters who disagree no hint of reasons that might justify the positions they support, slogans and sound

7. Garsten, Saving Persuasion, 7.

bites give voters nothing meaningful upon which to reflect, and thus seem extremely unlikely to induce persuasion on the merits. Or perhaps candidates avoided the issues altogether, devoting their campaign efforts instead to negative attacks on each other's honesty and integrity.

Certainly most politically aware Americans have experienced campaigns that seem to fit this description. But is it true, even in a campaign such as this, that *no* persuasion of any kind occurs? Suppose, for example, that many voters are unaware before the campaign begins of the identity of the parties' nominees. Once the campaign begins, they learn that Smith is the Democrat and Jones is the Republican. That being all they need or care to know, these voters then decide how they are going to vote on the basis of the candidates' party affiliations. If I am a committed Democrat, and I swing my allegiance to Smith upon learning that he is my party's nominee, can it truly be said that I have in no way been "persuaded" to vote for Smith?

One might respond that this is not an example of "persuasion" but, invoking a categorization common in the political science literature, merely of "informing." I have not changed any belief or opinion, but have merely learned a fact the possession of which permits me to apply a preexisting disposition to a new set of political circumstances. But the distinction between "merely" informing and persuading is itself one that also is vulnerable to collapse upon closer examination. Suppose instead that I am a committed, single-issue, pro-life voter and that I routinely vote for whichever candidate most strongly opposes abortion. I accordingly review the candidates' campaign literature for their positions on abortion, conclude that Jones is more strongly pro-life than Smith, and decide as a result to vote for Jones. Have I merely been "informed"—here are the facts about their positions—or have I been "persuaded"?

The distinction is hardly clear-cut. True, I have not altered my opinion during this campaign either on the merits of abortion or on the desirability of choosing among candidates solely on the basis of where they stand on one issue out of many. But I have been induced to vote for one candidate over the other based on the candidate's positions, taken and disseminated during the campaign, on the merits of important issues. I have not *changed* my opinions on the merits of the issues *in response* to anything that has been said during the campaign, and in that sense have not been "persuaded" to change my views. But I have been "persuaded" *to vote* for one candidate instead of another on the basis of substantive considerations.

These situations pose difficulties for the persuasion/no persuasion and inform/persuade frameworks because the provision of information can never be totally divorced from the process by which people formulate their beliefs and conclusions. "Facts" do not exist in a vacuum; they are capable of having political relevance, and hence political meaning, only in reference to some preexisting conceptual framework. It follows that political facts can be, in an important sense, persuasive—but only insofar as they support propositions that count as reasons to vote for or against someone. A fact can never be wholly divorced from the conceptual framework into which it fits.

Even ostensibly more "scientific" distinctions, like the distinction between endogenous and exogenous formation of political opinion, suffer from similar problems. The idea of campaign-endogenous opinion formation presupposes the possibility that voters will formulate their intentions about how to vote during the campaign rather than before it. But what can this mean? Surely no human being generates anew an entire set of political beliefs during each and every campaign season. This means that voters inevitably take many of their beliefs—indeed, virtually all of the conceptual superstructure that permits them to function in the political world—with them into the campaign. But if they take their beliefs with them into the campaign, how then can any decision they make during the campaign about how to vote properly be characterized as campaign-endogenous? By definition, such a decision is made substantially, and possibly almost entirely, on the basis of campaign-exogenous considerations.

We need not solve these puzzles, however, because there is a better way to conceive of what campaign critics are doing when they invoke these descriptive distinctions. All of these ways of thinking about campaigns refer not so much to genuinely opposed categories of political behavior so much as they refer to a widely shared ideal of political conduct that serves as a standard of reference against which campaigns may be judged. To the extent that critics focus on whether campaigns are based on issues or personality or whether they are thick or thin, deliberative or tabulative, persuasive or informative—all are different ways of saying that there are better and worse ways to make democratic decisions at election time, and therefore better and worse kinds of campaigns, that do a better or worse job of steering citizens toward the better kind of decision process. What makes campaigns better or worse along any of these dimensions of characterization concerns to a great extent what people talk about, how well they listen and reflect, and how seriously they take the electoral process. On the whole, then, the Campaign Critique in all its permutations expresses a relatively clear and consistent preference for campaigns that talk about substance over style; that appeal to deeply held rather than superficially held beliefs; that deal with politically important issues rather than trivial ones; and that attempt sincerely to change people's more deeply held beliefs rather than merely to inform or motivate them.

Granted, the distinction I have just described is far from scientific; it is instead one of practical judgment in a particular civic context. The ultimate point of reference for the exercise of such judgment, moreover, seems to be a conception of the obligations that voters bear as citizens of a democracy. Implicit in this conception is something like a belief that democratic citizens are obliged to take seriously their role as voter, to care deeply about the long-term health of the polity, and to make decisions rationally, based on the best possible facts and reasons. Consequently, for a citizen to make decisions based on superficial considerations, or on considerations of candidate image, or solely on the basis of party affiliation, or solely on the basis of private, personal interests, is, in enough cases to make a difference, to behave in a way that falls short of the standards that a proper regard for the duties of citizenship demands. All the negative dimensions of the most commonplace dichotomous characterizations of campaign behavior can thus be understood simply as expressing a judgment that citizens have to some significant degree deviated from the ideal.

The central concern of this book is to flesh out and explore the details of this ideal of democratic citizenship in election campaigns. In the chapters that follow, I trace the ideal to its source, demonstrate its thorough infiltration of legal norms, evaluate its feasibility in light of the findings of empirical social science, and test it against the requirements of democratic theory. I conclude, in the end, that the concerns for democracy manifested in the Campaign Critique are valid but misdirected. Such concerns are misdirected because they rest on an unrealistic conception of what campaigns are capable of accomplishing, and because they misdiagnose the problems *observable* in campaigns as problems *of* campaigns. The real challenges to democratic self-governance lie elsewhere, outside the confined and in many ways highly artificial boundaries of the formal campaign itself.

Plan of the Book

A fundamental premise of the book's argument is that actual contemporary election campaigns fall short of prevailing public understandings of what the electoral process ought to be. To establish this premise, Chapter 1 reviews the evolution of public conceptions of campaign politics and the emergence of the contemporary deliberative model by taking the reader on a brief tour through the social history of American election campaigns. The account begins with eighteenth-century republicanism, according to which campaigning was thought to be inappropriate for qualified candidates, and voters were thought incapable of meaningfully contemplating questions of public policy. By the early nineteenth century, in contrast, campaigns were conceived mainly as a form of public entertainment, and voting was understood as intensely partisan and largely personal. It was not until the late nineteenth and early twentieth centuries, with the rise of Progressivism, that election campaigns began to be associated with meaningful public deliberation on political issues. For Progressives, the hallmark of citizenship was intelligence rather than passion, information rather than enthusiasm, and it followed that the appropriate way to appeal to this new breed of democratic citizenry was to engage its intelligence through reasoned persuasion directed to ascertaining the Truth. As a result, the prevailing public experience of election campaigns today is characterized by high expectations that the central feature of campaigns will consist of reasoned persuasion of the electorate, accompanied by profound disappointment at the failure of campaigns to live up to this widely held expectation.

Taking as its starting point Chapter 1's documentation of a serious disjunction between American political ideals and reality, Chapter 2 asks whether this disjunction might have its roots in any kind of flaw in our legal institutions. Do we have, that is to say, a constitutional infrastructure well-suited to summoning forth the kind of electoral politics to which we aspire? I argue that although the American constitutional regime pays emphatic lip service to the ideal of reasoned persuasion in elections, its actual institutional arrangements in fact presuppose just the opposite—election campaigns that are thin rather than thick, aggregative rather than persuasive. In social science terminology, American constitutional law rests on the presupposition that public opinion is exogenous to political campaigns rather than endogenous to them. Consequently, the legal structure of American politics is weighted heavily toward the premise that the central purpose of an election campaign is not to provide a forum in which citizens can reflect upon and arrive at deliberatively sound political opinions, but rather is simply to tabulate as accurately as possible the opinions that citizens already hold at the inception of the campaign. Chapter 2 documents this claim with examples drawn from the laws of ballot access, campaign finance, and party association.

The failure of the law's doctrinal structure and outcomes to support its publicly professed commitments could be a sign of a problem. Is it? Chapter 3 addresses this question by reviewing the social science literature on how people arrive at political opinions. This literature demonstrates dramatically that the actual persuasion of voters plays virtually no meaningful role in American election campaigns because it is next to impossible to persuade voters during an election campaign of anything they do not already believe. As I have already indicated, it is important to be clear that what is meant by persuasion in this context is an approach toward an ideal in which voters are induced to reflect upon, and if necessary to alter, preexisting policy positions and sometimes even the deeply held political beliefs upon which those positions rest. This is the kind of persuasion contemplated by the dominant, conventional social and political understandings of election campaigns and embraced by contemporary doctrines of constitutional law. Chapter 3, then, demonstrates that, according to recent findings in social science research, persuasion of the thicker sort contemplated by publicly proclaimed democratic ideals almost never happens during election campaigns, and indeed is typically impeded by numerous obstacles rooted in the structure of human cognition and social relations.

This conclusion, in turn, raises another question: should we care? Certainly on the face of it, the marginal role that thick deliberation and persuasion actually play in democratic electoral campaigns seems to contradict the most fundamental requirements of democratic theory. Chapter 4 argues, however, that it does not: in fact, there is nothing in any of the major prevailing theories of democracy that makes thickly deliberative election campaigns an absolute or even particularly pressing condition for democratic legitimacy.

In standard liberal theories of democracy, the importance of campaigns is limited mainly to providing an opportunity for the exchange and collection of information sufficient to make an informed choice among the competing candidates for office. But if voters have collected sufficient relevant information and reflected upon it between elections, or during earlier elections, or in the course of activities unrelated to electoral politics, liberal theories of democracy do not require campaigns of any particular deliberative thickness. In more communitarian and participationist conceptions of democracy, election campaigns may serve theoretically valuable functions, but their significance varies inversely with the availability of alternative forums for political participation and deliberation. Elections and their associated campaigns can provide opportunities for meaningful engagement and participation, but if sufficient opportunities for engagement and participation exist outside the electoral context, participatory and communitarian theories of democracy lay down no great theoretical imperative requiring election campaigns themselves to serve as the dominant venue for political participation and deliberation.

Finally, and perhaps somewhat counterintuitively, contemporary theories of deliberative democracy also impose no theoretical requirement of election campaigns of any particular deliberative thickness. Citizen deliberation is obviously important in theories of deliberative democracy, and when we think of political deliberation we tend to think immediately of election campaigns as opportunities for deep engagement on the big social questions of the day. But while deliberatively thick campaigns might satisfy the requirements of deliberative democracy, they are not *necessary* so long as opportunities for meaningful deliberation are available in other settings. Indeed, one of the striking features of recent work on ground-level applications of deliberative democracy is its tendency to bypass election campaigns altogether in favor of governmental structures that provide citizen input directly into ongoing policy debates associated with daily governance.

If neither the legal-institutional infrastructure, the empirical evidence, nor democratic theory provides support for the socially dominant conception of election campaigns as forums for meaningful debate and persuasion, then it is time to take another look at the baseline conception itself. Chapter 5 does so by reexamining the prevailing critique of American elections, which deems our campaigns democratically inadequate largely because they are insufficiently deliberative. This critique, I argue, is better conceived as drawn not from some formal requirement of law or democratic theory, but as a contingent, pragmatic response to an extremely powerful social fact: the heavy majoritarian bias of public political opinion. I suggest that the persistent contemporary longing for campaign-endogenous public opinion is rooted in a long-standing elite frustration and impatience with the course and slow pace of social and political reform in the United States. American social critics are committed to democracy but wish that it would issue in different and faster results. They therefore long for a kind of electoral democracy that would genuinely (though only modestly) destabilize majoritarian public opinion. The Campaign Critique, in other words, expresses a wish that public opinion be campaign-endogenous because campaigns in which citizens actually open themselves to a deep form of persuasion hold out the only reasonable hope that social and political change may occur in a mass democracy at any rate faster than glacially.

Having identified the problem, Chapter 5 then goes on to ask whether and by what means it might be possible to make our election campaigns what their critics evidently would prefer them to be: recurring occasions for the modest destabilization of majoritarian public opinion. I conclude that the prospects for doing so are dim, and that those measures which might most contribute to the successful destabilization of public opinion raise troubling issues of liberty and autonomy for democratic citizens.

In light of this conclusion, Chapter 5 then reverses field to give more serious consideration to the system of campaigns we seem to have, one that appears to aim no higher than the mounting of campaigns that are primarily tabulative—that count up public opinion as it already exists. Here I review some of the implications for constitutional doctrine and legal policy that might flow from an officially sanctioned public embrace of the tabulative campaign, and discuss how we might think about election law if we lower our expectations to strive only to ensure nothing more than that campaign-exogenous public opinion is tabulated as accurately as possible.

This chapter and the book conclude by arguing that the Campaign Critique rests on a fundamentally mistaken premise. The premise is not that the practice of American democracy suffers from flaws that impair its ability to live up to our highest aspirations; this I believe to be fundamentally true. The mistaken premise, rather, is that the problems critics observe in our election campaigns are problems *of* the campaigns. For the most part, they are not. The real problems lie principally *outside* the electoral arena, in the way that public opinion is shaped and formed every day, in the arena of ordinary life. The most significant problems we encounter within the electoral arena—and there are many—tend to reflect, doubtless with some accuracy, problems of democratic opinion formation that have their source outside the electoral arena. The book therefore concludes by reviewing some areas on which the concerns of election critics might more profitably focus, including the structure and regulation of mass media, and structural resource inequalities that may unfairly grant some more influence than others over the formation of public political opinion between elections.

ONE

The Political Campaign: Emergence of the Deliberative Ideal

WE TAKE IT FOR GRANTED TODAY that campaigns for elective office ought to be deliberative. Candidates, we believe, ought to inform voters of the facts, offer thoughtful positions on serious issues, and work hard to persuade voters of the merits of their positions and qualifications so as to earn any support they receive. Voters, for their part, are supposed to listen carefully, deliberate among themselves, weigh the choices reflectively, and cast a vote that expresses their most considered views. As obvious as this may seem to us, however, the prevailing deliberative model did not always occupy the prominent place it now holds in the public imagination. My purpose in this chapter is to put the current model in historical perspective by showing how it emerged from prior, very different models of the ideal election campaign. My argument, in brief, is that public conceptions of election campaigns have changed tremendously since the founding, and the present conception of the campaign as a forum for meaningful public deliberation and persuasion solidified only in the early twentieth century. This new standard of political behavior not only required much more of both voters and politicians than previous standards, but was accompanied nearly as soon as it was introduced by the corresponding belief—new in the history of American democracy—that voters and candidates routinely fail to live up to their democratic obligations. The new standard, that is to say, introduced to the American public the idea that democracy is hard. Democratic self-rule is not simply a reward that is somehow showered upon the deserving; on the contrary, for democracy to be adequately realized in any polity, citizens must roll up their sleeves and work up a sweat.

Eighteenth-Century Republicanism

The kind of campaign to which we now aspire—in which candidates appeal directly to voters by offering competing policy platforms which voters then independently evaluate and compare—would have seemed both absurd and alarming to Americans of the eighteenth century, if indeed they could have conceived of such a practice. Although by the founding Americans had already practiced a form of democratic self-government for 150 years, their practices were guided by an inherited ideology of republicanism. This system of thought, built on mutually reinforcing principles of social and political hierarchy, attributed little innate capacity for self-government to ordinary people and consequently accorded them a minor and distinctly subordinate role in electoral politics.

At the heart of republican electoral practice lay the belief that the people are incompetent to evaluate either public policy or the job performance of hierarchically superior government officials.[1] Instead, republicanism credited the people with a much narrower and more limited kind of skill and judgment—the ability to judge character. Although the people could not judge a man on the basis of what he might do in office, they were nevertheless well-qualified to judge whether he was likely to do it honestly and virtuously. Montesquieu put it thusly:

> The people are extremely well qualified for choosing those whom they are to intrust with part of their authority. They have only to be determined by things to which they cannot be strangers, and by facts that are obvious to sense. They can tell when a person has fought many battles, and been crowned with success; they are, therefore, capable of electing a general. They can tell when a judge is assiduous in his office, gives general satisfaction, and has never been charged with bribery: this is sufficient for choosing a praetor. They are struck with the magnificence or riches of a fellow-citizen; no more is requisite for electing an edile [executive]. These are facts of which they can have better information in a public forum than a monarch in his palace. But are they capable of conducting an intricate affair, of seizing and improving the opportunity and critical moment of action? No; this surpasses their abilities.[2]

---

1. Brown, *The Strength of a People*, 44.

2. Montesquieu, *The Spirit of the Laws*, Bk. II, ch. 2, 9–10. *See also* Letter from Thomas Jefferson to Dupont de Nemours (Apr. 24, 1816) (claiming that the people are competent as judges of fact and choose representatives based on their knowledge of human character), cited in Koch, *The Philosophy of Thomas Jefferson*, 153.

Republicanism held, moreover, that ordinary people were slaves to their passions[3]; that was why, in Madison's words, "democracies have ever been spectacles of turbulence and contention."[4] Consequently, the eighteenth-century electorate was thought to have no appropriate role to play in the initiation of policy.[5] Instead, the citizen of this era "was entrusted with the responsibility of identifying and evaluating his superiors,"[6] those with a legitimate claim to leadership.[7] On matters of policy and governance, these elites were to guide the masses,[8] who were expected to respond by deferring to the applied judgment of their betters.[9]

These principles were put into practice in the U.S. Constitution, which created overtly republican institutions of governance that, as Madison frankly admitted, were designed to effect "the total exclusion of the people in their collective capacity" from the reins of government.[10] Thus, in the original scheme, the Senate and the President were elected indirectly, utilizing mechanisms that were thought to be most likely to produce the wisest and most virtuous officials.[11] The Electoral College, in particular, was structured so as to make the choice of President depend upon the detached deliberation of wise and virtuous electors rather than on popular judgments about the merits of particular candidates or policies.[12] On the state level, comparatively few were even permitted to vote, an arrangement that the U.S. Constitution adopted by simply incorporating state voting eligibility rules for purposes of federal elections.[13]

---

3. Ketcham, *Presidents above Party*, 78.
4. Madison, *The Federalist Papers*, No. 10.
5. Dinkin, *Voting in Provincial America*, 6.
6. Beeman, "Deference, Republicanism, and the Emergence of Popular Politics in Eighteenth-Century America," 407.
7. *See also* Manin, *The Principles of Representative Government*, 94.
8. Brown, *Strength of a People*, 95.
9. Bagehot, *The English Constitution*, 14; Wood, *The Creation of the American Republic*; Watson, *Jacksonian Politics and Community Conflict*; Altschuler and Blumin, *Rude Republic*, 15; Brown, *Strength of a People*, 44; Schudson, *The Good Citizen*, 14.
10. Madison, *The Federalist Papers*, No. 63, 387 (emphasis deleted). The Progressives were openly critical of the Framers on this point, often describing them and the Constitution in ways that could not be more different from the kind of pious reverence characteristic of today's originalist discourse. *See, e.g.*, White, *The Old Order Changeth*, 3, 34, 38.
11. Madison, *The Federalist Papers*, No. 57; *see also* Bessette, *The Mild Voice of Reason*, 19.
12. Madison, *The Federalist Papers*, No. 68.
13. Keyssar, *The Right to Vote*; U.S. Const. art. I, § 2.

Republican principles also were manifest in the actual practice of elections during the eighteenth century and into the first two decades of the nineteenth. During the colonial period, Americans received an English tradition in which officeholding was understood to be a privilege of social rank. In this system, the selection of parliamentary candidates was managed by gentlemen in a way calculated to confirm the social order. Indeed, for much of parliamentary history, the contested legislative election was a selection procedure of *last* resort; its use acknowledged a failure of consensus that suggested a breakdown of social order in a represented locality.[14]

In colonial America and the postrevolutionary United States, elections were generally conducted under similar circumstances. Americans of this period lived in a world of "intricate networks of personal loyalties, obligations, and quasi-dependencies."[15] In this world, politics was a gentlemen's avocation[16] in which candidates, typically from locally prominent, wealthy, and well-established families,[17] were "put forward" by their similarly situated backers.[18] Election to office constituted a kind of recognition of the station of local leading men and a reaffirmation of the social hierarchy,[19] and therefore frequently went uncontested.[20]

Elections in this period were not, indeed could not have been, about issues in the contemporary sense. Eighteenth-century governments were trivially small by modern standards so they did little that might generate controversy, and in any case "custom and usage" rather than self-conscious policy choices ordinarily guided the management of public affairs.[21] Maintaining social unity was exceedingly important in the eighteenth-century American locality, and contested elections undesirably disturbed the local harmony.[22] Because "the routine conduct of politics . . . was not

---

14. Kishlansky, *Parliamentary Selection*, 16, 22, 25, 27, 37, 61–62, 73.

15. Wood, *The Radicalism of the American Revolution*, 57.

16. Schudson, *The Good Citizen*, 31.

17. *Ibid.*, 5.

18. McCormick, *Second American Party System*, 20.

19. Pole, *Political Representation in England and the Origins of the American Republic*, 151, 158, 159; Watson, *Jacksonian Politics and Community Conflict*, 107; Schudson, *The Good Citizen*, 4, 20, 22.

20. Formisano, *The Transformation of Political Culture*, 30; Schudson, *The Good Citizen*, 20.

21. Zuckerman, *Peaceable Kingdoms*, 34.

22. Dinkin, *Voting in Provincial America*, 4; Schudson, *The Good Citizen*, 12, 18; Troy, *See How They Ran*, 12; Zuckerman, *Peaceable Kingdoms*, 37–38, chs. 2–3.

really the people's business,"[23] ordinary Americans did not require information of the kind that participation in an issue-oriented politics would demand.[24] To the extent that issues arose on the national scene, as they did by 1800, when the first national party system appeared, national politics consisted mainly of appeals not to the people, but to local elites, who then influenced local voters through traditional relations of hierarchy and deference.[25]

Finally, republicanism deeply shaped the nature of the eighteenth-century election campaign. Because the public had such a circumscribed role in political affairs, public interest in elections was low.[26] If voters were presented with a choice of candidates, the only issue for their contemplation was one of character.[27] Virtually no activity took place that contemporary voters would recognize as campaigning. Gentlemen did not "run" but "stood" for office.[28] Any kind of overt electioneering was looked upon with disfavor and alarm, for it suggested an unseemly and potentially dangerous degree of personal ambition.[29] These conventions greatly constrained the kind of campaign activities to which candidates for office might resort. Those who wished actively to contest an office were limited to using surrogates to press their case.[30] When candidates encountered voters, they might offer at most a handshake and a personal greeting,[31] and at election time might engage in the leveling democratic ritual of "treating"—offering voters food and drink, known colloquially as "swilling the planters with bumbo."[32]

Because there were no political parties in eighteenth-century America, candidates lacked party platforms upon which to run.[33] Not only did campaigning in anything resembling its modern form not exist, such campaigning

---

23. Altschuler & Blumin, *Rude Republic*, 15.

24. Schudson, *The Good Citizen*, 26, 27; Brown, *The Strength of a People*, 33.

25. Bender, *Community and Social Change in America*, 102.

26. Formisano, *The Transformation of Political Culture*, 27; Gienapp, "Politics Seem to Enter into Everything," 15; Dinkin, *Campaigning in America*, 1.

27. Wilentz, *The Rise of American Democracy*, 52; Dinkin, *Campaigning in America*, 18; Dinkin, *Voting in Provincial America*, 51–52, 73.

28. Troy, *See How They Run*, chs. 1–2; Ketcham, *Presidents above Party*.

29. Heale, *The Presidential Quest*, 12–14; Troy, *See How They Run*, 8.

30. Dinkin, *Campaigning in America*, 6; Dinkin, *Voting in Provincial America*, 57.

31. Dinkin, *Campaigning in America*, 3, 12.

32. *Ibid.*, 8.

33. This does not mean, of course, that Americans of this era lacked a politics; it means only that their politics operated very differently from how it operates now, in a system in which political parties are available. *See* Hall, *Politics without Parties*.

would have flown in the face of prevailing conventions of political and civic virtue. As M.J. Heale has said of candidates for the presidency, a candidate was "enjoined by the political imperatives of the day *not* to address himself to the people."[34] If we can be sure of anything about election campaigns in republican America, it is that persuasion of voters on the merits of the issues of the day played no role in electoral politics. Persuasion was something reserved for other gentlemen, in the legislature; it was not for the electorate.

The Nineteenth Century: Partisan Loyalty

It is not entirely clear whether the eighteenth-century mode of electoral politics collapsed suddenly or evolved gradually. During the bitterly contested election of 1800, political organizations centered around prominent leaders—most significantly Jefferson and Hamilton—organized, acquired political identities as Republicans and Federalists, and engaged in open and ideological contestation for the presidency, making use, for example, of caucuses, rallies, partisan newspapers, and other techniques that later became standard tools of American political parties.[35] The degree to which this behavior anticipated the well-organized party system that later arose, and thus departed from prevailing republican norms, is unclear. Although Republicans and Federalists campaigned publicly for support in a way previously unknown in national politics,[36] most historians seem to think that the process employed tended generally to utilize rather than circumvent existing conduits of personal influence by established elites.[37]

What is clear, however, is that some time during the 1820s, the pace of change in American political practices began to accelerate dramatically. Republicanism during this period was quickly eclipsed by a radically new set of political beliefs and conventions that altered the face of American politics. Although change occurred on many fronts, the nature of the transformation

34. Heale, *The Presidential Quest*, 2. This was, however, not universally true at the local level. In Maryland, for example, a tradition arose in which candidates for local office debated each other publicly. Larson, *A Magnificent Catastrophe*, 185–89.

35. Larson, *A Magnificent Catastrophe*.

36. *See* especially Wilentz, *The Rise of American Democracy*, chs. 2–3.

37. Wilentz, *The Rise of American Democracy*, 50–52; Formisano, *The Transformation of Political Culture*, ch. 5; McCormick, *The Second American Party System*, 343.

can perhaps be most concisely conveyed with some numbers. Between 1800 and 1824, about one-quarter of the eligible electorate turned out to vote in presidential elections, and turnout in this period never exceeded about 40 percent.[38] By 1840, in contrast, turnout suddenly spiked to over 80 percent—and this of an electorate greatly expanded by the relaxation during the Jacksonian period of state voter eligibility laws. In every presidential election for the balance of the nineteenth century, voter turnout ranged between roughly 70 and 80 percent before beginning a slow decline during the twentieth century.[39]

These levels of voter turnout, impressive though they are, actually fail to capture the full magnitude of the nineteenth-century change in political practices, for voters of the 1840s through the 1890s not only turned out at the polls, but participated in politics with a depth and intensity unmatched during any other period in American history. These voters identified strongly with political parties, participated in party activities, attended speeches and rallies, marched in or cheered their candidates at parades, and belonged to political clubs. In Robert Wiebe's words, "[n]ot only did *everybody* participate but everybody *participated*."[40]

These facts have generated an intense and frequently complicated debate among historians about their meaning. In its broadest contours, the debate revolves around the following question: Did a politics that was nearly ideal *by modern standards* exist during the nineteenth century, from which we have subsequently lapsed? Or did political practices conforming to modern political ideals develop later—or never develop at all? The better view, it seems to me, is that nineteenth-century political practices differed in fundamental ways from contemporary ones, and that high nineteenth-century levels of turnout and participation consequently indicate something very different—and, from the perspective of the present, far less significant—than the raw numbers alone might suggest.

In many respects, the emergence in the 1830s and 1840s of a nineteenth-century style of politics that became the dominant form of electoral practice for the next half century looks very much like the birth and subsequent flourishing of contemporary democratic ideals and practices. The table was set

38. Burnham, "The Turnout Problem," 113.

39. *Ibid., passim.*

40. Wiebe, *Self-Rule*, 61.

for a new, more inclusive style of politics during the early nineteenth century by a sharply increased demand for and expansion of the franchise, mainly through the elimination of property and taxpaying requirements.[41] At the same time, the eighteenth-century social practice of deference began to erode in the 1820s[42] in favor of a growing egalitarian belief in the political competence and virtue of the common man.[43]

By the 1830s, two well-organized mass political parties, the Democrats and Whigs, competed regularly for office at the state and national levels.[44] Party nominating conventions began in the 1820s and 1830s to articulate positions on national issues and to communicate these positions to their members and supporters in the form of a convention "address."[45] By 1844, both parties routinely adopted formal platforms intended to communicate their positions to the public at large.[46] Candidates, too, began to communicate with the electorate, first by making at least some of their positions known in private correspondence intended for public consumption[47] and later by stumping and public debating.[48] The parties eventually became especially active in taking their message directly to the people, sponsoring all manner of events, including rallies, speeches, debates, and parades.

This kind of party competition not only became regularized by the mid-nineteenth century but was far more pervasive and involving than is party competition today. The really intriguing feature of nineteenth-century politics is not that parties held rallies, but that the rallies were remarkably well-attended, drawing enormous crowds at a time when populations were

---

41. Keyssar, *The Right to Vote*, 33–52.

42. Wood, *Radicalism of the American Revolution*, chs. 13–19; Wiebe, *Self-Rule*, ch. 1.

43. Watson, *Liberty and Power*, 5; Meyers, *The Jacksonian Persuasion*, 19–21; Remini, *The Jacksonian Era*, 26.

44. Holt, *Rise and Fall of the American Whig Party*; Formisano, *The Birth of Mass Political Parties*, 3.

45. *E.g.*, Heale, *The Presidential Quest*, 51–58; Holt, *Rise and Fall of the American Whig Party*, 15, 45; McCormick, *Second American Party System*, 204.

46. Benson, *The Concept of Jacksonian Democracy*, 219.

47. Troy, *See How They Ran*, 23–25; Heale, *The Presidential Quest*, 92–95, 107, 114–16; McCormick, *Second American Party System*, 201.

48. Dinkin, *Campaigning in America*, 36, 51, 66; Gienapp, "'Politics Seem to Enter into Everything,'" 40; Heckman, *Lincoln vs. Douglas*, ch. 1. These practices took much longer to develop for presidential candidates than for candidates for lower office. The Lincoln–Douglas debates, it must be remembered, took place in connection with a race for a senatorial seat.

sparsely scattered and transportation was at best inconvenient and at worst arduous. Similarly, the surprising thing is not that party events featured a program of speakers, but that the speeches went on for hours, and audiences listened patiently for the better part of a day. It is striking not that parties staged torchlight parades through urban areas, but that literally thousands marched in these parades, and many more lined the route to watch.[49] And of course all of this activity culminated in massive turnouts on election day. Politics, moreover, went on year-round, for it was not until the twentieth century that election schedules became standardized, with elections falling mainly in November and perhaps a few lesser offices contested in March or April. During most of the nineteenth century, elections in many places occurred throughout the year.[50]

These factors, then, might seem to mark the nineteenth century as a kind of golden age of democratic politics, with intensely competitive parties constantly courting an electorate that was deeply engaged in politics throughout the year. Voters of the nineteenth century must, it seems, have lived and breathed politics in just the way that contemporary critics of American democracy recommend.

This impression, however, cannot withstand closer scrutiny. Consider, for example, the famous Lincoln–Douglas debates of 1858, long held up as "the model for what political argument ought to be, the standard from which we somehow have fallen and the ideal that we should seek to restore."[51] This series of seven debates was attended by a total of perhaps 90,000 people, with crowds at the best-attended debates approaching 15 or 20,000.[52] Yet the throngs who attended these events could not have been there for the reasons that we instinctively associate with voter attendance at such events: to listen to the speeches, make up their minds, and then cast a vote for the candidate who made the better case. First, Lincoln and Douglas were competing for a seat in the U.S. Senate. In 1858, senators were elected by the state legislature, not the state's voters. Second, it is extremely unlikely that the great majority of the people who attended the debates could even have heard them; no

---

49. During the 1864 election in New York City, for example, 60,000 Democrats marched to Times Square to support McClellan at a time when the entire population of the city was just over 800,000. And that was just the Democrats! Baker, "The Ceremonies of Politics."

50. Kornbluh, *Why America Stopped Voting*, 11; Polakoff, *The Politics of Inertia*, ch. 1.

51. Zarefsky, *Lincoln, Douglas and Slavery*, ix.

52. Heckman, *Lincoln vs. Douglas*, 80, 88, 109, 118, 122.

unamplified human voice in a crowded outdoor venue could have reached 15,000 people.[53] If most of those who attended the debates could neither hear the speeches nor vote for either candidate, why did they attend?

Or consider this contemporary account of the behavior of people attending an 1840 rally at which Henry Clay spoke:

> At the huge Southwestern Convention in August 1840, when 30,000 turned out to hear Henry Clay, "[m]en acted as if possessed, some of them embracing each other in transports of rapture, others with tears in their eyes choking with emotion. . . . [W]omen . . . were as ungovernable in emotions as the sterner sex, and several fainted, overcome by an excess of zeal and enthusiasm."[54]

Clay was undoubtedly a great statesman and accomplished speaker, but could anyone's views on internal improvements and tariff policy really bring men to tears and make women faint? This kind of excitement, as Richard Carwardine has observed, is more commonly "associated with religious enthusiasm,"[55] and indeed political organizers of the mid-nineteenth century often deliberately designed their events to resemble evangelical revival meetings.[56]

The closer one looks, the less nineteenth-century politics seems to have involved much in the way of public deliberation on issues and policies. Although campaigns clearly generated a great deal of excitement, this excitement seemed to revolve more around the hoopla and spectacle of the campaign than its substance. Commonplace nineteenth-century campaign events included picnics, barbecues, and tree plantings; songs, slogans, and glee club performances; displays of live animals; orations and brass bands.[57] "Long and extravagant processions, bibulous banquets, and mass meetings

---

53. Schudson, *The Good Citizen*, 135–36. In addition, Douglas was said to have become quite hoarse by the last debate, "'his voice almost extinct.'" Heckman, *Lincoln vs. Douglas*, 126, quoting Gustave Koerner, *Memoirs of Gustave Koerner*, 1809–1896, Vol. II, 67, Thomas J. McCormack ed., Cedar Rapids: Torch Press, 1909.

54. Carwardine, *Evangelicals and Politics in Antebellum America*, 53, quoting James Phelan, *History of Tennessee* (Boston, 1889), 391, quoted in Alexander, "Presidential Election of 1840," 36.

55. *Ibid.*

56. *Ibid.*, ch. 2.

57. Dinkin, *Campaigning in America*, 36, 65, 69; Heale, *The Presidential Quest*, 107; Gienapp, "Politics Seem to Enter into Everything," 34.

stretching over a number of days became regular features of presidential campaigns, as did memorabilia of all kinds, from medallions, satin ribbons, and bandanas to hand-mirrors, shaving-soap and knives, bearing the likenesses or names of the candidates."[58] Parties staged huge torchlight parades, reviewed by the candidate from his balcony like a general reviewing his troops, culminating in mass rallies, fireworks, and a serenade to the candidate.[59] Partisans competed in contests to raise huge poles up to 100 ft. high.[60] Party enthusiasts rolled giant leather balls inscribed with party slogans across the countryside.[61] Other events featured blackface minstrel shows and even, on at least one occasion, Chang and Eng, the famed Siamese twins—literally a freak show.[62]

The extensiveness and dominance of these kinds of activities even led historian William Gienapp, a committed adherent of the view that the nineteenth century was a political golden age, to observe: "Whether such events were conducive to a careful discussion of the issues is problematic. Campaign hoopla generated popular interest, but at times this pageantry took precedence over the dissemination of political information."[63] Yet Gienapp underestimated the force of his own conclusion: nineteenth-century politics, even at its best, was rarely substantive.

There is little disagreement on the propositions that ideology played no significant role for the general public in political contests before about 1840,[64] and that by the Gilded Age national politics had become "virtually issueless."[65] In the famous words of the astute British observer Lord James Bryce, written in 1888, "Distinctive tenets and policies, points of political doctrine and points of political practice, have all but vanished. . . . All has been lost, except

58. Heale, *The Presidential Quest*, 106.

59. Baker, *Affairs of Party*, 294–301.

60. Dinkin, *Campaigning in America*, 38.

61. Holt, *Rise and Fall of the American Whig Party*, 105–06.

62. Wilentz *The Rise of American Democracy*, 503.

63. Gienapp, "Politics Seem to Enter into Everything," 35. Notwithstanding such moments of doubt, Gienapp argued, in the end, that "the nineteenth-century electorate was more committed, more informed, more issue conscious" than voters of the twentieth century. *Ibid.*, 61.

64. *E.g.*, McCormick, *The Second American Part System*, 91, 271; Wilentz, *The Rise of American Democracy*, 307.

65. Altschuler & Blumin, *Rude Republic*, 225; Dinkin, *Campaigning in America*, 91.

office or the hope of it."[66] Nor is there any significant dispute that American politics was dominated for the middle two decades of the nineteenth century by very real, substantive, and publicly engaging issues: secession, slavery, and reconstruction.[67] The only real area of dispute seems to be whether the politics of the late 1830s through the 1850s—the period of the second party system, during which Whigs and Democrats competed for state and national offices—can plausibly be characterized as ideological and issue-driven. Although a few historians contend passionately that this was the case,[68] the weight of opinion, and the better view, seems to be that the politics of this period had more in common with the republican approach that it displaced than the issue-centered approach that emerged during the early twentieth century.[69]

Consider, for example, the behavior of presidential candidates during this period. The republican taboo on presidential campaigning that prevailed in the eighteenth century held firmly through almost the entire nineteenth century[70] so candidates of this period would not and did not campaign for office. Indeed, Whig candidates maintained that they wanted to be chosen "spontaneously," in the republican manner, and therefore refused to make promises or pledges,[71] depriving voters of any reliable way to evaluate the positions of the candidates on the issues, had they been so inclined. In his letter accepting nomination as the 1840 Whig presidential candidate, William Henry Harrison would not even go so far as to "declare the principles upon which the Administration will be conducted" should he be elected,[72] as this would compromise his impartiality as President.[73] Furthermore, the

---

66. Bryce, *The American Commonwealth*, Vol. 2, 21.

67. Even the great skeptics Altschuler and Blumin concede this. Altschuler and Blumin, *Rude Republic*, ch. 5. J. Mills Thornton argues that the only real issue ever in Alabama antebellum politics was slavery. Thornton, *Politics and Power in a Slave Society*, 32.

68. *See* especially Holt, *Rise and Fall of the American Whig Party*; Howe, *The Political Culture of the American Whigs*; Silbey, *The American Political Nation*; Jensen, *The Winning of the Midwest*.

69. Skeptics include Schlesinger, *The Age of Jackson*; Pessen, *Jacksonian America*; Altschuler and Blumin, *Rude Republic*; Watson, *Jacksonian Politics and Community Conflict*; Formisano, *The Transformation of Political Culture*; Heale, *The Presidential Quest*; Keller, *Affairs of State*; Bensel, *The American Ballot Box*, and many others.

70. Troy, *See How They Ran*.

71. Heale, *The Presidential Quest*, 130.

72. Troy, *See How They Ran*, 22, quoting letter from Harrison to John Owen, 19 Dec. 1839.

73. *Ibid.*

parties during this period tended to nominate "available" men—appealing, electable candidates without extensive public records—rather than the great ideologues and statesmen of the day.[74]

Even if one does not go as far as, say, Edward Pessen, who argues that the parties of the 1840s lacked any ideological coherence, were essentially indistinguishable in their positions, and were motivated solely by ambition,[75] the content of nineteenth-century political campaigns does not suggest that they were weighted toward serious public contemplation and discussion of important issues. Often, the parties worked hard to obfuscate any differences between them,[76] and they frequently campaigned in different regions and to different audiences on drastically different positions.[77] As in earlier times, questions of character—indeed, overt and energetic character assassination—often dominated campaign discourse.[78]

None of this is very surprising in view of the characteristics of the electorate or the practice of voting itself in the nineteenth century. Most voters, when they were even aware of the issues, neither understood nor held any meaningful beliefs about them.[79] Many suffered from civically debilitating handicaps such as illiteracy, poverty, and cultural isolation that precluded them from acquiring political information or forming meaningful political views.[80] Nineteenth-century voters thus tended to be unsophisticated and consequently "'disposed to accept every wild statement.'"[81]

Nineteenth-century patterns of partisan affiliation tend to reinforce this view. Whereas voters responding primarily to issues might be expected to switch party affiliation from election to election or office to office according to the substance of candidate and party positions, the partisan affiliation of nineteenth-century voters generally was extremely stable and intense. Party affiliation was typically handed down from father to son and widely shared

---

74. Holt, *Rise and Fall of the American Whig Party*, 89; Troy, *See How They Ran*, 45; Dinkin, *Campaigning in America*, 49.

75. Pessen, *Jacksonian America*, 156, 160, 211, 215–16, 224–33, 247.

76. Holt, *Rise and Fall of the American Whig Party*, 183.

77. Gienapp, "'Politics Seem to Enter into Everything,'" 49.

78. Holt, *Rise and Fall of the American Whig Party*, 185–86; Watson, *Jacksonian Politics and Community Conflict*, 77–80; Dinkin, *Campaigning in America*, 55.

79. Bensel, *The American Ballot Box*, viii–ix, x, 296; Formisano, *The Birth of Mass Political Parties*, 12.

80. *Ibid.*, 3.

81. Formisano, *The Transformation of Political Culture*, 325, quoting a 1902 political memoir.

within social groups.[82] This in itself is not inconsistent with issue voting so long as families and social groups tended to share politically salient interests that were reflected consistently in the substantive positions of the parties they supported. Yet the more fine-grained studies of nineteenth-century partisan affiliation cast doubt on such consistency. Paula Baker's study of political life in late nineteenth-century Schoharie County, New York, finds generally that "partisan alignments were chaotic: the same social or economic groups supported different parties in different communities for disparate reasons." She concludes that "[m]en's relationship with others in the community, rather than membership in social groups, shaped partisan choices."[83] Partisan identity, in other words, was influenced more by patterns of partisanship within the voter's immediate social network than by the substantive interests the voter might share with others situated similarly but residing in different communities with different historical patterns of partisanship.

The nature of voting in the nineteenth century similarly worked systematically against the emergence of a genuinely issue-oriented campaign politics. The nineteenth-century polling place was often "anarchic," and in many election places "physical and verbal intimidation shaped the public space outside the voting window."[84] Voting was by no means a private act, as it is now, but was performed in public, in full view of all manner of interested and sometimes unsavory characters. Parties printed their own tickets, and although voters were free to alter these ballots as they saw fit, to do so without being noticed would have been difficult and required some courage. Bribery, too, was common: for many, "the act of voting was a social transaction in which they handed in a party ticket in return for a shot of whisky, a pair of boots, or a small amount of money."[85] Official investigations of disputed late nineteenth-century elections disclosed that at least one-quarter of voters questioned had never even bothered to read their ballots.[86] As Richard Bensel sums up:

> The sheer physicality of voting underscores the presumption that men's opinions on policy issues were fixed by their ethnic and cultural identities,

---

82. Jensen, *The Winning of the Midwest*, 7.

83. Baker, "The Culture of Politics in the Late Nineteenth Century," 178. *See also* Benson, *The Concept of Jacksonian Democracy*.

84. Bensel, *The American Ballot Box*, 13.

85. *Ibid.*, ix.

86. Altschuler & Blumin, *Rude Republic*, 265.

> along with previously acquired loyalties to party organizations. Because their opinions were fixed, winning became a matter of raising the practical barriers for opponents and lowering them for friends. Men placed their bodies in the path of opponents attempting to approach the voting window. They shoved, poked, threatened, grabbed, and sometimes stabbed or shot those they saw as politically damned. But, whatever they did, men at the polls rarely engaged in an open and free debate of the issues that divided them. In sum, the . . . polling place, in nineteenth-century America, was often one of the less democratic sites in the nation.[87]

All of these considerations cast considerable doubt on the possibility that nineteenth-century politics gave any pride of place to the reasoned persuasion of voters, at least to a degree greater than now occurs, and in all likelihood such persuasion played a considerably smaller role than it presently does. If this is so, how then do we explain the high levels of voter turnout and participation of the nineteenth century? If people did not participate in politics because of a commitment to collective political action based on shared ideological beliefs, why did they participate? Social and political historians tend to answer this question in several ways.

First, politics was simply an enjoyable form of public entertainment, often "the best show in town."[88] Nineteenth-century life could be hard. For rural voters, the hoopla and spectacle of political campaigns "provided relief from the isolation and toil of farm life"; for city dwellers, it provided "fellowship and an escape from an environment that could be dehumanizing."[89] It is no coincidence that many of the commonplace entertainments associated with nineteenth-century campaign hoopla also could be found at the local county fair.[90]

Second, participation in politics provided an affirming experience of social solidarity. Many writers have likened the kind of enthusiasm with which nineteenth-century Americans supported their political parties to the kind of enthusiasm with which contemporary Americans support their home football or baseball teams.[91] As Michael Schudson evocatively puts it, "your

---

87. Bensel, *The American Ballot Box*, 290.

88. Schudson, *The Good Citizen*, 136.

89. Kornbluh, *Why America Stopped Voting*, 30.

90. Altschuler & Blumin, *Rude Republic*, 62–63.

91. *E.g.*, Gienapp, "Politics Seem to Enter into Everything," 32; Schudson, *The Good Citizen*, 146.

party [was] your party, just as, in our own day, your high school is your high school."[92] Participation in public political rituals also allowed voters to affirm their identities as members of a community. The fact that "membership in the community [was], in part, . . . contingent on the revelation of one's partisan preferences, on the demonstration of one's political involvement," was secondary; the important thing was to experience a gratifying sense of solidarity with one's neighbors and political equals.[93] Finally, widespread public participation in political events permitted the enactment of an important social ritual of democracy in which the people quite literally demonstrated their approval of the chosen candidates, conferring a popular imprimatur that legitimized the candidates' entitlement, if elected, to rule in the people's name.[94]

Third, nineteenth-century political parties relied heavily on effective mobilization of their supporters. Party agents were numerous, and in an era of unregulated partisan political activity, they resorted without compunction to favors, bribery, and if necessary to physical force to get their charges to the polls.[95] But social pressures may have played an equally important role in maintaining high levels of voter turnout. As Altschuler and Blumin suggest, the vigor of activists and the watchfulness of local party agents may have combined with the lack of anonymity in small-town America so that in many places "it may well have been more bothersome not to vote than to have voted."[96] Indeed, they go on to speculate, the very landscape of post-1840, antebellum America may have played a role in the high turnout of the period: "this world of farms and villages along good country roads may have been the ideal human landscape for maximizing voter participation."[97]

If in the age of republicanism the main obligation of political citizenship was deference, during the period from about 1840 through roughly the 1880s or 1890s, the primary obligation of political citizenship was partisan

92. Schudson, *The Good Citizen*, 6.

93. McGerr, *The Decline of Popular Politics*, 40.

94. *Ibid.*, 30, 41; Baker, *Affairs of Party*, 264.

95. Bensel, *The American Ballot Box*.

96. Altschuler & Blumin, *Rude Republic*, 71.

97. *Ibid.*, 72.

loyalty:[98] "Loyalty and regularity, not information, were the political virtues."[99] Unlike today, independent voters were rare[100]; indeed, political independence and associated changes in partisan leanings were viewed with great suspicion.[101] As an Alabama newspaper editor wrote in 1850, "men who claim to be independent of party 'are hermaphrodites in politics' and therefore 'productive of no good.'"[102]

One final piece of evidence counsels in favor of this account: it coincides with accounts of nineteenth-century political citizenship against which the Progressives revolted and which they ultimately succeeded in displacing.[103]

Emergence of the Modern Ideal

As the nineteenth century drew to a close, numerous mutually reinforcing trends led to a rapid decline of the characteristic nineteenth-century style of politics in favor of a style that is clearly recognizable to contemporary Americans, and from which American politics has not since fundamentally deviated.[104] A new public political ideology, associated with the Mugwumps and then the Progressives, arose that stressed reason and political independence over partisan loyalty. These ideological developments were accompanied by significant institutional reforms and corresponding changes in the

98. Formisano, *The Transformation of Political Culture*, 279–80; Formisano, *The Birth of Mass Political Parties*, 57.

99. Schudson, "Politics as Cultural Practice," 178.

100. Gienapp, "Politics Seem to Enter into Everything," 60.

101. Formisano, *The Transformation of Political Culture*, 279–80.

102. Thornton, *Politics and Power in a Slave Society*, 44, quoting Montgomery Advertiser, Feb. 27, 1850.

103. Other explanations sometimes offered for nineteenth-century voting patterns focus on ethnocultural and religious influences. Kleppner, *The Third Electoral System*; Silbey; *The Partisan Imperative*; Jensen, *The Winning of the Midwest*; to a lesser extent Formisano, *The Birth of Mass Political Parties*, ch. 9, and Watson, *Jacksonian Politics and Community Conflict*. These theories, however, can at most explain why some groups of voters supported one party rather than another; they cannot explain why voters chose to attend partisan events and to vote rather than to stay home. To resort to such explanations to explain high turnout and participation collapses them into the same kind of social solidarity theories to which they typically stand opposed.

104. Taylor, *Citizenship and Democratic Doubt*, 20.

style of public politics, including important changes in the style and content of political campaigns. Such changes were also accompanied by powerfully reinforcing developments in communications, technology, and society—by the emergence, that is, of modernity itself.

Dissatisfaction with the practice of nineteenth-century politics began to appear in the 1870s, manifesting itself in a shift toward what has often been called the "educative" campaign.[105] Samuel Tilden's 1876 presidential campaign assembled a candidate briefing book, circulated speeches, drafted editorials, and sent out speakers with the self-conscious objective of "substituting seemingly reasoned, objective argument for the emotional, irrational appeal of spectacular partisanship."[106] By 1884, both parties had gravitated toward this model,[107] and James G. Blaine, the Republican candidate, went so far as to declare that an election was a "search for truth"[108]—a new, even revolutionary idea in democratic politics. The nineteenth-century model was permanently buried during the 1896 campaign when William Jennings Bryan, the Republican nominee, conducted a whistle-stop campaign of public speaking that covered 27 states, 18,000 miles, and featured 600 speeches heard personally by five million Americans.[109] Although the Democratic candidate, William McKinley, followed the older model of a more restrained candidacy, he nevertheless responded with a "front-porch" campaign that also aimed to educate and inform the electorate.[110] So pervasive and powerful was this shift in electoral tactics that by 1892 the parties had begun to abandon as ineffective the familiar spectacle of nineteenth-century campaign politics, and campaign hoopla was entirely defunct by 1920.[111]

These stylistic changes were driven, or at least supported and justified, by the reformist ideology of the Progressives, who, in the late nineteenth and early twentieth centuries, mounted an energetic and highly effective movement against the nineteenth-century politics of partisan loyalty. At the heart of Progressive thought lay the belief that public affairs in a complex world

105. McGerr, *The Decline of Popular Politics*, ch. 4; Dinkin, *Campaigning in America*, ch. 5.

106. McGerr, *The Decline of Popular Politics*, 73.

107. *Ibid.*, 76–78.

108. Troy, *See How They Ran*, 85.

109. Keller, *Affairs of State*, 582; Troy, *See How They Ran*, 104.

110. Keller, *Affairs of State*, 583.

111. McGerr, *The Decline of Popular Politics*, 70; Reynolds, *Testing Democracy*, 1.

must be conducted rationally and for the common good. Progressives argued that politics in the nineteenth century had become perverted: whereas politics ought to be conducted to achieve the good of all, nineteenth-century politics was aimed at achieving only the good of some—fellow partisans, party bosses, the rich, or corporate interests.[112] Ultimately, the Progressive conception of democratic politics was rooted in a spiritual faith in the perfectibility of man and the belief that politics ought to be an instrument for achieving that perfection. "Democracy must stand or fall," wrote the Progressive theorist Herbert Croly, "on a platform of possible human perfectibility."[113] "What a democratic nation must do," he continued, "is not to accept human nature as it is, but to move in the direction of its improvement."[114]

Progressives supplemented this conception of politics with a corresponding conception of political citizenship. On the Progressive view, the political obligations of citizens were civic rather than partisan.[115] Citizens were obliged to place the public good over any form of private good, including not only personal self-interest but the interests of groups with which they might be affiliated such as their party or ethnic group.[116] To discharge this responsibility required of citizens something that had not previously been demanded of them: hard work, discipline, and self-denial.[117] "The theory of democracy upon which the entire progressive movement is based," wrote movement historian Benjamin Parke De Witt, "is that every normal citizen who is mentally and morally fit not only has the right, but is also under a duty to participate in the solution of political problems."[118] Responsible citizenship thus required citizens not merely to attend party events, cheer their candidates, and cast a vote, but to study and reflect upon questions of public policy, which in turn imposed on citizens an obligation to become informed.[119]

---

112. Croly, *The Promise of American Life*, 214; De Witt, *The Progressive Movement*, 23, 113.

113. Croly, *The Promise of American Life*, 400.

114. *Ibid.*, 413.

115. Schudson, *The Good Citizen*, 147.

116. Croly, *The Promise of American Life*, 214, 418; Taylor, *Citizenship and Democratic Doubt*, 42; Hofstadter, *The Age of Reform*, 259, 261; Judd, *Politics of American Cities*, 94.

117. Croly, *The Promise of American Life*, 22; Taylor, *Citizenship and Democratic Doubt*, 25.

118. De Witt, *The Progressive Movement*, 190.

119. Reynolds, *Testing Democracy*, 119; Schudson, *The Good Citizen*, 185; Hofstadter, *The Age of Reform*, 261.

Progressivism, in short, sought to "transform voting from a social to a civic act, rationalizing electoral behavior."[120]

The Progressive conception of citizenship fit hand in glove with its conception of governance. Like political theorists before them, Progressive reformers argued that public officials were obliged to manage public affairs for the common good.[121] What distinguished the Progressive view from its predecessors, however, was the way in which Progressives believed that measures promoting the common good could be identified—scientifically, through the impartial application of reason. Progressives acknowledged that problems of governance could be complex, but argued that scientifically grounded expertise could furnish solutions to most problems.[122] Politics should therefore elevate to office qualified experts rather than party favorites. Citizens themselves were not expected to possess the expertise actually to solve public problems, but they were required to possess knowledge sufficient to permit them to judge the plausibility of solutions offered for their contemplation by appropriately qualified experts. If citizens needed help or encouragement to do their part, the answer was not patronage or other forms of bribery, but education.[123]

These ideological commitments caused Progressives to reject outright the party-based political system of the nineteenth century. The boss-dominated, urban political machine of the late nineteenth and early twentieth centuries was, Progressives believed, a kind of political organization that, wrongfully and at great civic cost, "interpreted political and civic relations chiefly in terms of personal obligations, and placed strong personal loyalties above allegiance to abstract codes of law or morals."[124] Party loyalty on the late nineteenth century model was, according to Progressives, simply irrational; votes, Progressives contended, should be cast on the basis of merit, not loyalty.[125] The ability of parties to mobilize a mass membership based on nothing more than naked loyalty impaired the possibility of rational self-government for

---

120. Schudson, *The Good Citizen*, 147.

121. Wiebe, *The Search for Order*.

122. Croly, *The Promise of American Life*, 329, 433; Haber, *Efficiency and Uplift*, 103; Taylor, *Citizenship and Democratic Doubt*, 1, 51–52; Wiebe, *The Search for Order*, 161–62.

123. Wiebe, *The Search for Order*, 160–61; Reynolds, *Testing Democracy*, 120.

124. Hofstadter, *The Age of Reform*, 9.

125. Judd, *The Politics of American Cities*, 94.

the common good by "diluting the votes of informed and intelligent citizens with those of men who supinely submitted to machine dictation."[126] Progressives sought—successfully in the end—to replace the nineteenth-century model of partisan fidelity with a very different model in which an autonomous citizen independently evaluates candidates and policies.[127] Progressives therefore advocated ticket splitting and party switching, practices viewed during the prior half century as tawdry and vaguely sinister, and argued that voters should support a party's candidates only instrumentally, as a reward for good performance in office.[128]

Progressives did not merely complain about existing political practices; they mounted an extremely effective campaign of legal reforms to implement the kind of politics they preached. Perhaps the most significant such reform was the introduction of the Australian ballot system, in which voting takes place in secret rather than in open view, and official ballots are printed not by parties but by the government.[129] Where voting under the old system had been a communal activity cementing partisan fraternity and social solidarity, voting under the Australian system emphasized the autonomy and isolated sovereignty of "a private individual making rational choices about policy preferences."[130] Progressives also introduced civil service reforms that drastically curbed patronage appointments, depriving parties of one of their principal tools for maintaining loyalty and mobilizing supporters.[131] Voter registration requirements and publicly printed ballots made voting more difficult by placing greater responsibility on the voter to secure eligibility, and by requiring voters to make decisions considerably more complex than choosing which party's premarked ballot to submit.[132] Progressives also pressed their attack on the power of parties by introducing nonpartisan elections, today the most common format for elections at the local level.[133] In the end, these innovations transformed elections from intimate, boisterous,

126. Reynolds, *Testing Democracy*, 126.

127. Crenson & Ginsburg, *Downsizing Democracy*, 15.

128. McGerr, *The Decline of Popular Politics*, 55–58; Reynolds, *Testing Democracy*, 97–99.

129. Buenker, "Sovereign Individuals and Organic Networks," 187; McGerr, *The Decline of Popular Politics*, 62–65.

130. Schudson, *The Good Citizen*, 170.

131. Crenson & Ginsburg, *Downsizing Democracy*, 20–29.

132. Reynolds, *Testing Democracy*, 119; Schudson, *The Good Citizen*, 185.

133. Cassel, "The Nonpartisan Ballot in the United States."

celebrations of partisan solidarity into "impersonal, state-administered affairs."[134]

Progressives were assisted in the achievement of their reform agenda by contemporaneous changes in American society that worked independently to undermine nineteenth-century practices of partisan politics. In nineteenth-century America, politics had been one of the principal forms, and in some places nearly the only form, of public entertainment. By the early twentieth century, however, other forms of entertainment routinely competed for public attention. The availability of vaudeville, amusement parks, theaters, dance halls, circuses, baseball, boxing, bicycles, and eventually movies, phonographs, automobiles, and radio cut deeply into the dominance of politics as a source of public diversion.[135]

Progressivism also fell into step with a broader cultural change, the emergence of a distinction between "highbrow" and "lowbrow" culture. As Lawrence Levine has demonstrated, forms of entertainment that during most of the nineteenth century had been understood as "popular," and therefore available and accessible to the masses, underwent a process of "sacralization" in which they were appropriated by social elites, who claimed that such entertainments could be appreciated only by a cognoscenti who understood them and approached them with a suitable reverence and seriousness of purpose.[136] Shakespearean theater, opera, and symphonic music became "the possession of the educated portions of society," who disseminated these arts "for the enlightenment of the average folk who were to swallow [the arts] not for their entertainment but for their education, as a respite from—not as a normal part of—their usual cultural diet."[137] Progressive political reforms worked much the same transformation on politics: no longer a forum for earthy, lowbrow fellowship, politics and political discourse were to be approached seriously and soberly, and consumed for purposes of enlightenment and education, in the "respectable" discharge of a weighty civic obligation.[138]

---

134. Reynolds, *Testing Democracy*, 117.

135. Dinkin, *Campaigning in America*, 96, 98; Kornbluh, *Why America Stopped Voting*, 115; McGerr, *The Decline of Popular Politics*, 148; Schudson, *The Good Citizen*, 177.

136. Levine, *Highbrow/Lowbrow*.

137. *Ibid.*, 31.

138. Reynolds, *Testing Democracy*, 57.

At the same time, rapid technological changes during the early twentieth century further undermined the intimacy, community, and party-centeredness of democratic politics. New means of communication such as the phonograph, movies, and radio allowed candidates to reach mass audiences from great distances, and without the intermediation of local party agents to spread and supervise the communication of the party's message.[139] These developments made campaign politics more centralized, less local, and consequently less personal, and ultimately initiated a transformation of the voter from a direct, active participant in partisan campaign politics to a spectator.[140] The same advances in communication, accompanied by an evolving nationalization of public affairs, also began to break down the insularity of local community, diminishing the usefulness of partisan politics as a ritual of local communal solidarity.[141] And by the early twentieth century, "many Americans found that partisan affiliation did not reflect the full array of their concerns," and so began to disengage from parties—as well as from electoral politics and voting—in favor of other avenues of political influence, such as nongeographical special interest groups.[142]

Together, these changes in political style, democratic ideology, and social context gave rise to a new kind of electoral campaign. This kind of campaign focused on the presentation of issues.[143] Its objective was no longer primarily to mobilize loyal partisans through appeals to party loyalty and communal solidarity, but to attract the votes of autonomous, politically independent voters through persuasion.[144] Candidates brought this campaign of issue-based persuasion neither to local elites nor to party agents, whose support in earlier eras had been essential to bringing along the great mass of the electorate, but, increasingly, directly to the individual voter himself. No longer a kind of prize to be won through the agency of some social or partisan mass power broker, each man (and later each woman) came to be conceived as his own personal power broker—an independent, democratic sovereign whose

---

139. Dinkin, *Campaigning in America*, 100, 127, 132; Kornbluh, *Why America Stopped Voting*, 113.

140. Reynolds, *Testing Democracy*, 117.

141. Kornbluh, *Why America Stopped Voting*, 117; Bender, *Community and Social Change in America*, 108–10; Wiebe, *The Search for Order*.

142. Kornbluh, *Why America Stopped Voting*, 116.

143. McGerr, *The Decline of Popular Politics*, vii; Schudson, *The Good Citizen*, 428; Troy, *See How They Ran*, 125, 131.

144. Dinkin, *Campaigning in America*, 96; Schudson, *The Good Citizen*, 165.

support was to be earned on the merits rather than taken for granted as a social fact.

The Twentieth Century: Campaigns Fail to Measure Up

The Progressive conceptions of the voter as a rational, independent sovereign, and of the campaign as a civic forum for informing and persuading an intelligent and critical public, invested individual voters with a power and elevated them to a status that they had never before enjoyed. Yet, paradoxically, this change in public conceptions precipitated a crisis of democracy from which the nation has never recovered. By raising the bar—by setting for candidates and voters a demanding standard of knowledge, attentiveness, diligent reflection, and impartial self-sacrifice—Progressivism opened the door to a new phenomenon in the history of American democracy: the possibility that our actual practice of politics might fall short of our ideals.

The lapse was almost immediate. If the educative campaign was well-established by the late Progressive era, when Woodrow Wilson occupied the White House,[145] by about 1920 it had already begun to decline in favor of a new, more scientifically sophisticated and more cynical style of campaigning sometimes known as the "merchandising" or "advertising" campaign.[146] In this style of campaigning, a precursor of the modern, media-driven campaign of sound bites and staged "photo ops," the techniques of an increasingly sophisticated marketing industry were appropriated by politicians to sell themselves. Campaigns "entered a new realm of contrived images and salesmanship"[147] in which they began to employ public relations professionals to craft images and messages tailored for easy public acceptance.[148] George Gallup developed accurate, scientific polling in the 1930s, and the first political consulting firm was formed in 1933 to apply these techniques self-consciously to electoral campaigns.[149] Technology was thereafter

---

145. Troy, *See How They Ran*, 129–32.

146. Jensen, *The Winning of the Midwest*, ch. 6; Dinkin, *Campaigning in America*, ch. 6; McGerr, *The Decline of Popular Politics*, ch. 6.

147. McGerr, *The Decline of Popular Politics*, 171; see also Troy, *See How They Ran*, 146–48.

148. Dinkin, *Campaigning in America*, 129.

149. *Ibid.*, 138, 129.

deployed not so much to reach and educate a rational public as to manipulate a seemingly gullible one—a twentieth-century tool used for nineteenth-century humbug.

The fast-growing disjunction between public political ideals and the reality of everyday electoral practices created the conditions in which it became possible to recognize a previously unknown and unsuspected pathology of democracy: the problem of political "irrationality." The novelty of the problem did not lie principally in the failures of politicians to live up to the highest ideals of progressive democracy; Americans had been complaining about the inadequacies of political candidates since the first contested campaigns.[150] What was new, rather, was the emerging suspicion that it was *voters*—not candidates—who were failing to live up to democratic ideals. When little was expected of voters, they could hardly help but carry their civic burden. But where much was expected of voters, suddenly the possibility arose that fulfilling the duties of responsible democratic citizenship might lie beyond the interests—or worse, the abilities—of the ordinary citizen.

As the twentieth century wore on, voters began to fall short of public standards of political behavior in numerous ways. First, they ceased to vote in numbers even remotely approaching nineteenth-century levels. In the 1896 presidential election, about 80 percent of eligible voters turned out at the polls. By 1904, turnout fell to about 65 percent and dropped below 50 percent in 1920 and 1924, never again exceeding about 63 percent, which it reached briefly in the election of 1960.[151] Second, the electorate withdrew from politics in many other ways. Voters ceased attending party events. They no longer stayed as well-informed; newspaper readership, for example, declined.[152] Citizens chose to spend time in private rather than in public pursuits.[153] Voters became passive spectators of political events conducted by others. By mid-century, critics in the West professed serious concerns about the capacity of ambitious leaders (such as those in interwar Germany and Italy and Cold-War-era Communist nations) to mislead and take advantage of a lazy, gullible public.

In 1960, the ideal of the autonomously independent, rational democratic citizen was dealt a devastating blow by the publication of *The American Voter*,

150. Troy, *See How They Ran*, ix.

151. Burnham, "The Turnout Problem."

152. Bogart, *Press and Public*, 16.

153. Putnam, *Bowling Alone*.

a landmark work of political science that documented in shocking detail the ignorance, inattentiveness, and irrationality of the American electorate.[154] *The American Voter* showed not just that average voters were not fully informed about the issues and the candidates, but that they were woefully ignorant of fundamental facts about the political world, including the basics of contemporary public issues, the most rudimentary policy commitments of the parties and candidates, and even the function and powers of the elective offices they voted to fill.[155] If voters did not know these facts, it seemed, they must necessarily lack the capacity for rational decision making in the political arena.

We live, accordingly, in an era that has developed a new tradition—a tradition of democratic anxiety and disappointment.[156] That our campaigns fail to meet the standards and ideals that we have for more than a century professed seems obvious. That part of the problem lies in the unwillingness of politicians to rise to the level of our ideals is likewise an article of faith.[157] But there is something more—a sneaking suspicion that the poor quality of our campaign politics may ultimately be attributable to shortcomings of the electorate itself; that in the end, our electoral politics falls short of our ideals because we are not capable of meeting those ideals; that candidates give us poor campaigns because they are only responding to public demand; that we have, in short, the politics we deserve.

The Current Standard: Political Ideals in the Twenty-First Century

What, then, is the standard against which election campaigns are judged today? What, in the mind of the twenty-first century American public, are the characteristics of the ideal campaign? There is, alas, no official statement of public opinion on this question, so it can be answered only inferentially. Yet I think it is possible to say, without significant controversy, that the Progressive ideal worked its way so deeply into American political consciousness that it,

---

154. Campbell et al., *The American Voter.*

155. These results have been often replicated. *See, e.g.*, Smith, *The Unchanging American Voter*; Delli Carpini & Keeter, *What Americans Know About Politics.*

156. Sandel, *Democracy's Discontent*, 3.

157. Hibbing & Theiss-Morse, *Stealth Democracy.*

or something very much like it, continues to dominate public aspirations for democratic politics.[158] As a result, Americans today, like their intellectual forebears of a century ago, tend to believe that the ideal voter labors under burdensome obligations to become and remain informed about public affairs; to pay close and continuous attention to politics and the actions of elected officials; to evaluate the proposals and performance of candidates and officials dispassionately; to remain open to new ideas and solutions to public problems; and to place the good of all above private advantage in political decision making. The ideal candidate, in turn, must behave in ways that permit the ideal citizen to discharge his or her obligations. Candidates, consequently, must do their utmost to inform voters about the pressing issues of the day, propose solutions to public problems, and through reasoned persuasion convince voters to elect them to office. A campaign, on this view, is thus a forum for reasoned discourse, debate, and persuasion on the merits of public issues.[159]

The evidence for this claim is admittedly impressionistic, but it is there. Consider, for example, public attitudes toward political parties. The defining virtue of nineteenth-century political citizenship, partisan loyalty is today dead and buried. American are now highly suspicious of parties, and tend to view party disagreements over policy as little more than special-interest bickering.[160] Roughly 40 percent of voters now identify themselves as independent.[161] Two out of three American voters routinely vote a split ticket.[162] Voters prefer, by a nearly two-to-one margin, divided over unified party control

158. According to Bob Pepperman Taylor, for example, the Progressives "for better or for worse and as much as any other generation in American history, set the stage for our own public life." Taylor, *Citizenship and Democratic Doubt*, 20. *See also* Levine, *The New Progressive Era.*

159. In one of the few recent attempts to assess empirically the quality of contemporary campaigns, Maisel, West, & Clifton use for their normative baseline what they call the "reform" belief that "a 'good' campaign involves substantive campaigns that present options to voters in a way that allows them to vote for candidates with whom they agree on fundamental matters." Maisel, West, & Clifton, *Evaluating Campaign Quality*, 10. Another recent study evaluating campaign quality begins from the normative premise that "the kind of electoral politics that most Americans want [is] principled policy debates that clarify what is truly at stake in every national election." Buchanan, *Presidential Campaign Quality*.

160. Hibbing & Theiss-Morse, *Stealth Democracy*, ch. 6.

161. Stanley & Niemi, *Vital Statistics on American Politics*, 114, Table 3-1.

162. Roper Poll, Feb. 1996, cited in Ladd, 1996 Vote, 14.

of the national executive and legislative branches.[163] Today's voters thus clearly feel free, and perhaps obligated, to judge candidates individually on the merits of their qualifications rather than solely in reference to their professions of partisanship.

Or consider the kinds of critiques of contemporary campaigns that appear routinely in the popular press. Perhaps no campaign event has come in for more sustained and unified criticism than the quadrennial presidential debates. "Elections," according to one prominent editorial page, ought to be "town meetings to form a more perfect community,"[164] and presidential debates, which "ought to be about the choices of ideas in the marketplace of politics,"[165] should therefore play an important role in the public processes of electoral democracy. Instead, critics from all points on the ideological spectrum agree that the presidential debates fall far short of this standard. To liberal columnist Frank Rich, the presidential debates are "Oprahfied, prescripted, content-free" events that "have more in common with 'The Gong Show' than with the three-hour intellectual exchanges of Lincoln and Douglas."[166] To conservative columnist George Will, the presidential debates are "tossed salads of brevity" that consist "primarily [of] the regurgitation of market-tested paragraphs."[167] Even among voters, barely half describe presidential debates as even "somewhat helpful" in informing their voting decisions.[168] None of this would surprise political philosopher Ronald Dworkin, who argues that "our national politics fails the standards of even a decent junior high school debate," contributing to a political life so debased as to "threaten our standing as a genuine democracy."[169]

The poor quality of the debates has led thoughtful commentators to ask questions that carry more than a whiff of despair. Have we, one asks, "lost the ability in our public discourse to speak to one another in a way that moves ideas forward, that can result in enlightenment"?[170] "Is Persuasion Dead?"

---

163. Harris Poll, Oct. 19, 2006 (46 percent to 25 percent).

164. Editorial, "Refining the Debates."

165. McCarthy, "A 'Minor' Problem With the Debates."

166. Rich, "The Next Infomercials."

167. Will, "The Uselessness of Debates."

168. Pew Research Center for the People & the Press survey conducted by Princeton Survey Research Associates, Nov. 10–12, 2000.

169. Dworkin, *Is Democracy Possible Here?*, 127, 130.

170. Sexton, "That Was No Debate."

inquires another, who goes on to ask: "Is it possible in America today to convince anyone of anything he doesn't already believe?"[171]

Yet if recent campaign debates among presidential candidates have been inadequate to the task—if they have fallen short of the requirements of the ideal campaign—what is the solution? Tellingly, the prevailing answer seems to be more and better debates. In 1968 and 1972, the presidential candidates debated once. In 1976, there were six debates: three during the primaries and three during the general election. By 1980 the total number of debates rose to eight, and in 1984 the candidates debated 14 times (11 primary, 3 general).[172] During the 2008 presidential campaign, the Democratic and Republican National Committees together sponsored a total of 47 official debates among the primary candidates, including a much-hyped format cosponsored with the popular video website YouTube, in which questions were posed by ordinary voters instead of journalists. The candidates also engaged in numerous unofficial debates as they barnstormed the country. And of course, the primary debates were followed by the usual series of general election debates by the party nominees, so that by the end of the campaign an attentive (or perhaps more accurately, obsessed) voter might easily have had the opportunity to take in more than 50 candidate debates.[173]

This enthusiastic commitment to the face-to-face debate as a mandatory feature of a proper election campaign suggests strongly an underlying belief that campaigns are and must be forums for the reasoned persuasion of voters. When 69 percent of voters believe "not much" or "nothing at all" of what they hear in televised political advertisements,[174] and nearly half of all voters rate television news and newspapers as doing either a poor or only fair job of presenting the candidates and the issues,[175] the public, the parties, and the candidates all seem to agree that a campaign must include some event at which the candidates can present their substantive views directly to the electorate in a manner that enables voters to make sound political judgments.[176]

---

171. Miller, "Is Persuasion Dead?"

172. Jamieson & Birdsell, *Presidential Debates*, App. 1: 222–27.

173. Fallows, "Rhetorical Questions"; Commission on Presidential Debates, www.debates.org; Todd & Felton, "Clocking the Candidates."

174. USA Today/Gallup Poll. Oct. 6–8, 2006.

175. The Harris Poll. Nov. 13–18, 2000.

176. Jamieson & Birdsell, for example, claim that presidential debates take place in "a climate more conducive to political learning than any other that the typical voter will seek or chance upon." Jamieson & Birdsell, *Presidential Debates*, 5. Alan Schroeder characterizes

If we pass from the views of the public to those of highly informed professionals, much the same picture appears. It is the business of political scientists to study campaigning and other aspects of political behavior, and to do so meaningfully they must employ some benchmark to orient their inquiries, for without such a benchmark they would have no way of knowing what phenomena are worth studying. How, then, do professional political scientists think about election campaigns? Their answer has been remarkably consistent for the last half century. According to the authors of a classic 1954 study of voting behavior, "[t]he democratic citizen is expected to be well informed about political affairs. He is supposed to know what the issues are, what their history is, what the relevant facts are, what alternatives are proposed, what the party stands for, what the likely consequences are."[177] Leading political scientists working today overwhelmingly share this view. "Politics, at its core, is about persuasion," insists one prominent research team.[178] "Political campaigns," according to another, "are expected to inform voters about issues of the day, to reduce their dependence on simplistic labels, and to enable them to reach reasoned choices."[179] "[T]he purpose of a campaign," claims another leading political scientist, "is to provide voters with good and convincing reasons to vote for their candidate."[180]

The public seems to have internalized this view. Those who abstain from electoral politics seem generally to feel a kind of guilty awareness that they have shirked a civic duty. One voter interviewed by the *Los Angeles Times* who left his house intending to vote but instead ended up at the gym probably summed up the feelings of many: "I know it's terrible."[181] At the same time, those who pay close attention to electoral politics and vote regularly are likely to congratulate themselves on discharging their civic obligation. The American public, in other words, seems to adhere to this day to the conception of democratic citizenship forged by the Progressives.

---

the debates as "'last-minute cram sessions for preparing the voting public.'" Schroeder, *Presidential Debates*, 207 (quoting Doris M. Graber, *Mass Media and American Politics* (Washington, D.C.: CQ Press 1997), 257).

177. Berelson, Lazarsfeld, & McPhee, *Voting*, 308.

178. Mutz, Sniderman, & Brody, *Political Persuasion*, 1.

179. Ansolabahere & Iyengar, *Going Negative*, 37.

180. Campbell, *The American Campaign*, 52.

181. Warren, "Election 2002," 2:1.

We seem to believe that, as democratic citizens, we labor under a not insignificant burden to be attentive, well-informed, rational participants in the political life of the nation. Yet, as we ourselves seem inclined to acknowledge, when judged by this standard our electoral politics fails to measure up.

TWO

Election Law and the Formation of Public Opinion

NOT LONG AFTER IT FIRST APPEARED, the deliberative ideal of election campaigns began, as social ideas often do, to infiltrate the law. Today, a rhetorical commitment to the importance of persuasion in electoral campaigns thoroughly suffuses our legal institutions. It is present in the ideology of the marketplace of ideas, which presupposes a meaningful competition among political ideas in which citizens choose among those ideas on the basis of their persuasiveness.[1] It is equally present in the theory of the First Amendment, long associated with the philosopher Alexander Meiklejohn, that the primary purpose of free speech is to enable citizens of a democracy to govern themselves intelligently.[2] The Supreme Court has explicitly elevated the process of persuasion in election campaigns to the status of constitutional doctrine: "The primary goal of all candidates," the Court has held, "is to carry on a successful campaign by communicating to the voters persuasive reasons for electing them."[3] "Competition in ideas and governmental policies," says the Court, "is at the core of our electoral process and of the First Amendment freedoms."[4] For that reason, "the First Amendment . . . has its fullest and most urgent application precisely to the conduct of campaigns for political office."[5]

On the face of it, this kind of emphatic commitment to free and open political expression suggests a constitutional regime of electoral politics that accords a central role in election campaigns to the process of persuasion. Election campaigns, however, do not take place in the abstract world described by broad, cross-cutting constitutional principles; they take place

1. *See, e.g.*, Ingber, "The Marketplace of Ideas"; Strauss, "Persuasion, Autonomy, and Freedom of Expression."

2. Meiklejohn, *Free Speech and Its Relation to Self-Government.*

3. Buckley v. Valeo, 424 U.S. 1, 101 (1976) (per curiam).

4. Williams v. Rhodes, 393 U.S. 23 (1968).

5. Monitor Patriot Co. v. Roy, 401 U.S. 265, 272 (1971).

in the real world of concrete legal and political institutions. If we examine the constitutional regimes shaping our actual electoral institutions, we shall see that they operate on a set of very different principles. In particular, much of the constitutional architecture structuring the electoral process is based not on a robust commitment to electoral persuasion but on its opposite—on the premise that very little of what we might think of as persuasion is to be expected in the electoral process. Thus, despite our gaudy commitment to persuasion as a principle of constitutional design, down in the constitutional boiler room our regulatory institutions do not expect persuasion, do little to encourage it, and may even operate in a way that suppresses it.

I shall illustrate this proposition by reference to four constitutional regimes that contribute significantly to the structure of contemporary American electoral politics: the rules by which candidates may earn a place on the ballot; the federal system of public financing of presidential elections; the associational rights of political parties; and the constitutional treatment of laws regulating the giving and spending of money in election campaigns.

Ballot Access Rules

In perhaps no area of constitutional jurisprudence is the disjunction between the Court's professed commitment to campaigns as forums for persuasion more at odds with its actual decisions than in the field of ballot access—the body of law that determines how and when candidates may obtain a place on the official election ballot. An election ballot is in a sense just a piece of paper, yet laws regulating the production of the ballot are among the most significant in an electoral democracy. Although such laws do not on their face purport to regulate much more than the terms upon which candidates may have their names printed on the ballot, in practice they exert an extremely powerful influence on the course of election campaigns. First and foremost, laws regulating access to the official ballot play a crucial gatekeeping role by establishing the conditions under which potential candidates for public office may become actual candidates.[6] Second, the necessity of

6. As Madison observed, "[a] Republic may be converted into an aristocracy or oligarchy as well by limiting the number capable of being elected, as the number authorised to elect." Madison, *Notes of the Debates in the Constitutional Convention*, Aug. 10, 1787.

complying with ballot access laws[7] means that ballot access rules often drive party and candidate decisions about the allocation of time, effort, and resources, especially early in the process of mounting a candidacy.

Although the Supreme Court has sometimes mentioned the gatekeeping function of ballot access laws as a reason for examining them closely,[8] in an extensive body of decisions adjudicating the constitutionality of state ballot access laws[9] it has focused its attention on a different aspect of ballot access rules: their implications for election campaigns. For more than 20 years, the Court has taken the position that the main constitutional interest in ballot access lies in its implications under the First Amendment for the ideological content of campaign discourse. In this area, the Court has held, "the rights of voters and the rights of candidates do not lend themselves to neat separation,"[10] and the principal reason for this interdependence is that "an election campaign is an effective platform for the expression of views on the issues of the day."[11] In consequence, the Court has long analyzed legal restrictions on the ability of candidates to secure a place on the ballot in terms of the First Amendment right of expressive association of candidates, their parties, and their supporters in the electorate.[12]

Much of the Court's language in the realm of ballot access expressly contemplates an ideologically focused campaign in which public opinion is formed endogenously, through a meaningful process of speech and persuasion.

---

7. Write-in voting is permitted in many states and can be used by voters and candidates as a way of circumventing ballot access laws, but no candidate would deem the possibility of waging a write-in campaign a meaningful substitute for a line on the official ballot form, as the Court has explicitly acknowledged. Anderson v. Celebrezze, 460 U.S. 780, 799 n.26 (1983) ("this opportunity [to cast a write-in vote] is not an adequate substitute for having the candidate's name appear on the printed ballot"). Nothing, moreover, requires states to permit any write-in voting at all. Burdick v. Takushi, 504 U.S. 428 (1992). Moreover, in many states candidates wishing to run write-in campaigns must themselves register as official candidates. *See, e.g.*, Mich. Comp. Laws Ann. § 168.737a(1) (West 1997); Ohio Rev. Code Ann. § 3513.041 (West 2006).

8. *E.g.*, Lubin v. Panish, 415 U.S. 709, 716 (1974) ("the voters can assert their preferences only through candidates or parties or both"); Bullock v. Carter, 405 U.S. 134, 143 (1972) (ballot access laws "limit the field of candidates from which voters might choose").

9. Ballot access, even for federal offices, is regulated almost exclusively by state law. States have the authority to regulate state and local level political processes as a matter of state sovereignty and self-governance. States have also been granted the authority to regulate federal congressional elections under Article I, § 4 of the U.S. Constitution and presidential elections under Art. II, § 1.

10. Bullock, 405 U.S. at 143.

11. Anderson, 460 U.S. at 788.

12. *Ibid.*, 787–88.

"Competition in ideas," the Court said in one of its earliest cases involving a constitutional challenge to ballot access restrictions, "is at the core of our electoral process."[13] For the Court, "an election campaign is a means of disseminating ideas"[14] and a "platform for the expression of views."[15] Formal candidates for office, the Court has often argued, play a critical role in the competition among ideas during a campaign because only such candidates are granted "the opportunity . . . to wage a ballot-connected campaign."[16] Nothing of course prevents candidates who are not listed on the ballot from waging a kind of rump campaign aimed at drawing attention to themselves or the issues they advocate, but a campaign that is connected to the ballot is more effective than one waged by unofficial candidates because, as the Court has observed, an official candidate listed on the ballot "serves as a rallying point for like-minded citizens."[17] To deny a party's candidates a place on the ballot makes their candidacies more hypothetical than real, thereby "eliminat[ing] the basic incentive that all political parties have" to advance their ideological goals[18] and impoverishing the campaign itself.

For these reasons, the Court has proclaimed its skepticism of state ballot access restrictions. Such restrictions, the Court has held, not only "jeopardize [a] form of political expression,"[19] but also impair the central function of campaigns to serve as forums for ideological persuasion on topics of public importance. The Court has therefore taken the position that if campaign discourse is to be "'uninhibited, robust, and wide-open,'"[20] election campaigns must not be "monopolized by the existing political parties."[21] Parties and

---

13. Williams v. Rhodes, 393 U.S. 23, 32 (1968).

14. Illinois State Board of Elections v. Socialist Workers Party, 440 U.S. 173, 186 (1979).

15. Anderson, 460 U.S. at 788.

16. Munro v. Socialist Workers Party, 479 U.S. 189, 199 (1986).

17. Anderson, 460 U.S. at 788. *See also* Buckley, 424 U.S. at 101 ("qualifying for the ballot [is] a step that, with rare exceptions, is essential to successful effort").

18. *Ibid.*, n.8.

19. Illinois State Board of Elections, 440 U.S. at 186. Political scientists have begun to provide empirical support for this contention. For example, Lacy and Burden found that Ross Perot's 1992 independent run for the presidency "increased turnout by nearly three percentage points, and one out of every five Perot supporters would not have voted had Perot not entered the race." Lacy and Burden, "The Vote-Stealing and Turnout Effects of Ross Perot in the 1992 U.S. Presidential Elections."

20. Anderson, 460 U.S. at 794, quoting New York Times Co. v. Sullivan, 376 U.S. 254, 270 (1964).

21. *Ibid.*

candidates must accordingly be "free to associate, to proselytize, to speak, to write, and to organize campaigns for any school of thought they wish,"[22] and to do so from the platform of a line on the official ballot. After all, the Court has noted, even losing candidacies have "contributed to [the public's] understanding of the issues;"[23] "Abolitionists, Progressives, and Populists have undeniably had influence, if not always electoral success."[24]

Despite the Court's expressed commitment to ballot access as a vehicle for securing the campaign-endogenous formation of public political opinion, state ballot access laws have, with the Court's approval, generally taken precisely the opposite approach. The main concern of today's ballot access laws typically is not to create a campaign in which many candidates and many points of view compete for public approval, but rather to *narrow* the scope of campaign discourse by restricting ballot access to candidates who support positions that *already* command substantial support among the electorate before the campaign has even begun. That is to say, most ballot access laws contemplate election campaigns weighted heavily toward the simple tabulation of public opinion that has been formed exogenously to the campaign.

Until the late nineteenth century, American election ballots were printed privately, by political parties.[25] The state provided a ballot box and tabulated the results, but any party could promote its candidates and supply its supporters with a ballot listing the party's candidates. As a result, ballot access in the contemporary sense was completely open. By the end of the nineteenth century, this system had proven itself so susceptible to corruption that, in a wave of reform that quickly swept the nation,[26] most states adopted the so-called "Australian ballot" system. Under this system, private ballots were disallowed, an official ballot was prepared by the state at public expense,

22. Jenness v. Fortson, 403 U.S. 431, 438 (1971).

23. Anderson, 460 U.S. at 798.

24. Illinois State Board of Elections, 440 U.S. at 185–86. *See also* Munro v. Socialist Workers Party, 479 U.S. 189, 200 (1986) (Marshall, J., dissenting) ("The minor party's often unconventional positions broaden political debate, expand the range of issues with which the electorate is concerned, and influence the positions of the majority, in some instances ultimately becoming majority positions").

25. Fredman, *The Australian Ballot*, ix, 21, 28; Bensel, *The American Ballot Box in the Mid-Nineteenth Century*, 14–17; Argersinger, "'A Place on the Ballot,'" 290.

26. See Fredman, *The Australian Ballot*, 46–63.

and voters cast their ballots in secrecy.[27] By taking over the production of the ballot, however, the state was forced to decide whom to list as official candidates for office. In South Australia and in Britain, both of which had previously adopted the system, virtually free ballot access was preserved by permitting candidates a place on the official ballot upon presentation of a nominating petition containing two or ten signatures, respectively.[28] In the United States, on the other hand, access to the official ballot has been from the beginning considerably more restrictive; a widely copied Massachusetts law of 1888, for example, required candidates for statewide office to submit nominating petitions containing 1,000 signatures.[29]

Today, most states regulate ballot access according to a simple principle: parties and candidates that, *prior to* campaigning for office, can demonstrate substantial existing support among the electorate are permitted a place on the ballot; parties and candidates that cannot demonstrate such support are excluded. Consider Connecticut's not atypical scheme of ballot access. Like many states, Connecticut distinguishes between a "major party" and a "minor party." A "major party" is any party whose candidate for governor at the last gubernatorial election polled at least 20 percent of the total votes cast or whose members comprise at least 20 percent of the total number of voters who have registered as members of a political party.[30] A "minor party" is any party whose candidate "for the office in question" received at least 1 percent of the total votes cast.[31] Under the statute, candidates nominated by parties that have qualified as major or minor are listed automatically on the ballot.[32] In contrast, candidates of parties that were not sufficiently popular at the most recent election to qualify as "minor," and candidates wishing to run as independents, must make a showing of current support by filing nominating petitions containing signatures equal to 1 percent of the number of votes cast at the preceding election for the office for which they are running, or 7,500, whichever is less.[33] Connecticut's scheme thus makes

27. Argersinger, "'A Place on the Ballot,'" 291.

28. Fredman, *The Australian Ballot*, 47.

29. *Ibid.*

30. Conn. Gen. Stat. § 9-372(5).

31. *Ibid.*, § 9-372(6).

32. *Ibid.*, § 9-379.

33. *Ibid.*, § 9-453d. Candidates nominated by major and minor parties are precluded from qualifying for the ballot by nominating petition. *Ibid.*, § 9-453t.

ballot access contingent upon a showing of electoral support well before the commencement of the official campaign.[34] In the case of major and minor party candidates, support is simply presumed on the basis of recent electoral performance. All other candidates must show substantial support by producing signed nominating petitions before being admitted to the ballot.

Connecticut's ballot access scheme is in some ways on the generous side. In some states, independent candidates and candidates representing parties that do not qualify for automatic ballot access must collect signatures of as many as 5 percent of the votes cast at the last election to obtain a ballot position.[35] Some states, moreover, impose additional geographical distribution requirements on signature gathering; in New York, for example, candidates for statewide office must not only collect a total number of signatures equal to 5 percent of the party's total registered membership, but must in addition collect a certain proportion of those signatures from each of one-half of the state's congressional districts.[36] Also, unlike Connecticut, which treats major and minor party candidates equally, some states subject minor parties to more onerous ballot qualification requirements.[37] In every state, however, the major parties enjoy a continuing presumption of access to the ballot on account of their prior record of electoral success.

The burden of these ballot access requirements on third-party and independent candidates should not be underestimated. To obtain signatures of even 1 percent of the electorate for statewide office can require in large states a heroic effort. In Florida until 1998, third-party and independent candidates for governor had to obtain nearly 200,000 signatures, a burden no candidate ever successfully carried.[38] Nominating signatures, moreover,

---

34. Nominating petitions must be filed no later than 90 days before election day. *Ibid.*, § 9-453i. *See also ibid.* § 9-423(a) (establishing second Tuesday in August as last date for party primary elections).

35. *See, e.g.*, Me. Ann. Stat. tit. 21-A, ch. 5, § 303(3) (for a new party seeking to obtain a ballot position through petitions, the petitions "must contain the signatures and legal addresses of voters equal in number to at least 5% of the total vote cast in the State for Governor at the last preceding gubernatorial election"). Maine does, however, offer an alternative avenue of ballot access for candidates running as independents. *Ibid.*, § 354.

36. N.Y. Election Law, § 6-136(1). The 5 percent requirement is, however, capped at 15,000 signatures. *Ibid.*

37. *See, e.g.*, American Party of Texas v. White, 415 U.S. 767 (1964).

38. Winger, "Ballot Access: A Formidable Barrier to Fair Participation." Florida substantially eased this requirement in 1998 after an initiative amendment to the Florida Constitution

are costly to obtain. Commercial signature-collection firms routinely charge more than $1 per signature,[39] meaning that small-party or independent candidates might conceivably exhaust a good portion of their campaign resources merely qualifying for the right to run, if indeed they have the resources to qualify at all.

The effect of these kinds of ballot access schemes is of course to make it extremely unlikely that any views will be presented to the electorate during the campaign that do not, prior to the campaign, already enjoy widespread public support. The typical ballot access regime thus serves not as an initial move in a campaign-endogenous process of open debate by diverse candidates and their supporters, but as a first-pass method of narrowing the scope of discussion to those ideas that are already widely held. This may well be a practical principle on which to run a smooth election campaign, yet it is an approach that undercuts at least to some degree the possibility of campaign-endogenous public opinion formation by limiting the slate of official candidates to those who already enjoy some popularity as the champions of positions that large numbers of voters exogenously hold.

Given the Court's strong rhetorical commitment to open ballot access as a means of encouraging campaign-endogenous opinion formation, one might expect it to take a dim view of these kinds of restrictions. It has not. The Court has, to be sure, invalidated certain state ballot access laws as unduly exclusionary on the grounds that they require the payment of excessive filing fees,[40] require candidates to announce their candidacy too early in the political season,[41] or interact so as to establish an indefeasible ballot

---

required equality of candidate ballot access. Winger, "How Many Parties Ought to Be on the Ballot?," 177 n.55.

39. In California initiative drives, the present going rate appears to be between one and two dollars per signature, *e.g.*, Marelius and Mendel, "Governor's Backers, Foes Scramble to Make Ballot" (reporting going rate of $1 to $1.50 per signature), but considerably higher figures have often been reported. *See, e.g.*, Salladay, "Game of the Name Is Profit" (reporting expenditures of $1 to $2 per signature); Hubbell and Gledhill, "Petition Circulators Cleaning Up" ($3 to $3.50 per signature); Skelton, "Gov.'s Performance in Role of 'Reformer' Seems a Little Strained" (up to $10 per signature).

40. Bullock v. Carter, 405 U.S. 134 (1972); Lubin v. Panish, 415 U.S. 709 (1974).

41. Anderson v. Celebrezze, 460 U.S. 780 (1983).

access monopoly in favor of the two major parties.[42] But the Court has never invalidated a ballot access restriction solely on the ground that it required an excessive showing of precampaign support, or that it treated the major, established parties more leniently in its access requirements than minor parties or independent candidates.[43]

In fact, the Court has quite enthusiastically endorsed state ballot access laws that restrict ballot positions to candidates who are able to show a significant level of exogenous public support. The Court has been quite clear on this point: "There is surely an important state interest in requiring some preliminary showing of a significant modicum of support before printing the name of a political organization's candidate on the ballot."[44] But what is the nature of the state's interest? On this question, the Court has been blunt: to admit to the ballot candidates who do not *begin* the campaign enjoying "a significant modicum" of public support would be to tolerate a kind of "ballot . . . clutter[ ]"[45] or "clogging of [the] election machinery" that would

42. Williams v. Rhodes, 393 U.S. 23 (1968).

43. *See* Jenness v. Fortson, 403 U.S. 431 (1971) (upholding Georgia ballot access requirement that independents collect signatures equal to 5 percent of the total number of voters eligible to vote at the last election); Storer v. Brown, 415 U.S. 724 (1974) (upholding California ballot access requirement that independent candidates collect signatures equaling five percent of total votes cast in the preceding election, during a 24-day period, exclusively from registered voters who vote in a party primary); American Party of Texas v. White, 415 U.S. 767 (1974) (upholding Texas ballot access scheme imposing successively more onerous requirements on major parties, minor parties, nonminor parties, and independents); Munro v. Socialist Workers Party, 479 U.S. 189 (1986) (upholding ballot access requirement that minor party candidates receive at least 1 percent of the total votes cast in the primary to qualify for a ballot position).

44. Jenness, 403 U.S. at 442. *See also* Lubin, 415 U.S. at 718 ("States may . . . impose on minor political parties the precondition of demonstrating the existence of some reasonable quantum of voter support by requiring such parties to file petitions for a place on the ballot signed by a percentage of those who voted in a prior election"); Storer, 415 U.S. at 733 (states may require independent candidates to "qualify for the ballot by demonstrating substantial public support"). The same interest, the Court has held, justifies a state ban on fusion candidacies, in which major party candidates run simultaneously on the ballot lines of minor parties. Failing to ban such candidacies would "undercut [the state's] ballot-access regime by allowing minor parties to capitalize on the popularity of another party's candidate, rather than on their own appeal to the voters, in order to secure access to the ballot." Timmons v. Twin Cities Area New Party, 520 U.S. 351, 366 (1997).

45. Munro, 479 U.S. at 196.

court "voter confusion" at best,[46] and would at worst open the door to "unrestrained factionalism"[47] and even "chaos."[48] Indeed, the Court has gone further: routine ballot access restrictions are constitutional because "a State has an interest, if not a duty, to protect the integrity of its political processes from frivolous or fraudulent candidacies."[49] A candidate, then, who enters a campaign hoping actually to persuade voters to a position that they do not in large numbers already hold before the campaign begins therefore does not display the "seriousness" necessary to justify a place on the ballot;[50] he or she is a "spurious candidate[]" that the state is justified in "weeding out."[51]

This is surely a remarkable judicial record. In the same group of cases in which the Court enthusiastically touts endogenous public opinion formation as the essence of electoral democracy, and acknowledges the connection between official candidacy and the ability to persuade, it simultaneously condemns an institutional arrangement—relatively unrestricted ballot access—that might well assist in producing just the kinds of campaigns the Court endorses.[52] It is one thing to fear electoral chaos and disorder[53] but quite another to equate it with the give and take of genuine persuasion during the campaign. On the other hand, a candidate's attempt to use his candidacy as a platform to persuade the electorate to a position it does not already hold looks disorderly only if one conceives of the true function of election campaigns as simply to record accurately the electorate's exogenously held preferences. With its ballot access jurisprudence, the Court

46. Bullock, 405 U.S. at 145.

47. Storer, 415 U.S. at 736.

48. *Ibid.*, 730.

49. Bullock, 405 U.S. at 145.

50. Lubin, 415 U.S. at 715; *see also ibid.* at 718 (producing signed petitions is a way for a candidate to "demonstrate the 'seriousness' of his candidacy").

51. Bullock, 405 U.S. at 146. The Court used virtually identical reasoning in upholding the decision of a public television station to exclude from a televised campaign debate among candidates for Congress all but the major party candidates. Arkansas Educational Television Comm'n v. Forbes, 523 U.S. 666 (1998).

52. Indeed, since the Court began deciding ballot access cases, states have interpreted its rulings to authorize *increased* restrictions on minor party and independent candidates. Winger, "The Supreme Court and the Burial of Ballot Access."

53. Pildes, "Democracy and Disorder" (arguing that much of the Supreme Court's election jurisprudence displays an underlying fear of democracy as excessively disorderly and chaotic).

has crafted legal institutions best suited to doing just that: tabulating campaign-exogenous public opinion.

Public Financing of Election Campaigns

In a series of statutes stretching back to 1966, Congress has provided for public financing of presidential election campaigns.[54] The present statutory scheme of public financing and the Supreme Court's reasoning in upholding it both bear striking similarities to the ballot access laws and cases just described. Under the law, candidates for President may receive public financing in amounts that differ depending upon the precampaign popularity of the political party of which the candidate is the nominee. For purposes of funding, a "major party" is one whose presidential candidate received at least 25 percent of the vote in the preceding presidential election;[55] a "minor party" is a party whose presidential candidate received between 5 and 25 percent of the vote in the last presidential election;[56] and a "new party" is any other political party.[57]

Under the statute, candidates nominated by a major party are eligible to receive for the general election the full amount of public funds to which the law entitles them.[58] In 2008, this amount was $84 million.[59] Minor party candidates, however, are not entitled to the full amount of public funds made available to candidates of the major parties; they are entitled instead only to a proportion of that amount corresponding to the ratio by which their party's candidate in the previous presidential election fell short of the average number of votes earned in that election by the candidates of the major parties.[60] Candidates of new political parties get no public financing up front, but are entitled to a postelection disbursement of public funds in proportion to the number of votes they

54. This history is recounted briefly in Buckley, 424 U.S. at 85 and n.114.

55. 26 U.S.C. § 9002(6).

56. *Ibid.*, § 9002(7).

57. *Ibid.*, § 9002(8).

58. *Ibid.*, § 9004(a)(1).

59. Federal Election Commission, Presidential Spending Limits for 2008, http://www.fec.gov/pages/brochures/pubfund_limits_2008.html.

60. 26 U.S.C. § 9004(a)(2)(A).

actually receive, provided they receive at least 5 percent of the total popular presidential vote.[61] Candidates who run as independents, without the backing of any political party, even a new one, may not receive public financing.[62]

Under this scheme, then, public campaign funds are allocated on the basis of a candidate's estimated precampaign support, creating a significant bias in favor of candidates who support positions that are widely held before the campaign commences. Although the federal public financing scheme is thus similar to the typical ballot access law, in which ballot access becomes easier as a candidate's estimated precampaign support increases, candidates for President who support less popular views actually suffer under this scheme from multiple disadvantages. First, because their views are not already widely held before the campaign begins, they must advance their positions through actual campaign-endogenous persuasion, requiring them to work harder during the campaign to earn votes. Second, again because their views are not exogenously popular, they have greater difficulty securing public funding for their election campaigns. Third, because they will have fewer resources at the outset of the campaign than candidates who enter it supporting exogenously popular views, they will be unable to keep pace with their competitors' spending, a disadvantage that, for reasons to be further elaborated below, will likely cause them to fall even further behind in appealing successfully for votes. In short, the bias under this financing system in favor of exogenously popular political opinion is severe.

The Supreme Court has had no difficulty sustaining this method of public financing. As in the ballot access area, the Court has identified the campaign-endogenous formation of public opinion through persuasive speech as the central value of concern: "Subtitle H [the public financing provision] is a congressional effort, not to abridge, restrict, or censor speech, but rather to use public money to facilitate and enlarge public discussion and participation in the electoral process, goals vital to a self-governing people."[63] Nevertheless, the Court dismissed challenges to the financing scheme's differential treatment of major and minor party candidates in terms similar to those it has employed in the ballot access arena: "Congress' interest in not funding hopeless candidacies with large sums of public money . . . necessarily justifies the withholding of public assistance from candidates without significant

61. *Ibid.*, § 9004(a)(3).

62. Given the possibility of some reimbursement for new party candidates under § 9004(a)(3), functionally independent candidates have a strong financial incentive to organize new parties as vehicles for their independent runs.

public support."[64] Clearly, if a candidacy that does not from the very outset of the campaign enjoy substantial public support is "hopeless," it can only be because persuasion of large numbers of voters during the campaign is simply impossible and therefore not to be expected—even with a full measure of public funding. This in turn suggests, of course, that the favored major party candidates, if they are sensible, are unlikely to spend their public campaign funds on attempts to persuade voters who do not already agree with them, but are more likely to invest that money in mobilization efforts designed to ensure that existing supporters turn out on election day to vote.

It is possible to design a system of public campaign financing on different premises. Under Maine's Clean Election Act, for example, *all* candidates who qualify for public funding receive equal amounts of public funds.[65] Candidates may qualify, moreover, irrespective of their party affiliation; indeed, they need profess no party affiliation whatsoever. All candidates need do to qualify is to raise a modest number of $5 contributions.[66] Upon qualifying, all candidates then have equal amounts of public funds and may not spend any additional private money. If persuasion of voters during a campaign through political speech is possible, then under the Maine system all candidates have in theory the same chance to persuade the electorate. Of course, candidates for Maine offices who begin the campaign espousing views that are already widely held among voters will have an advantage over candidates who advance less popular views. But the Maine system seems to take seriously the notion of campaign-endogenous opinion formation in a way that the federal system does not. I mention this not to praise the Maine approach over the federal approach but merely to emphasize the chief point: federal constitutional law bows frequently and reverentially to the concept of election campaigns as forums for political persuasion, yet in its actual operation institutionalizes a system in which significant, meaningful persuasion is not realistically to be expected, and in fact may at times be powerfully suppressed.[67]

---

63. Buckley, 424 U.S. at 92–93.

64. *Ibid.*, 96.

65. Maine Rev. Stat. tit. 21-A, ch. 14, § 1125(8).

66. *Ibid.*, § 1125(3).

67. In fact, the Court has gone further. In Arkansas Educational Television Commission v. Forbes, 523 U.S. 666 (1998), the Court upheld the decision of a government-financed public television station to exclude from campaign debates a candidate who did not command significant public support before the debate. As a result, candidates who do not express exogenously popular views, but hope instead to persuade the electorate

Political Party Associational Rights and the Responsible Party Model

The U.S. Constitution makes no mention of political parties, and the Framers harbored a well-known antipathy toward them,[68] yet political parties have nevertheless emerged as integral and indeed indispensable components of the American electoral process.[69] While not without their critics,[70] parties often are credited with performing numerous democratically valuable functions such as organizing electoral competition,[71] providing important information to the voting public,[72] mobilizing the electorate,[73] ensuring the responsiveness of elected officials,[74] and even organizing public understandings of the political world.[75] Because parties play such a substantial role in the organization and operation of the electoral system, and because that system is by definition a critical public institution of democratic self-governance, legislators have often viewed parties as fundamentally public organizations whose activities may be freely regulated to promote

---

during the campaign, not only can be kept off the ballot and denied public financing, but can actually be denied perhaps the only meaningful opportunity to persuade the electorate that the campaign season might offer. Former Minnesota governor Jesse Ventura, who won election as a minor party candidate of the Reform Party, claimed that being permitted to debate major party candidates early in the campaign season played an important role in his eventual electoral success. Ventura's account is retold in Issacharoff, Karlan, and Pildes, *The Law of Democracy*, 444–45.

68. According to one prominent commentator, the "root idea" of Anglo-American political thought concerning parties was that "parties are evil." Hofstadter, *The Idea of a Party System*, 9. A similar story appears in Leonard, *The Invention of Party Politics*, chs. 1–2.

69. "It should be stated flatly at the outset that . . . the political parties created democracy and that modern democracy is unthinkable save in terms of the parties." Schattschneider, *Party Government*, 1.

70. *See, e.g.*, American Political Science Association, "Toward a More Responsible Two-Party System," 15–24.

71. *E.g.*, Issacharoff, "Private Parties with Public Purposes," 276.

72. *E.g.*, Sorauf, *Party Politics in America*, 20; Campbell, *The American Voter*, chs. 6–8.

73. *See, e.g.*, Huckfeldt and Sprague, "Political Parties and Electoral Mobilization"; Caldeira, Clausen, and Patterson, "Partisan Mobilization and Electoral Participation."

74. Ranney, *The Doctrine of Responsible Party Government*, 10–14; American Political Science Association, "Toward a More Responsible Two-Party System," 15–19.

75. Rosenblum, "Political Parties as Membership Groups," 826 ("Alone among associations, then, parties offer a comprehensive map of the political world—cues and symbols and framing devices that extend across issues and candidates and over time").

public goals.[76] As a result, questions concerning the degree to which the activities of parties may be regulated by law appear regularly on the judicial docket.

In addressing these questions, the U.S. Supreme Court has looked to the Constitution for answers and has found them primarily in the First Amendment right of expressive association,[77] a doctrine that the Court has construed to provide parties with extremely robust immunity from unwanted government regulation. The Court first recognized the right of expressive association in a 1958 case, *NAACP v. Alabama*,[78] in which it characterized the NAACP as a group dedicated to public advancement of the shared political beliefs of its members. The freedom of speech, the Court implied, carries with it a correlative right to organize for the purpose of speaking effectively. Because, the Court said, "[e]ffective advocacy of both public and private points of view, particularly controversial ones, is undeniably enhanced by group association,"[79] the Constitution protects not only speech, but also the associative forms and relationships that permit individuals to enhance their speech through collective action. In later cases, the Court applied this analysis to political parties, which it has tended to view as paradigms of expressive associations:

> For more than [three] decades, this Court has recognized the constitutional right of citizens to create and develop new political parties. The right derives from the First and Fourteenth Amendments and advances the constitutional interest of likeminded voters to gather in pursuit of common political ends, thus enlarging the opportunities of all voters to express their own political preferences.[80]

76. As Samuel Issacharoff has observed, parties are sometimes treated by law as "the political equivalent of common carriers subject to ordinary regulatory oversight." Issacharoff, "Private Parties with Public Purposes," 278.

77. The right to expressive association is distinct from what the Court has called the right of intimate association. The latter is based not on the First Amendment, but on conceptions of personal autonomy in the choice of friends and intimate associates that are rooted in substantive due process. *See* Roberts v. United States Jaycees, 468 U.S. 609, 617–19 (1984).

78. 357 U.S. 449 (1958).

79. *Ibid.*, 460.

80. Norman v. Reed 502 U.S. 279, 288 (1992). Accord New York State Board of Elections v. Lopez Torres, 128 S.Ct. 791 (2008).

The Court has invoked the right to expressive association on numerous occasions to invalidate government regulations to which parties have objected.[81]

The main benefit that parties derive from the right to expressive association is the ability to control the content of their public communications. As speakers, parties enjoy the same freedom from censorship and content regulation that individuals possess directly under the First Amendment's first-order protection for freedom of speech.[82] The second-order right of expressive association, however, provides parties with the ability to control the content of their speech in another way: by controlling their membership.[83] Thus, parties may not only decide who can be a member, but also may decide, even over the objection of the state, who will be eligible to participate and vote in primary elections to select party candidates.[84] On this view, a party must be able to control its membership in order effectively to control its speech because the presence within an organization of individuals who do not share a commitment to its goals and positions can contradict or undermine the organization's message. This might occur when unwanted members deliver a contrarian message under the organizational banner,[85] or when their mere presence within the organization by itself delivers a message that conflicts with the one the organization wishes to send.[86]

Considered in isolation, application of the right of expressive association to political parties appears consistent with a constitutional commitment to

---

81. *E.g.*, Cousins v. Wigoda, 419 U.S. 477 (1974); Tashjian v. Republican Party, 479 U.S. 208 (1986); Eu v. San Francisco County Democratic Central Committee, 489 U.S. 214 (1989); California Democratic Party v. Jones, 530 U.S. 567 (2000).

82. Eu v. San Francisco County Democratic Cent. Comm., 489 U.S. 214 (1989).

83. Democratic Party of United States v. Wisconsin, 450 U.S. 107, 122 (1981) ("the freedom to associate for the 'common advancement of political beliefs' necessarily presupposes the freedom to identify the people who constitute the association, and to limit the association to those people only") (citation omitted). Parties cannot, however, exclude members on the basis of constitutionally prohibited criteria such as race. Smith v. Allwright, 321 U.S. 649 (1944).

84. *See* Tashjian v. Republican Party, 479 U.S. 208 (1986); California Democratic Party v. Jones, 530 U.S. 567 (2000).

85. Hurley v. Irish-American Gay, Lesbian and Bisexual Group, 515 U.S. 557 (1995).

86. Boy Scouts of American v. Dale, 530 U.S. 640 (2000). An especially cogent example of this is the 1992 decision of the Georgia Republican Party to forbid David Duke, a former leader of the Ku Klux Klan, from running in Georgia's Republican presidential primary, an act tantamount to expelling him from the state party. The Court of Appeals for the Eleventh Circuit sustained the party's action. Duke v. Cleland, 954 F.2d 1526 (11th Cir. 1992).

persuasion as a significant element of electoral competition. After all, the right of expressive association is based on the idea that individuals can speak more effectively, and thereby presumably reach and persuade more listeners, when they act in concert with others of similar views. Considered, however, in its institutional setting of electoral competition in a two-party system, the right of expressive association functions quite differently. In fact, the doctrine contributes significantly to the institutionalization of a system of party competition in which, paradoxically, deliberative persuasion of voters plays a minimal role. This is because, in elaborating and applying to political parties a robust right of expressive association, the Supreme Court has essentially constitutionalized under the First Amendment a version of the "responsible party" model of politics elaborated by American political scientists during the 1950s—a model that *rejects* the idea that meaningful voter participation is an important ingredient of electoral politics.

The Responsible Party Model

The responsible party model has its origins in Joseph Schumpeter's influential minimalist theory of mass democracy.[87] Schumpeter argued that the classic liberal theory of democracy, in which the legitimacy of government depends upon a system of active popular sovereignty implemented through democratic elections, rests on a blatant fallacy: that the people of a democracy select representatives to do their bidding and thus to implement their will.[88] This view is false, according to Schumpeter, mainly because the citizenry of a modern mass democracy does not in fact actively determine its wishes and then select leaders to implement its instructions, but instead does nothing more than passively authorize leaders to pursue policies chosen by those leaders. As Schumpeter famously summarized his critique: "the democratic method is that institutional arrangement for arriving at political decisions in which individuals acquire the power to decide by means of a competitive struggle for the people's vote."[89]

---

87. Schumpeter, *Capitalism, Socialism and Democracy*. Ranney traces the roots of the doctrine back considerably further, to Woodrow Wilson and A. Lawrence Lowell. *See* Ranney, *The Doctrine of Responsible Party Government*, 25–69.

88. Schumpeter, *Capitalism, Socialism and Democracy*, 250–68.

89. *Ibid.*, 269.

Shortly after its appearance, Schumpeter's theory was firmly embraced by mainstream American political science in the form of the "responsible party" model of democratic governance. According to Austin Ranney, its most articulate expositor, the responsible party model contemplates that the people do not actively participate in the formulation of collective policy goals, but rather exercise a form of much more indirect "*control* over the government in this sense: If half-plus-one of the people feel their wants are not being satisfied, they can, in peaceful and orderly elections coming at frequent intervals, replace the set of rulers in power with an alternate set."[90] This form of popular control requires political parties because only parties "can provide the coherent, unified sets of rulers who will assume collective responsibility to the people for the manner in which government is carried on."[91] The possibility of meaningful popular control over government, however, depends upon the people being presented with a clear choice:

> There must exist at least two (and preferable only two) unified, disciplined political parties. Each has its conception of what the people want and a program of various measures designed to satisfy those wants. In a pre-election campaign each attempts to convince a majority of the people that its program will best do what the people want done. In the election each voter votes for a particular candidate in his district, primarily because that candidate is a member of the party which the voter wants to take power, and only secondarily because he prefers the individual qualities of one candidate to those of the other. The party which secures a majority of the offices of government in the election then takes over the entire power of the government and the entire responsibility for what the government does. It then proceeds to put its program into effect.[92]

The Supreme Court's jurisprudence of political parties as expressive associations tracks closely the basic assumptions of the responsible party model. Under the doctrine of expressive association, a political party is defined as an organization devoted centrally to a set of ideas: it is an association of like-minded

---

90. Ranney, *The Doctrine of Responsible Party Government*, 10.

91. *Ibid.*, 12.

92. *Ibid.* A similar conception is articulated in the 1950 special report of the American Political Science Association's Committee on Political Parties. *See* American Political Science Association, "Toward a More Responsible Two-Party System," 15–24.

individuals dedicated to the advancement, ultimately through electoral success, of a set of policies to which all members subscribe—precisely what a party should be under the responsible party model.[93] Furthermore, under the doctrine of expressive association, a party has the right to exclude from membership and participation individuals who do not share its members' convictions, thereby allowing the party to maintain its ideological purity. This authority in turn ensures that parties will be able to differentiate themselves as sharply as possible, in turn providing the electorate with a set of clear and coherent alternatives—again, precisely the kind of boundary maintenance required by the responsible party model.[94] Indeed, it is doubtless no coincidence that the Court's jurisprudence of expressive association first emerged in the 1950s, contemporaneously with the emergence of the responsible party model in political science, and came to full flower during the 1970s and'80s, at a time when many political scientists began loudly to bemoan the decline of the party system and to call openly for its renewal.[95]

One of the distinguishing features of the responsible party model of election campaigns is the diminished and highly circumscribed role it prescribes in the electoral process for engagement and persuasion of individual voters. In its more extreme versions, the responsible party model attributes to the electorate virtually no capacity or independent agency: "the electoral mass," said Schumpeter, "is incapable of action other than a stampede."[96] Thus for Schumpeter, at least, a modern election campaign is not and cannot be an attempt to persuade the electorate through reasoned argument; it is at most

93. The Court recently made this extremely clear, if there had been any doubt, in Clingman v. Beaver, 544 U.S. 581 (2005), when it upheld Oklahoma's "semi-closed" primary system in which parties were prohibited from allowing any nonparty members other than independents to vote in their primaries. A voter's desire to vote in a party's primary while remaining affiliated with a different party, the Court reasoned, represents a nonideological form of association not entitled to constitutional protection: "Their interest is in casting a vote for [another party's] candidate in a particular primary election, rather than in banding together with fellow citizens committed to [that party's] political goals and ideals." *Ibid.*, 588.

94. The Court has affirmed the authority of the state to police the clarity of party identity. *See* Clingman v. Beaver, 544 U.S. 581 (2005) (state may bar a party from permitting members of other parties to vote in its primary); Timmons v. Twin Cities area New Party, 520 U.S. 351 (1997) (state may prohibit a party from designating as its candidate a person who is the candidate of another party).

95. *See, e.g.*, Broder, *The Party's Over*; Kirkpatrick, *Dismantling the Parties*; Crotty, *American Parties in Decline*; Wattenberg, *The Decline of American Political Parties*.

96. Schumpeter, *Capitalism, Socialism, and Democracy*, 283.

an attempt to induce a stampede.[97] The political scientists who built the responsible party model on Schumpeter's foundation did not share to the same degree Schumpeter's apparent contempt for the capacity of the modern democratic citizenry.[98] Yet even so, like Schumpeter, they plainly contemplated a degree of citizen capacity for and engagement in electoral politics that falls considerably short of the role that citizens had previously been thought to play in prevailing democratic theories.

The diminished role of voters in the responsible party model results primarily from the diminished nature of the electoral decision that the model attributes to them. According to the model, democracy does not consist in unconstrained reflection and deliberation by the people followed by a popular choice among candidates competing to do the people's bidding. It involves instead something much less: unconstrained reflection and deliberation by political elites, organized in competing parties, followed by approval or disapproval by the electorate of the parties' proposed political programs. Indeed, a critical assumption of the responsible party model is that voters do not in general independently formulate opinions on matters of public policy because they lack the information, time, and expertise necessary to do so.[99] An election, on this view, is not—or certainly need not be—an occasion for serious public reflection, deliberation, and debate; it is instead nothing more than a very gross kind of referendum on the performance of the party currently in power. This is just the kind of decision that, on the model's assumptions, appropriately matches voters' capacities with their responsibilities as citizens: voters need not hold opinions on the desirability of particular policies, the nature of the common good, or any other aspect of public affairs; all they need to know is whether they generally approve or disapprove of the incumbent administration. So far as issues and positions are concerned, the parties do all the heavy lifting.[100]

---

97. As Schumpeter openly proclaimed: "The psycho-technics of party management and party advertising, slogans and marching tunes, are not accessories. They are of the essence of politics." *Ibid.*

98. The authors of the APSA report, for example, explicitly rejected a view of politics as simply the pure clashing of interest groups, American Political Science Association, "Toward a More Responsible Two-Party System," 16, 19, and spoke repeatedly of the need for the public to be able to make an "intelligent" choice, and of party differentiation as necessary for "reasonable and profitable discussion." *Ibid.*, 22.

99. Ranney, *The Doctrine of Responsible Party Government*, 10.

100. *See* Issacharoff and Ortiz, "Governing through Intermediaries."

Most important for present purposes, the responsible party model does not contemplate (though it does not preclude) a kind of election campaign in which voters come to their voting decisions during the campaign after some substantial deliberative process of persuasion through campaign speech. On the contrary, the purpose of an election, according to the responsible party model, is not to provide an opportunity for voters and other political actors to persuade the electorate what to believe, but is rather to give parties an opportunity to compete for votes by appealing to what voters *already* believe. The model, that is to say, presupposes that public opinion on electorally salient issues is formed exogenously to election campaigns, not endogenously during them. In fact, under the responsible party model, parties lack any incentive to use the campaign period to try to move voters off of their initial beliefs by persuading them to change their opinions: in the three or so months between a summer nominating convention and a November election, parties will surely have their hands full if they do nothing more than simply try to convince voters that they, better than the opposing party, will satisfactorily fulfill the wishes of the voters as the voters exogenously understand their own wishes. This kind of an appeal, to be sure, involves a kind of persuasion, but it is persuasion of a distinctly thin variety, lying far from the deliberative ideal, that demands little of either voters or party speakers.

The Limits of Parties' Internal and External Communications

Thus far, I have argued that the First Amendment right of expressive association contemplates the campaign-exogenous formulation of public political opinion primarily by showing its congruity with the responsible party model. But we can reach the same conclusion about the doctrine by examining directly the ways in which it institutionalizes communications both among party members and between members of competing parties.

According to the Court, the justification for recognizing a right of expressive association is that groups enjoy an advantage over unaffiliated individuals in getting their opinions accepted in the marketplace of ideas. Although the Court has often been vague about the precise nature of this advantage, it seems to derive mainly from the ability of groups to pool resources:[101]

101. Federal Election Comm'n v. National Conservative Political Action Committee, 470 U.S.

presumably, groups of like-minded individuals can take advantage of economies of scale and effort in crafting a message that is sound and persuasive, and can disseminate their message more efficiently and consistently, and to a wider audience than could the group's members individually. The advantages of association, in other words, are measured in the enhanced capacity of the speech to persuade.[102]

In an election campaign, however, where the expressive associations are the two major political parties, a different dynamic arises, one not particularly well-suited to the persuasion of voters during election campaigns. On the contrary, at every step of the electoral process the right of expressive association seems to work against and even to undermine the possibility of meaningful campaign persuasion. In the first place, if political parties really have significant advantages over individuals in the expression of political views, then the best and possibly the only way for the great majority of individuals successfully to engage in persuasive campaign speech is to affiliate with the political party that best matches their views. This institutional arrangement, however, immediately imposes potentially serious constraints on the number and kinds of opportunities during which persuasion of voters by campaign speech can reasonably be expected. Specifically, it tends to reduce the opportunities for meaningful campaign persuasion mainly to two occasions: (1) during the process by which individuals affiliate with a party—that is, speech between the party and its members; and (2) in the course of

---

480, 494 (1985) (public interest organizations are "mechanisms by which large numbers of individuals of modest means can join together in organizations which serve to '[amplify] the voice of their adherents'") (quoting Buckley v. Valeo, 424 U.S. 1, 22 (1976) (per curiam)); Citizens Against Rent Control v. City of Berkeley, 454 U.S. 290, 294 (1981) (the "value [of association for expressive purposes] is that by collective effort individuals can make their views known, when, individually, their voices would be faint or lost"); Colorado Republican Federal Campaign Committee v. Federal Election Comm'n, 518 U.S. 604, 637 (1996) ("Political associations allow citizens to pool their resources and make their advocacy more effective") (Thomas, J., dissenting).

102. This is a view that is traceable back at least as far as Tocqueville: "When an opinion is represented by [an association of individuals], it necessarily assumes a more exact and explicit form. It numbers its partisans and engages them in its cause; they, on the other hand, become acquainted with one another, and their zeal is increased by their number. An association unites into one channel the efforts of divergent minds and urges them vigorously towards the one end which it clearly points out." Tocqueville, *Democracy in America*, Vol. 1, 199. For a much more contemporary expression of the same sentiment by a leading political theorist, see Gutmann, "Freedom of Association: An Introductory Essay," 3.

interparty competition during the campaign for the votes of nonmembers—that is, speech between competing parties.

The first of these is not a likely venue for much that we would call persuasion. The process by which voters affiliate with political parties is largely mechanical and impersonal; affiliation usually involves little more than registering to join the party,[103] and perhaps contributing some money. Certainly, voters do not typically join political parties in the hope of changing the party's beliefs and positions; if anything, "affiliation" implies the contrary—a commitment by the voter to adhere to, or at least to support, the positions and candidates of the party, even if the voter's beliefs on some issues do not match the party's. Nor does affiliation involve much in the way of campaign persuasion by the party of its adherents. In most states and for most voters, affiliation of a voter with a party is something that occurs *before* the inception of the campaign, not during it.[104] Affiliation typically occurs, moreover, on the basis of the voter's precampaign opinion, and it typically endures long after any act of persuasion that may have initially caused the voter to join the party. As a result, parties do not typically bother trying to *persuade* their own membership during election campaigns; they generally take the agreement of their members for granted.[105] Furthermore, the possibility that a party's members might encounter campaign speech designed to persuade them to deviate from the party's commitments is greatly minimized by the party's ability, through exercise of the right of expressive association, to exclude from membership those who do not share its views. This ability of parties to enforce internal ideological purity thus *reduces* the kinds of intellectual

---

103. New York's provision is typical: "At the time a voter is registered or completes an application for registration he may mark his party enrollment within the circle or box underneath or next to the party of his election on the application form." N.Y. Election Law § 5-300. *See* Garrett, "Is the Party Over?," 100–103.

104. This is true by definition in most instances because, in order to vote in a party's primary, a voter must have joined that party before the primary, which occurs by definition before the general election campaign, the main expected venue for public speech designed by parties intended to persuade voters to its positions. More important, voters tend to register for a political party and then remain a member of that party without ever reassessing their affiliation, even when they find themselves voting for candidates of other parties. *See, e.g.*, Finkel and Scarrow, "Party Identification and Party Enrollment." Thus, persuasive speech between a party and its membership during an election campaign is rarely a factor in a voter's decision to support any candidate.

105. Parties do not by any means take for granted that their members will actually turn out and vote, and much of their activity is devoted to activating their loyal adherents. But this has very little to do with persuasion and much more to do with mobilization.

encounters among party members that might prompt them to reflect on their preexisting beliefs, and in so doing to open themselves to persuasion. In short, the process of party affiliation is not likely to involve much in the way of persuasion, and if it does, it is extremely unlikely to involve persuasion by way of the party's own speech during election campaigns.

The more important point, however, does not concern intraparty speech but speech between parties; the First Amendment right of expressive association is less about the persuasion of existing party members than it is about the ability during election campaigns of parties to persuade voters who are not already their members. Yet how likely is it for a party, in the exercise of its right of expressive association, actually to persuade nonmembers to its views? Under the circumstances in which a two-party system actually operates, the prospects seem slight.

In a two-party system, the principal potential audience for a party's persuasive speech consists naturally of members of the other major party.[106] However, on the set of assumptions that undergird the First Amendment right to expressive association, members of the opposition party are unlikely candidates for persuasion. As we have seen, parties, according to this doctrine, are groups of like-minded voters who are committed to a set of shared ideas. Party affiliation, on this view, is thus not an organizational or social act, but an ideological one. Because they have already affiliated themselves based on ideological preference, then, members of the opposition party have by definition made a commitment to a set of beliefs and positions that will, in the main, differ from the beliefs and positions of which the speaking party wishes to persuade them. Members of one party are therefore already inoculated to a considerable degree against the views of the other party.[107]

---

106. The theory behind the two-party system does not really contemplate the existence of independent voters. As the theory has been elaborated, no voter ought to have an incentive to refrain from party affiliation or at least to have no such incentive that differs from the incentives most voters have to abstain entirely from politics. Downs, *An Economic Theory of Democracy*. Of course, independents do exist in a formal sense as registered independents or as registered voters who have declined formally to join a political party, but most formal independents are not ideologically independent in that they tend to lean habitually toward one of the major parties. True independents, in the sense of voters who are, at every election, equally likely to vote for any party, are extremely rare. Keith et al., *The Myth of the Independent Voter*.

107. *See, e.g.*, Clingman v. Beaver, 544 U.S. 581, 604 (2005) (O'Connor, J., concurring) ("a party's inability to persuade a voter to disaffiliate from a rival party would suggest not the presence of anticompetitive regulatory restrictions, but rather the party's failure to win the voter's allegiance").

Moreover, under the doctrine of expressive association, parties can make their members virtually immune from persuasion by insulating them from expressions of contrary views. By policing its internal ideological purity, a party can ensure, first, that all party members will be reasonably like-minded, and therefore will not challenge one another's beliefs; and second, that the party membership will select only candidates who share the members' collective views, and who will consequently project messages during the campaign with which party members already agree, thereby confirming their beliefs.

If the audience for each party's speech consists primarily of those who are already affiliated with another party, are committed to a different set of ideological views, and have the capacity to avoid unwanted encounters with alternative points of view, of what, on this model, is campaign speech likely to consist? Surely such a system is unlikely to produce mass raiding by persuasion of each party's membership by the other. A much more likely result is that such a system of mass organizational speech will quickly degenerate into a shouting match directed at a small minority of voters who are either uncommitted[108] or who are among the least strongly committed to their own parties.[109] This may well describe our present electoral politics, but it hardly seems to satisfy the model contemplated by the First Amendment—and, ironically, by the right of expressive association—of the election campaign as an occasion for democratic self-governance by a broad-based regime of meaningful, reasoned persuasion.

In short, so long as political parties operate under the current robust version of the right of expressive association, about the only thing the party system can realistically hope to be is an accurate and efficient electoral sorting mechanism that matches voters, mainly on the basis of their campaign-exogenous ideological commitments, with appropriate candidates. In other words, in a two-party system operating under a strong right of expressive

---

108. The number of truly uncommitted voters usually is far smaller than the number of formally unaffiliated voters because most independents habitually lean ideologically toward one or another of the major parties. Keith et al., *The Myth of the Independent Voter*. Such voters may thus plausibly be described, on the assumptions of the expressive association doctrine, as sharing an ideological commitment with formally affiliated members of the party toward which they habitually lean.

109. As Campbell has observed, a campaign "can only realistically hope to change the preferences of the subset of voters who lack a pre-campaign commitment or whose commitment is so tenuous that they might be persuaded to change . . . ." Campbell, *The American Campaign*, 30–31.

association, the most realistic goal to which election campaigns can aspire is not persuasion but a rough kind of matching function. Persuasion is not of course ruled out, but it is neither expected nor likely to occur.

Campaign Finance and the First Amendment Privilege for Widely Held Ideas

In its cases dealing with campaign finance, as in its ballot access and party association cases, the Supreme Court has punctiliously observed a rhetorical commitment to the deliberative ideal. Ever since its historic decision in *Buckley v. Valeo*,[110] still its most significant campaign finance decision, the Court has begun its analysis from the premise that government regulation of the giving and spending of money in election campaigns "operate[s] in an area of the most fundamental First Amendment activities" because it affects "[d]iscussion of public issues and debate on the qualifications of candidates."[111] The Court in *Buckley* expressed particular hostility toward restrictions on campaign spending because they "reduce[] the quantity of expression by restricting the number of issues discussed, the depth of their exploration, and the size of the audience reached."[112] A campaign, the Court asserted, is an occasion for voters to "evaluate the candidates' personal qualities and their positions on vital public issues"[113] through competition among candidates to provide the voters with "persuasive reasons for electing them."[114]

In later campaign finance cases, the Court has repeatedly emphasized the central role of persuasion in the electoral process. It has observed, for example, that "advertising may influence the outcome of the vote" by "persuad[ing] the electorate."[115] It has protected the ability of campaign speakers to tailor their message to make it more persuasive.[116] It has affirmed that campaign appeals for money often are " 'intertwined with . . . persuasive speech seeking

110. 424 U.S. 1 (1976) (per curiam).

111. *Ibid.*, 14.

112. *Ibid.*, 19.

113. *Ibid.*, 53.

114. *Ibid.*, 101.

115. First Bank of Boston v. Bellotti, 435 U.S. 765, 789 (1978). *See also* McConnell v. Federal Election Comm'n, 540 U.S. 93, 261 (2003) (Scalia, J.) ("ads do persuade voters").

116. McIntyre v. Ohio Elections Comm'n, 514 U.S. 334, 342 (1995).

support for . . . particular views.'"[117] And it has indicated a concern for persuasion in the electoral process in its approval of regulatory measures designed to "ensure that competition among actors in the political arena is truly competition among ideas."[118]

Despite this commitment, the First Amendment doctrines crafted by the Court to evaluate laws regulating campaign finance do not, in their actual operation, presuppose anything like the electoral persuasion the Court's language seems to take for granted. This is especially ironic because the Federal Election Campaign Act of 1974 (FECA),[119] which the Court gutted in *Buckley*, was, as originally conceived by Congress, very much concerned with securing a prominent role for persuasion in electoral campaigns. As a result, in *Buckley*—the fountainhead of constitutional campaign finance jurisprudence—the Court in the name of electoral persuasion destroyed a scheme of campaign regulation that might conceivably have promoted persuasion, and replaced it with one in which electoral persuasion is quite unlikely to play any meaningful role.

As Congress wrote it in 1974, FECA set ceilings on the amount of money that individuals could contribute to candidates for federal office, on the amount that individuals could spend independently on behalf of candidates, and on overall campaign spending by candidates for federal office.[120] It also expanded public financing of presidential campaigns, required public disclosure of campaign contributions and expenditures, and established the Federal Election Commission to oversee and enforce the legislation.[121] The critical idea unifying the various provisions of FECA was equality of resources. Aimed in large part at eliminating the kind of campaign spending abuses that emerged during the 1972 election cycle,[122] the statute was designed

---

117. McConnell v. Federal Election Comm'n, 540 U.S. 93, 139 (2003), quoting Schaumburg v. Citizens for a Better Environment, 444 U.S. 620, 632 (1980).

118. Federal Election Comm'n v. Massachusetts Citizens for Life, Inc., 479 U.S. 238, 259 (1986).

119. Pub. L. No. 92-225, 86 Stat. 3 (1971), as amended by Pub. L. No. 93-443, 88 Stat. 1263 (1974) (codified as amended at 2 U.S.C. §§ 431–56 (1982) and in scattered sections of Titles 18 and 47 of the U.S. Code).

120. Pub. L. 93-443, Title I.

121. *Ibid.*, Title II.

122. These are comprehensively spelled out in the final report of the Senate Select Committee on Presidential Campaign Activities, S. Rep. No. 93-981, 93rd Cong., 2d Sess. (June 1974).

to produce a regime in which each candidate, regardless of his or her resources or enthusiasm, ideally would spend roughly the same amount of money on trying to get elected, and in which interested voters likewise would contribute to and spend on behalf of their chosen candidates equally.

Equalizing campaign resources does not, of course, by itself guarantee that election campaigns will be contested on the basis of deliberative persuasion through competition in ideas. Congress clearly was concerned, in its legislative deliberations, not just with inequality of resources, but also with what Senator Edmund Muskie, an unsuccessful candidate for the 1972 Democratic presidential nomination, termed "a wave of superficial advertising more appropriate to soap or cereal than national politics."[123] No provision of FECA, of course, purported to prevent candidates from attempting to court voters with slick, content-free advertising. Nevertheless, Congress was apparently convinced that limiting and equalizing campaign resources would create an environment in which ideological persuasion was more likely to emerge as the governing norm. As Senator Bob Dole argued, "[t]he great growth of campaigning expense . . . generates almost irresistible pressures on campaigns away from lengthy, rational and thoughtful presentation of issues and alternatives. It instead fosters shallow, briefly-presented and emotional exploitation of personalities, images and catch-words."[124] Or, as a report accompanying an early version of the bill that became FECA claimed:

> This will make possible parity of exposure on [mass] media as between candidates competing for the same Federal elective office. Thus, such candidates will be competing for the votes of the electorate on their merits rather than on the basis of exposure as in the case of such commodities as toothpaste, soft drinks and beer, aspirin and razor blades.[125]

Evidently, the theory behind FECA was that the equalization of campaign resources would promote deeper, more deliberative forms of persuasion in two ways. First, equalizing resources would reduce candidates' incentives to compete for votes on the basis of slick advertising and exposure. Presumably, rational voters can be won over only by substantive appeals on the merits of

123. 117 Cong. Rec. 29,321 (1971).

124. *Ibid.*, 30,074.

125. H.R. Rep. No. 565, 92d Cong., 1st Sess. 19 (1971).

politically salient issues; it is the votes of irrational voters that may be "bought," so to speak, by nothing more than superficial, expensive packaging.[126] Equalizing candidates' resources thus puts them on an equal footing in competing for both rational and irrational votes, and this equality in turn improves the substance and rationality of election campaigns by depriving any candidate of the ability to compete unfairly for irrational votes in virtue of having greater resources to devote to the kind of expensive, showy appeals to which certain voters, in the view of Congress, unfortunately respond.[127] Second, by thus reducing candidates' incentives to compete for irrational votes, Congress may have hoped that superficial sloganeering would cease altogether to become an attractive campaign tactic, thereby clearing the field for the kind of substantive, persuasion-oriented campaign discourse that members of Congress clearly wished to encourage.

Finally, FECA's emphasis on equality of resources among candidates and voters suggests an underlying congressional belief that the proper unit of currency in election campaigns should be ideas, and that each idea is entitled to an equal hearing. If spending money bears some rough relation to the ability to persuade by increasing either the depth in which ideas may be communicated or the breadth of their dissemination, then limiting the amount of money that voters and candidates may spend restricts the ability of rich individuals to dominate the marketplace of ideas by reaching deeper and more extensively into the market than other individuals who back competing ideas. In such a system, each idea gets to make its best pitch, so to speak, using the resources allowed it, and must then stand aside and let other ideas be heard.[128] In the end, the voters choose among the ideas they have encountered, and since each idea has had an equal opportunity to persuade them, voters are presumably more likely to judge those ideas on their merits.[129]

---

126. Ortiz, "The Democratic Paradox of Campaign Finance Reform," 913.

127. Gardner, "Neutralizing the Incompetent Voter."

128. Justice Scalia has referred derisively to this idea as the "illiberal free-speech principle of 'one man, one minute.'" Austin v. Michigan State Chamber of Commerce, 494 U.S. 652, 684 (1990).

129. Four members of the present Court appear to share these assumptions. As Justice Stevens recently wrote in dissent in Davis v. FEC, "the imposition of reasonable limitations [on contributions] would likely have the salutary effect of improving the quality of the exposition of ideas. After all, orderly debate is always more enlightening than a shouting match that awards points on the basis of decibels rather than reasons." 128 S. Ct. 2759, 2779 (2008).

In *Buckley v. Valeo*, the Court tore a gaping hole in the congressional plan by invalidating its most important components—the ceilings on campaign expenditures by candidates and individuals—while leaving in place the Act's restrictions on campaign contributions to candidates. The Court justified its ruling on the ground that restricting the amount of money that candidates and voters can spend on speech is tantamount to restricting the amount of their speech itself: "A restriction on the amount of money a person or group can spend on political communication during a campaign," the Court said, "necessarily reduces the quantity of expression by restricting the number of issues discussed, the depth of their exploration, and the size of the audience reached"[130]—such limits, that is, impair the quality of campaign deliberation. In a now-famous analogy, the Court said dismissively that "[b]eing free to engage in unlimited political expression subject to a ceiling on expenditures is like being free to drive an automobile as far and as often as one desires on a single tank of gasoline."[131] Although even electoral campaign speech may be restricted for a sufficiently compelling reason,[132] the Court found the government's asserted justifications insufficient. The Court reserved its greatest antipathy for the government's argument that FECA's spending limitations were justified by an interest in "equalizing the relative ability of individuals and groups to influence the outcome of elections," a concept the Court deemed "wholly foreign to the First Amendment."[133]

The contribution limitations fared better for two reasons. First, said the Court, limitations on financial contributions to candidates do not restrict speech to the same extent as do limitations on the expenditures used to purchase speech: such a limitation "entails only a marginal restriction upon the contributor's ability to engage in free communication [because the contribution] serves as a general expression of support for the candidate and his views, but does not communicate the underlying basis for the support." Consequently, "[t]he quantity of communication by the contributor does not increase perceptibly with the size of his contribution, since the expression rests solely on the undifferentiated, symbolic act of contributing."[134]

130. 424 U.S. at 19.

131. *Ibid.*, n.18.

132. *Ibid.*, 44–45.

133. *Ibid.*, 48–49. The Court recently reaffirmed this aspect of *Buckley* by an 8 to 1 vote in an otherwise splintered decision in Randall v. Sorrell, 126 S.Ct. 2479 (2006).

134. *Ibid.*, 20–21.

Second, the Court found this relatively slight diminution in the quantity of electoral speech justified by the government's interest in "limit[ing] the actuality and appearance of corruption resulting from large individual financial contributions."[135]

The Court's reasoning in *Buckley*, then, reflects a strongly held belief that the First Amendment contemplates election campaigns in which speech is aimed at persuasion, and in which the timing, amount, and content of electoral speech is to be determined entirely by the speaker. Government, in this view, simply may not take any action to interfere with the process by which candidates and voters persuade each other during election campaigns. The way the Court applied these principles in *Buckley* thus left in place substantial restrictions on the ability of voters to transfer resources to candidates, yet lifted all restrictions on the ability of candidates to spend as much money as they could accumulate, whether from their own bank accounts or from their supporters. Ironically, this judicial reengineering left Americans with a system of campaign finance regulation that, in its actual operation, works in a way very much at odds with the goals the Court claimed it was trying to achieve. By applying a constitutionalized preference for persuasive campaign speech to a statutory system designed to achieve it, the Court unfortunately created a system in which persuasion cannot realistically be expected to play a significant role in election campaigns. Following *Buckley*, our institutions of campaign finance now in effect treat public opinion as campaign-exogenous.

The Court's First Amendment jurisprudence of campaign finance is built around two fundamental assumptions. The first assumption is that a candidate's *expenditure* of money during an election campaign translates into votes. The assumed relationship is certainly rough, but it is also roughly linear: the more candidates spend, the more votes they are likely to get.[136] In assuming this relationship, it bears mentioning that the Court does not, or at least need not, indulge any particular assumption about how, precisely, dollars translate into votes. Dollars might earn votes by purchasing reasoned persuasion in

135. *Ibid.*, 26. Because this justification sufficed, the Court had no occasion to consider the sufficiency of the government's equalization-of-influence rationale. *Id.* However, in Randall v. Sorrell, 126 S.Ct. 2479 (2006), the Court for the first time acknowledged a lower limit to permissible limits on financial contributions to candidates.

136. See, most recently, Randall v. Sorrell, in which stringent contribution limitations were invalidated partly on the ground that challengers would be unable to raise sufficient funds to mount effective challenges to incumbents, 126 S.Ct. at 2499 (opinion of Breyer, J.) (such limits threaten to "inhibit effective advocacy"). The proposition that money

substantive campaign communications appealing to the common good; or by funding voter manipulation strategies launched in well-packaged, suggestive advertising that appeals to subrational biases or naked self-interest; or by some other mechanism not well understood. Whatever the linkage, however, the Court—along with Congress—assumes that money works in campaigns, and that there is a rough proportionality between spending and votes.[137] It is this assumption that drives the Court's doctrinal commitment to the principle that campaign spending by candidates for elective office, or their supporters, cannot in any circumstances be limited.[138] Candidates, the Court presumes, simply must be entitled to spend as much as they want in order to secure as many votes as they can get. Spending limitations, on this view, severely disrupt the campaign process by limiting the ability of candidates to campaign as hard, as intensely, and as thoroughly as they wish.

The second assumption driving the Court's campaign finance jurisprudence is that a candidate's *receipt* of money during an election campaign reflects support for that candidate, and that this support indicates to some degree acceptance of the candidate's ideological and policy positions by the contributors who provide the funds. As the Court has put it, "[a] contribution

---

attracts votes is a widely accepted, though often implicit, premise among political theorists, *see, e.g.*, Rawls, *Political Liberalism*, 360–61; Thompson, *Just Elections*, 112–14; legal scholars, *see, e.g.*, Sunstein, *Democracy and the Problem of Free Speech*, 99; Strauss, "What is the Goal of Campaign Finance Reform?"; Briffault, "Public Funding and Democratic Elections"; judges, *see, e.g.*, Skelly Wright, "Politics and the Constitution," 1004; Attorney General of Canada v. Harper, 2004 SCC 33 (upholding limits on independent political spending as equalizing political influence); and of course the members of Congress who enacted FECA. *See, e.g.*, H.R. Rep. No. 93-1239, Report of the Committee on House Administration, Federal Election Campaign Act Amendments of 1974, 93d Cong., 2d Sess. 3 (1974) ("Under the present law the impression persists that a candidate can buy an election by simply spending large sums in a campaign"). Political science research seems to support this unobjectionable proposition. *See* Morton and Cameron, "Elections and the Theory of Campaign Contributions," 81 ("the massive quantities of monies gathered by candidates do seem to increase the probability of election of the receiving and spending candidates, incumbent or challenger"); Jacobson, "Measuring Spending Effects," 212–13.

137. Occasionally the concern is expressed that the spending-to-votes conversion ratio differs systematically for different classes of candidates—for example, that incumbents find it easier to translate their spending into votes, or that minor party candidates must spend more than major party candidates to achieve the same benefit. *See, e.g.*, Buckley v. Valeo, 424 U.S. 1, 31-35 (1976) (per curiam). Although some members of the Court have occasionally raised these issues, such concerns have never worked their way systematically into the Court's First Amendment jurisprudence, which generally assumes a rough, across-the-board parity among candidates.

138. The one exception to this rule is campaign spending by corporations and labor unions, discussed below.

serves as a general expression of support for the candidate and his views."[139] In this sense, contributing to a candidate is constitutionally similar to joining a political party: both represent a kind of loose affiliation based on shared political beliefs.[140] As with spending, the relation between contributions and support is assumed to be rough, but also linear: the more support candidates enjoy among the electorate the more contributions they will receive, and the more contributions they receive the more widespread we may assume their support to be. Indeed, the Court is so strongly committed to its conception of the proportionality of support to contributions that it has used that relation as a justification for permitting an outright ban on certain kinds of campaign contributions.

Public concern with the influence of money in electoral politics emerged in the late nineteenth century contemporaneously with "[t]he concentration of wealth consequent upon the industrial expansion in the post-Civil War era."[141] By the height of the Progressive Era, this concern focused especially on the role of large corporations, which were widely thought to have exercised undue influence on electoral politics in many states.[142] In response to these concerns, Congress and some states enacted laws aimed at restricting the ability of corporations to participate in politics. The first such federal statute, the Tillman Act of 1907,[143] barred corporate contributions to any candidate for federal office, a prohibition that has been carried forward in successive federal statutes including the Corrupt Practices Act of 1925[144] and the Federal Election Campaign Act of 1971,[145] and remains on the books to this day.[146] The Supreme Court has consistently upheld such prohibitions.[147]

---

139. Buckley, 424 U.S. at 21.

140. "Making a contribution, like joining a political party, serves to affiliate a person with a candidate." *Ibid.*, 22.

141. United States v. International Union, UAW, 352 U.S. 568, 570 (1957).

142. De Witt, *The Progressive Movement*, 113; Hofstadter, *The Age of Reform*, 5; Harris, *California Politics*, 3–7.

143. 34 Stat. 864 (1907).

144. 43 Stat. 1070 (1925).

145. 86 Stat. 20 (1971).

146. *See* 2 U.S.C. § 441b(b)(2)(C).

147. *See* Burroughs v. United States, 290 U.S. 534 (1934); United States v. International Union, UAW, 352 U.S. 568 (1957); Federal Election Comm'n v. National Right to Work Committee, 459 U.S. 197 (1982).

The main concern underlying congressional efforts to exclude corporate money from electoral politics is not that ideas backed by corporate speech are unworthy of public consideration; corporate speech, the Court has held, is as capable as speech from any other source of contributing to lively public debate on important political issues, and therefore enjoys the same protection under the First Amendment as political speech by individuals.[148] Instead, according to the Court, the concern has been that corporations, because of "the special advantages which go with the corporate form of organization," are able to accumulate "substantial aggregations of wealth,"[149] and that their access to such wealth could provide corporations with "an unfair advantage in the political marketplace."[150] Laws banning electoral spending and contributions by corporations, the Court has explained,

> aim at . . . the corrosive and distorting effects of immense aggregations of wealth that are accumulated with the help of the corporate form and that have little or no correlation to the public's support for the corporation's political ideas. . . . [Such laws ensure that electoral] expenditures reflect actual public support for the political ideas espoused by corporations.[151]

The problem, then, is not that corporate-backed speech and corporate-backed candidates should not be heard, but rather that they should not be

---

148. First National Bank of Boston v. Bellotti, 435 U.S. 765 (1978); Massachusetts Citizens for Life v. Federal Election Comm'n, 479 U.S. 238 (1986).

149. Federal Election Comm'n v. National Right to Work Committee, 459 U.S. 197, 207 (1982).

150. Massachusetts Citizens for Life, 479 U.S. at 257. For a different account of the rationale behind Progressive-era restrictions on corporate political expenditures, see Winkler, "Other People's Money" (arguing that the main rationale for such prohibitions was to protect corporate shareholders, not the political marketplace).

151. Austin v. Michigan Chamber of Commerce, 494 U.S. 652, 660 (1990). This concern has been sufficient to permit an outright governmental ban on independent corporate expenditures in support of candidates for federal office, a much more serious kind of limit than caps on contributions to candidates because, in the Court's view, limitations on independent spending suppress speech much more directly than limitations on contributions. Buckley, 424 U.S. at 19–21. Recently, in Federal Election Comm'n v. Beaumont, 539 U.S. 146 (2003), the Court confirmed what seemed obvious: if concern over possible dangers to the electoral process arising from corporate aggregations of wealth is sufficient to justify prohibiting independent corporate expenditures on behalf of candidates, then the same concern is *a fortiori* sufficient to justify prohibitions on corporate contributions to candidates.

heard excessively—more than they in some sense "should" be heard—and that the degree to which an idea "should" be heard during an election campaign corresponds to the degree of "actual public support" for the idea in question. That is why, in the Court's view, limiting the introduction of corporate wealth into the electoral arena serves ultimately to preserve "the integrity of the marketplace of ideas."[152] In the end, then, the Court's jurisprudence of campaign contributions rests on a highly significant premise: the belief that how well candidates *should* be doing in election campaigns depends to some degree on how well they are *already* doing.

Contrary to the Court's rhetoric, its two major assumptions—that campaign spending is correlated to votes and that campaign contributions are correlated to support—together presuppose, and to some extent institutionalize, a system of electoral politics in which election campaigns are highly unlikely to serve as occasions for the endogenous formation of public opinion. Instead, election campaigns are much more likely to function in a way that simply identifies, and transforms into political authorization, exogenously formulated opinions that voters bring with them to the campaign phase. This is because, under the constitutional rules developed by the Court, political ideas that are the most popular and widely held *before the campaign starts*, and the candidates who espouse them, will begin with an enormous advantage—the pole position, so to speak. The Court's First Amendment jurisprudence, that is to say, goes a long way toward guaranteeing that ideas

---

152. Massachusetts Citizens for Life, 479 U.S. at 257. Although the same reasoning certainly justifies regulatory limits on contributions to candidates by rich *individuals*, the Court has instead upheld limitations on individual contributions by reference to their potential both to corrupt candidates through the exchange of contributions for *quid pro quo* political favors, and to create an appearance of such corruption. *E.g.*, Buckley, 424 U.S. at 26. The Court's failure to look beyond the corruption justification has led to a strange doctrinal anomaly: its refusal to permit regulatory limits on the amount of money that individual candidates can spend on their own campaigns. *Ibid.*, 53–54. The Court has invalidated such restrictions essentially on the ground that candidates cannot, by contributing unlimited personal resources to their own campaigns, corrupt themselves. *Ibid.*, 53. Or, as Justice Scalia tartly pointed out in his dissent in Austin: "Why is it perfectly all right if advocacy by an individual billionaire is out of proportion with 'actual public support' for his positions?" Austin, 494 U.S. at 685 (Scalia, J., dissenting). In its most significant campaign finance decision since Buckley, however, McConnell v. Federal Election Comm'n, 540 U.S. 93 (2003), the Court has suggested that its thinking may be evolving in a way that recognizes some equivalence in "the role that corporations, unions, and wealthy contributors play in the electoral process." *Ibid.*, 122. *See also ibid.*, 138 ("§ 323, in the main, does little more than regulate the ability of wealthy individuals, corporations, and unions to contribute large sums of money to influence federal elections, federal candidates, and federal officeholders").

that are formed and widely held exogenously to the campaign will prevail during the campaign.

The process works in the following way: if, as the Court assumes, money is what enables candidates to deliver campaign speech, then any contribution received by a candidate before or shortly after the inception of the official campaign must by definition be donated on the basis of a point of view that is exogenous to—has been formulated before the commencement of—the election campaign. It follows that candidates who enter the campaign supporting positions that are the most popular before the campaign begins will have an initial advantage. First, they will attract more donations than their opponents before the campaign starts and during its earliest phase. Then they will use this money to communicate ideas that already enjoy widespread support among the electorate. Such ideas will likely appeal to more voters than competing, less popular ideas advanced by other candidates, an effect that may be expected to elicit further rounds of financial contributions from ideological supporters. This additional support will multiply the initial advantage these candidates already enjoy by allowing them to communicate their message more broadly and intensely. These further rounds of communication then produce further rounds of contributions, producing additional communication, and so on.[153]

This cycle, moreover, is unlikely to be disrupted because, by upholding contribution limits but invalidating spending limits, the Court has ensured that those who happen to have access to great sums of money—the rich—will be unable to finance broad dissemination during a campaign of an idea that is not already popular.[154] On its own assumptions, then, the Court's ideal campaign finance system is likely to operate more as a vehicle for identifying and ratifying exogenously held public opinion than as a vehicle for the endogenous formulation of public opinion through reflection and deliberation during the campaign process. Any candidate who attempts to promote political ideas endogenously through a process of exposure and debate during

153. Malbin, "A Public Funding System in Jeopardy," argues that this phenomenon is made even worse by the front-loading of presidential primaries, which requires candidates to raise money extremely early in the campaign to have any chance of gaining the kind of public exposure and attention necessary to mount a successful campaign.

154. The only exception is if the rich person decides to run for office personally. This is because, under *Buckley*, government may not limit how much money individuals spend out of their own pockets on their own campaigns. 424 U.S. at 51–54. However, not every rich person with an idea—even a good idea—is able or willing to run for public office.

the campaign itself will start off at a great, and possibly insurmountable, disadvantage. For the Court, however, this is as it should be because, as we have seen, in the Court's view the extent to which an idea "should" be communicated during an election campaign is proportional to the degree of support that the idea already enjoys among voters.

Campaign speech, then, does not on this model serve primarily as a transmitter of ideas, or as a mechanism for the forging of majority opinion. Rather than serving as a producer of inputs to an electoral system antecedent to the "real" electoral system of balloting and counting, campaign speech itself in a sense *is* the electoral system.[155] It is tabulative; it functions as a way of toting up who supports what view, not as the medium in which support for competing points of view is determined in the first instance. Campaign speech, under the First Amendment, is thus the end of a process rather than its beginning.

155. In this sense, campaign speech functions in a way not all that dissimilar from the ancient Spartan practice of "The Shout," in which the group that shouted the loudest was able to carry an election for its candidate. Plutarch, "Lycurgus," 35; Fishkin, *The Voice of the People*, 23.

THREE

Campaigns and the Stability of Political Opinion

IF MY ANALYSIS OF BALLOT ACCESS, public and campaign finance, and party association rules is correct, then it is difficult to resist the conclusion that the laws regulating our election campaigns give us a set of electoral institutions distinctly at odds with our publicly proclaimed commitments. In our social and historical understandings and even in our legal rhetoric, we proclaim our commitment to an ideal of politics in which election campaigns are deliberatively thick, and persuasion is accorded a central role. Yet in their actual operation, our electoral institutions seem to reflect a very different assumption that campaigns will be, and possibly even a surreptitious desire that they should be, largely devoid of meaningfully deliberative persuasion. Perhaps the least that can be said is that the law has so badly bungled its efforts to institutionalize persuasion as a routine element of election campaigns that it has succeeded in accomplishing the exact opposite of what it set out to do. Certainly, any candidate who wants to take his or her case directly to the people by persuading them during an election campaign of something they did not already believe faces huge and possibly insurmountable legal obstacles. From the point of view of our democratic commitments, then, our election law appears to present serious problems that ought to be fixed.

This is, however, precisely the conclusion that I believe we should resist. In this chapter, I raise the possibility that the problems with our campaigns identified by the Campaign Critique do not originate in our legal institutions, which are in all likelihood reasonably well-adapted to facilitate whatever kind of endogenous persuasion an election campaign is capable of accomplishing. Rather, I shall suggest, the problem lies in our social understanding of election campaigns, and of what they are capable of accomplishing; it lies, that is to say, in the Critique itself.

Empirical Social Science and the Ideal of Persuasion

Despite their reputation as clear-eyed cynics, political scientists seem by and large to subscribe as much as anyone else to the Campaign Critique. Certainly, political science as a discipline appears to have no quarrel with the normative ideal of thick, deliberatively persuasive election campaigns. When they speak about normative ideals at all, political scientists tend to agree that responsible citizenship imposes a substantial burden. For example, in a passage widely quoted by political scientists, the authors of a classic study of voting behavior contended:

> The democratic citizen is expected to be well informed about political affairs. He is supposed to know what the issues are, what their history is, what the relevant facts are, what alternatives are proposed, what the party stands for, what the likely consequences are.[1]

Indeed, one can dip into the literature almost at random and find similar accounts of the characteristics of the ideal democratic citizen. Such citizens are said to "pay attention, understand, weigh the possibilities, and structure their policy preferences in accord with their attitudes and interests."[2] The ideal citizenry, it is said, "has informed opinions but is tolerant of alternative perspectives and amenable to change in the face of a compelling argument."[3] In the ideal democracy, "political issues are fully explored, and political debates are fully aired. In such a society, citizens are open to persuasion but sympathetic to ongoing disagreement, the social boundaries of political

1. Berelson, Lazarsfeld, and McPhee, *Voting*, 308. Indeed, the duties of citizenship are sometimes experienced as distinctly unpleasant. *See* Lane, "The Joyless Polity," 353.

2. Claassen and Highton, "Does Policy Debate Reduce Information Effects in Public Opinion?," 410.

3. Chong and Druckman, "Framing Theory," 121.

4. Huckfeldt, Johnson, and Sprague, *Political Disagreement*, 1.

5. These articulations of the Campaign Critique, like the popular ones mentioned in the Introduction and the criticisms, reviewed in Chapter 1, leveled by Progressives at nineteenth-century forms of campaigning, are strongly oriented toward the rational. A new and growing body of political science work, however, has rediscovered a point made by Aristotle more than two millennia ago: emotion plays a strong and vital role in the intellectual process of persuasion; the two are not distinct. *See* Brader, *Campaigning for Hearts and Minds*; Marcus, Neuman, and Mackuen, *Affective Intelligence and Political Judgment*. This work answers a plea by some democratic theorists to reintroduce conceptions of emotion

viewpoints are fluid and shifting, and individuals encounter the full spectrum of issue positions and political viewpoints."[4] Progressive reformers could scarcely have put it any better.[5]

The story of contemporary empirical political science, however, has been its discovery, followed by its continuing, relentless confirmation of the immense gap between the normative ideals of democratic citizenship and the actual behavior of the American electorate. Some of the earliest and best-known findings, replicated regularly ever since, concerned the public's profound ignorance of political issues, parties, candidates, and the institutions of governance, as well as its inattentiveness to politics and its apparent inability to reason coherently on political subjects.[6] Less widely know outside the field, however, are several related bodies of work on the way in which people form political opinions and on the mechanisms by which political knowledge is acquired and disseminated. This work powerfully confirms the main premise of the Campaign Critique by tending to demonstrate that nothing like the kind of deep, deliberative persuasion contemplated by prevailing social ideals takes place during campaigns, or indeed that it ever has. Even more damning is a growing and impressive body of recent work in political psychology and social network theory suggesting strongly that persuasion, as the term is commonly used, is more than exceedingly rare—it is for structural reasons highly unlikely to occur during the course of an election campaign. Persuasion, especially in the ideal sense of people coming to

---

into the ideal of democratic citizenship, from which it has long been banished. *See, e.g.*, Garsten, *Saving Persuasion*; Marcus, *The Sentimental Citizen*. I do not discuss this body of work here because it does not affect any of my conclusions. Persuasion in the conventionally ideal sense, I argue here, does not occur during campaigns. Even if the definition of persuasion is broadened to include emotion-driven conversions, however, it still does not occur during campaigns. Whether voters are persuaded by reason, emotion, or some combination, the persuasion that leads them to their political beliefs overwhelmingly occurs outside the arena of the formal campaign.

6. Campbell et al., *The American Voter*; Smith, *The Unchanging American Voter*; Delli Carpini and Keeter, *What American Know About Politics and Why It Matters*. More recently, a significant salvage operation has been mounted aimed at showing that the ignorance and irrationality of American voters are merely apparent, and that they in fact know enough and reason well enough to fulfill their responsibilities as democratic citizens. *See, e.g.*, Popkin, *The Reasoning Voter*; Page and Shapiro, *The Rational Public*. These efforts, however, do not by any means argue that the behavior of American voters approaches anywhere near the ideal contemplated by the Campaign Critique; they argue only that the ways in which voters admittedly fall short of the ideal do not threaten core democratic values. Some recent work, on the other hand, suggests that voters may know more than pollsters typically are able to determine because of many respondents' low motivation to exert effort in answering survey questions. Prior and Lupia, "Money, Time, and Political Knowledge."

accept beliefs that they did not already embrace before a campaign began, is thus perhaps the last thing we should expect a campaign to be able to accomplish.

It is important to be clear here. The social science literature does not say—and I do not wish to be understood as characterizing it to say—that people are never persuaded, whether in the ideal sense or in some other lesser sense by political information and arguments, whether provided by candidates, officials, voters, or other political actors. The literature does, however, make an extremely powerful case that people almost never change their beliefs and opinions to any significant degree *during campaigns*. Nothing in the social science literature suggests that persuasion of the kind commended by the ideal never can occur, and much shows that it clearly does. What the literature does tend to show, however, is that in any given citizen's life the engaged, deliberatively reflective alteration of political opinion is unusual and infrequent, and that the norm is for political opinion to form early, to evolve very gradually, to be largely immune from significant, much less sudden and dramatic revision, and for campaigns to play at most a minor role in the formation of public political opinion, either at the individual or collective levels. Consequently, if our campaigns fall short of our democratic aspirations, it is far from clear that much of the blame can be placed at the feet of our legal institutions.

The Effect of Election Campaigns on Voting Decisions: The "Minimal Effects" School

Beginning around the middle of the last century, political scientists studying the American electorate began to find, over and over again, that few voters change their minds during election campaigns. At the same time, sophisticated election forecasting models began to emerge that were capable of predicting election outcomes with considerable accuracy on the basis of variables that were in place well before the onset of formal campaigns. These developments soon gave rise to a powerful inference that campaigns play virtually no meaningful role in determining who wins public office—the so-called "minimal effects" thesis. The leading studies in this body of work, typically relying on aggregated data concerning large numbers of voters, found repeatedly that influences unrelated to the actual campaigns—the health of the national economy, for example, or recent job growth, or whether an incumbent is running for reelection—are capable of so fully determining election outcomes as to compel the conclusion that it is these factors, rather than anything candidates do or say during campaigns, that actually drive the electoral process.[7] On this view, voters will, for example, "vote their pocketbooks"[8] no matter how the candidates campaign, a tendency so strong that political scientists sometimes feel entitled to say things like: "for all the difference it made, America could have skipped the 1984 campaign . . . : Ronald Reagan would [still] have won an overwhelming victory."[9]

Studies of the behavior of individual voters showed much the same thing. In their classic studies of Ohio and New York voters during the 1940s, Berelson and Lazarsfeld found that "the time of final decision, that point after which the voter does not change his intention, occurred *prior* to the campaign for most voters—and thus no 'real decision' was made *in* the campaign in the sense of waiting to consider alternatives."[10] About two-thirds of those who voted in November, the authors found, did not shift their position at all from what it had been before the campaign began.[11] Moreover, about 70 percent of all voters, including those who claimed to be undecided before and during the campaign, nevertheless voted in a way that "corresponded to the vote tendencies prevailing among groups with social characteristics similar to their own," a fact that the authors interpreted to demonstrate that "[t]he predispositions of such people were so deeply rooted that they could not be readily converted" by campaign speech.[12] In other words, even voters who say they have an open mind during a campaign, and who almost certainly believe they have open minds, end up voting in a way that could readily have been predicted before the campaign on the basis of their religious affiliation, socioeconomic status, or occupation.

More recent studies of individual voter behavior seemed to confirm these results. For example, in a study of the 1980 presidential campaign, Finkel

---

7. *See, e.g.*, Markus, "The Impact of Personal and National Economic Conditions on the Presidential Vote"; Holbrook, *Do Campaigns Matter?*

8. *See, e.g.*, Campbell et al., *The American Voter*.

9. Pomper, *The Election of 1984*, 70. Similarly: "The important determinants of the 1984 election were in place long before most people heard of Geraldine Ferraro [the Democratic vice presidential candidate], long before the candidates squared off in front of television cameras and long before Americans met the bear in the woods [a character in a Reagan television ad]." Rosenstone, *Forecasting Presidential Elections*.

10. Berelson, Lazarsfeld, and McPhee, *Voting*, 18.

11. *Ibid.*, 18–19.

12. Lazarsfeld, Berelson, and Gaudet, *The People's Choice*, 95.

found that "the overwhelming majority of individual votes could be predicted from attitudes such as party identification and presidential approval that were measured *before* the political party conventions. Changes in orientations during the general election period had little impact on vote choices at both the individual and aggregate level."[13] A recent comparative review of the literature on vote changing found that no more than 6 to 8 percent of voters in American presidential elections changed their minds about which candidate to support during the final month of the campaign.[14] Even studies that conclude campaigns do have some effect on election outcomes find such an effect only at the margins. Holbrook's analysis of twentieth-century presidential elections found that campaigns produced a net change in outcomes ranging between –.01 and 2.59 percentage points from the results that would have been expected on the basis of variables unrelated to campaigns—"not very impressive," in his estimation.[15] Similarly, Goldstein and Freedman's analysis of campaign spending in the 1996 U.S. Senate elections begins from the premise that "even the weakest Senate incumbents usually start out with a base of at least 45% of the vote,"[16] meaning that a Senator's principal goal is to acquire only an additional 5 percent, and suggesting strongly that roughly 90 percent of the Senate vote is essentially precommitted and unmovable before the campaign begins.

Of course, saying that campaign persuasion is typically not determinative of electoral outcomes, or that voters are rarely persuaded by campaign speech, is not the same thing as saying that campaign persuasion never occurs, or that it can never play a decisive role in electoral politics. Obviously, if some persuasion does occur during election campaigns, then it could be decisive in very close contests.[17] Nevertheless, the fact that campaign

---

13. Finkel, "Reexamining the 'Minimal Effects' Model in Recent Presidential Campaigns," 2.

14. Blais, "How Many Voters Change Their Minds in the Month Preceding an Election?"

15. Holbrook, *Do Campaigns Matter?*, 31. *See also* Bartels, "Message Received," in which the author, like a physicist inferring the existence of unobservable particles, infers the theoretical possibility of strong media effects from the fact that we observe them so rarely. In a more recent study, Bartels found that campaign persuasion is essentially nonexistent across most measures. Bartels, "Priming and Persuasion."

16. Goldstein and Friedman, "New Evidence for New Arguments: Money and Advertising in the 1996 Senate Elections," 1100.

17. Campbell argues that campaigns are not usually decisive in the sense of determining the outcome of elections, but he also argues that systematically identifiable factors in presidential campaigns determine on average about 4 percent of the vote, and that unsystematic campaign influences on average account for about 1.5 percent of the vote.

persuasion could conceivably play a marginal role in deciding close electoral outcomes in some races takes us far afield from the socially dominant conception of persuasion as the most significant element, and indeed the *raison d'être*, of election campaigns. Indeed, it must be stressed that the phenomenon studied by political scientists in the minimal effects tradition is the degree to which campaigns cause people to change their *votes*—never mind changing their *beliefs*, which is after all what persuasion in the ideal sense is supposed to involve. This is important for assessing the degree to which campaigns approach the conventional ideal, for voters obviously can be induced to change their votes without also changing their underlying beliefs. A voter who prefers tax cuts, for example, might be induced to support A instead of B if information provided in a campaign convinced her that A is the stronger antitax candidate, but this is a rather low-level kind of persuasion concerning the operative facts that does not involve any change in underlying concepts or structures of political belief. And if, according to the minimal effects thesis, voters almost never change their votes during a campaign, it can hardly be argued that they are persuaded to change their beliefs with anything approaching the same frequency, minimal as it is.

Recently, however, a newer body of findings has emerged that some political scientists enthusiastically believe tends to undermine the minimal effects thesis. This research has identified several characteristics of political communication—most notably its "agenda-setting," "framing," and "priming" characteristics—that can affect how voters receive information and how they then go on to use it in making political decisions. Whatever the implications

---

J. Campbell, *The American Campaign*, 188. However, because presidential campaigns often are very close, Campbell maintains that "campaigns have probably been decisive in roughly one out of every five elections." *Ibid.*, 189. Campbell's analysis, however, should not be taken to support the conclusion that campaigns have decisive effects because of their persuasive effect on voters; it shows at most that campaign outcomes may be determined by voting decisions made *during the campaign phase*. This is a very different proposition because it does not exclude the possibility that late-deciding voters decide on the same campaign-exogenous grounds as early-deciding voters but simply do so later. The figure in Campbell's analysis that might most logically be taken to represent some kind of persuasion is his estimation of "unsystematic" campaign effects, which he puts between one and two percent. By this, Campbell means voting decisions not predictable from the voter's partisan affiliation, attitude toward the incumbent administration, or economic situation. Even here, however, Campbell's figure would almost certainly overstate the campaign-endogeneity of public opinion, because what makes races capable of being close enough to permit unsystematic campaign effects to be decisive is that candidates seeking to persuade voters position themselves at the inception of the campaign as close as possible to the position of the median voter, as that position is determined based on voters' campaign-exogenous political opinions.

of these findings, I believe the enthusiasm of its proponents is misplaced, at least as such findings are relevant to the main point here, which concerns the degree to which actual campaign practice falls short of the deliberative ideal. At this point, however, I want to defer consideration of the new campaign effects findings in order to review a different body of literature based on sociological and cognitive considerations. This body of work is not in any way contradicted by the newer campaign effects literature, and it demonstrates clearly and dramatically just what campaign persuasion is up against and why it is so unlikely to occur: because of the powerful stability of political opinion.

The Sources of Political Knowledge

One reason the minimal effects results seem so surprising, and so inconsistent with generally held views about the role of persuasion in democratic politics, is because of the way the research problem often is framed. If the political knowledge relevant to a voting decision is defined as the information supplied to voters by candidates and partisans during formal election campaigns, and the barrage of such information during the campaign is shown to have no significant impact on voters' ultimate decisions, then the only possible explanations seem to be that voters are either inattentive or incompetent, or both, and that campaigns are as a result essentially meaningless. Yet this is clearly a poor way to frame the problem: it is obvious that the knowledge necessary to formulate a political opinion or a voting decision consists of far more than simply the information supplied to voters during the course of election campaigns. Campaign information is just, and only, information—inputs. What voters do with that information—how they understand it, react to it, process it—depends entirely on the predispositions, inclinations, beliefs, preferences, habits, and other qualities that individual voters bring to the task. But the information-processing equipment that voters bring *to* campaigns is by definition something they have created *before* the campaign. Unless the typical voter, like some pathetic character in an Oliver Sacks essay, lacks any kind of long-term memory or coherent, stable personality, it is inevitable that some extremely significant aspect of how voters react to information they acquire during an election campaign will be determined exogenously to that campaign.

An example may help to clarify this proposition. Suppose it is August 2004, and George W. Bush wants my vote in November. Of what would he have to persuade me during the campaign to get it? Suppose I am inclined to vote against him because I am a Democrat. If the basis of my party affiliation is ideological, Bush could in theory obtain my vote by persuading me on the merits that his own programs and positions are meritorious and that they are superior to the positions of his opponent. If he were clever, he might try to convince me that his own programs and proposals will actually succeed better in accomplishing goals to which I, as a Democrat, am ideologically committed than will the programs advocated by the Democrats themselves. This is the conception of an election-campaign-as-ideological-contest found in dominant social understandings and in the First Amendment rhetoric of free speech.

But what if I am a Democrat not only because of my ideological commitments, but because of habit, or family tradition, or because of judgments based on prior experience with officials of both parties? To persuade me to vote for him, Bush would have to undertake something much more difficult: he would need to persuade me not merely that his own programs and positions are meritorious, but that I should abandon a habitual mode of behavior; or that I should deviate from a family tradition stretching back three generations; or that I have drawn the wrong conclusions from decades of prior political experience. These are much more deeply held and ingrained habits of thought and behavior than are ideologically driven disagreements on policy means and ends. Or suppose that I am disinclined to vote for Bush because I disapprove of his decision to invade Iraq. If my disapproval is based on my belief, say, that Bush used bad judgment by too readily accepting intelligence reports claiming that Iraq possessed weapons of mass destruction, then perhaps he might persuade me to vote for him merely by demonstrating that his judgment was reasonable given the information he had. But if my disapproval of his decision rests on my relative valuations of the loss of American life compared to the likely potential benefits of establishing a democratic regime in Iraq, or on my predisposition to be averse to risking innocent lives in military actions, Bush's task would again be much more formidable and perhaps impossible. Can a presidential candidate possibly convince a voter over the course of an election campaign to abandon risk aversion as a principle of decision making? It seems highly unlikely.

A recent but now substantial body of political science literature, particularly work by scholars open to sociological and psychological approaches to the study of opinion formation, incorporates these kinds of considerations into the analysis of voting behavior. This path was charted more than 50 years ago when Berelson and Lazarsfeld recognized that "[t]he individual's vote is the product of a number of social conditions or influences: his socioeconomic and ethnic affiliations, his family tradition, his personal associations, his attitudes on the issues of the day, his membership in formal organizations."[18] More recently, Milburn has explained:

> Attitudes and behavior are a function of an interactive process between the internal—or what people carry around with them: personality, knowledge, and belief structures—and the external—or what is brought to them from the outside: the influence exerted by other individuals in conversations and through the mass media. Thus there is a dialectical and ongoing interactive process between internal and external forces.[19]

Or, as Zaller has succinctly put it: "Every opinion is a marriage of information and predisposition."[20] These approaches, in other words, recognize that a voter's decision to vote for a specific candidate often represents the most recent stage in a lengthy and complex ongoing process that long precedes the onset of the particular election campaign providing the occasion for casting the vote in question.

One of the most commonly identified sources of political predispositions is childhood socialization. Research on partisan identification—the inclination to support one party or another—has long shown that one of the best predictors of an individual's party affiliation is the party affiliation of his or her parents.[21] Some have argued that a durable impression may be made on a child as the result of "discussing his choice with a strongly partisan parent who is, most of the time, unwavering in his convictions."[22] Others suggest that intergenerational stability in partisan preference may be more plausibly attributed to the effect of shared backgrounds and experiences.[23] Studies of political behavior consistently find a "marked lack of independence in [the] political beliefs, opinions, and behavior of people who share a common social

---

18. Berelson, Lazarsfeld, and McPhee, *Voting*, 37.
19. Milburn, *Persuasion and Politics*, 1–2.
20. Zaller, *The Nature and Origins of Mass Opinion*, 6.
21. A. Campbell et al., *The American Voter*, 146–48; Jennings and Niemi, *The Political Character of Adolescence*, 37–62; Jennings and Niemi, *Generations and Politics*, 89–93, 152–56, 37–62.
22. McPhee, Ferguson, and Smith, "A Theory of Informal Social Influence," 83.
23. *E.g.*, Milburn, *Persuasion and Politics*, 37.

environment."[24] It is thus possible that children grow into voters of a particular political persuasion because they find themselves in social and economic circumstances similar to those of their parents. Whatever the explanation, however, the evidence is strong that voters learn much of what they believe about politics in childhood and maintain those beliefs throughout their lives.

Another obvious and important campaign-exogenous influence on political opinion is experience. Page argues that although most citizens get most of their electoral information through the media, this information is "supplemented and amplified to varying degrees by personal experience and by conversations with friends, neighbors, and coworkers."[25] Popkin advances what he calls a "by-product theory of political information: the information that people acquire to negotiate their daily lives is later applied to their political judgments and choices."[26] Zaller hypothesizes that a voter's "predispositions are at least in part a distillation of a person's lifetime experiences, including childhood socialization and direct involvement with the raw ingredients of policy issues, such as earning a living, paying taxes, racial discrimination, and so forth."[27] In one of the few systematic attempts to sort out the relative influence on political beliefs of formal information and personal experience, Neuman, Just, and Crigler found that people "freely mix together exemplary events and ideas drawn from their own life experiences, books, motion pictures, and entertainment television as well as the traditional news media as they explain their thinking on political topics."[28] The point, then, is that if voters' experiences play any kind of significant role in the process by which they formulate political opinions, and ultimately voting decisions, then it is inevitable that such decisions will be made in a way that is to a significant degree exogenous to the campaign itself.[29]

---

24. Huckfeldt and Sprague, *Citizens, Politics, and Social Communication*, 46–47. *See also* McPhee, Ferguson, and Smith, "A Theory of Informal Social Influence," 75 ("people in close contacts for long periods, such as husbands and wives or parents and children, are found to have remarkably nonindependent preferences").

25. Page, *Who Deliberates?*, 6.

26. Popkin, *The Reasoning Voter*, 22.

27. Zaller, *The Nature and Origins of Mass Opinion*, 23.

28. Neuman, Just, and Crigler, *Common Knowledge*, 111–12.

29. As Miller and Shanks put it, the overall message of this body of research is one of "inherent stability in contrast to occasional change." Miller and Shanks, *The New American Voter*, 494.

The Stability of Political Beliefs

What we have seen so far may help explain why voters are not, at the inception of an election campaign, blank slates upon which candidates can write whatever they wish. It does not necessarily explain, however, why voters are so resistant to persuasion during a campaign. Having an opinion is not the same thing as sticking to it, and is certainly not the same thing as sticking to it in the face of exposure to an overwhelming amount of campaign speech designed to persuade. Here, a substantial body of very helpful social science literature provides considerable insight into the durability of campaign-exogenous political opinion. These studies demonstrate that attempts to persuade voters during election campaigns face extremely significant obstacles in the form of cognitive biases, information-processing strategies, and social dynamics that together work with exceptional power to stabilize an individual's beliefs.

Cognitive Biases

Cognitive biases are patterns or habits of thought that make it more or less likely that an individual exhibiting the bias will arrive at a particular conclusion or belief. One of the most dramatic findings of recent social science studies of political behavior is that perfectly normal individuals exhibit several kinds of cognitive biases that all work in the same direction: to reinforce existing beliefs. These biases operate at every step of cognition to filter out information that challenges preexisting beliefs and to thwart the acceptance of contrary ones.

To persuade another human being one must first get his or her attention. Yet most individuals exhibit a kind of selective attention that causes them to attend most carefully to information with which they are already familiar or with which they already agree, and to ignore unfamiliar or challenging information. As Miller and Krosnick explain, "attitude change is rare because preexisting attitudes guide individuals' exposure to and interpretation of" campaign messages.[30] These preexisting attitudes create "'selectivity effects' on information processing" under the influence of which individuals attend

30. Miller and Krosnick, "News Media Impact on the Ingredients of Presidential Evaluations," 79.

more closely and more enthusiastically to "information that fits with the person's attitudes."[31] Graber attributes this to a natural tendency to take the path of least resistance: in the face of a cascade of new information, individuals simply find it easier, she claims, to focus their attention on "familiar stimuli for which they already have well-developed schema."[32] As a result, Graber argues, "[m]ost political information is sloughed off,"[33] and predictably it is the new, the unfamiliar, and the challenging that is ignored.

Even when potentially challenging ideas penetrate the selective attention barrier, they are likely to be misinterpreted so as to make them seem more consistent with existing beliefs than is actually the case. Alternatively, one might say that new and challenging ideas receive attention only in virtue of having been initially misperceived as consistent with existing ones. Popkin argues that voters tend to misperceive information in their own favor by projecting their own predispositions onto the candidates.[34] Milburn describes this processing bias in the following way: "Messages that are very similar to a person's existing position will be seen as the same, and little or no change will take place [whereas] communications that are very different from the person's position will be seen as even further away . . . and little or no change will take place."[35] Thus, attitude-inconsistent messages are typically interpreted and recalled in ways that reinforce rather than challenge existing attitudes.[36] Indeed, voters actually find it more difficult even to recognize when someone disagrees with them than when someone agrees.[37]

Finally, attitude-inconsistent information that the voter actually manages to perceive and absorb is both more likely to be actively resisted,[38] and less

---

31. Weisberg and Greene, "The Political Psychology of Party Identification," 104.

32. Graber, *Processing Politics*, 19.

33. *Ibid.*

34. Popkin, *The Reasoning Voter*, 38.

35. Milburn, *Persuasion and Politics*, 111.

36. Miller and Krosnick, "News Media Impact on the Ingredients of Presidential Evaluations," 79.

37. Huckfeldt and Sprague, *Citizens, Politics, and Social Communication*, 141–42; Huckfeldt et al., "Ambiguity, Distorted Messages, and Nested Environmental Effects on Political Communication." Cognitive biases can be strong indeed. According to one recent study, a voter's party affiliation is generally more stable than his or her beliefs concerning core values such as equal opportunity, limited government, and moral tolerance. Goren, "Party Identification and Core Political Values." That is, party identification drives political ideology and not the other way around. An even more striking, though seemingly dubious claim is made by Alford et al., who suggest that political orientation may be partly genetic. Alford, Funk, and Hibbing, "Are Political Orientations Genetically Transmitted?"

38. Taber and Lodge, "Motivated Skepticism in the Evaluation of Political Beliefs."

likely to be retained or to be accurately recalled as inconsistent.[39] Inaccurate and incomplete recall, Graber maintains, is "the norm."[40]

Social Reinforcement Effects

"Politics," Huckfeldt and Sprague point out, "is a social activity."[41] It does not occur in the privacy of one's room or in one's head, but in a social setting involving interactions among many people. As with any social activity, the behavior of individuals in politics is influenced by other individuals with whom they interact, both individually and collectively. Like cognitive biases, these social forces can play a significant role in determining what ideas voters are exposed to and how they interpret those ideas.

In the first place, a voter's social environment has an important influence on what information he or she is likely to encounter: "the search for political information is conducted in a context biased by social structure." That is, one looks in one's own environment for information, where the information available to be found is already biased by the environmental setting, thereby causing perpetuation of the original bias. As a result, "[t]he rational actor is thus trapped by her place in social and economic structure, and particularly by the distinctive mix of information that attaches to that structural locale."[42] In this way, the social environment "tends to reproduce the existing distribution of opinion."[43]

This information-limiting effect is not merely something that happens *to* voters because they happen to live in a certain social setting; powerful social forces typically cause individuals to collaborate, so to speak, in the construction of a social environment in which they are less rather than more likely to encounter political opinions that differ from their own. For example, members of the same social group tend to share political opinions, and members of a social group have more contact with each other than with members of other groups.[44] Such contacts are therefore more likely to reinforce than to

39. Miller and Krosnick, "News Media Impact on the Ingredients of Presidential Evaluations," 79.

40. Graber, *Processing Politics*, 14.

41. Huckfeldt and Sprague, *Citizens, Politics, and Social Communication*, 124.

42. *Ibid.*, 50.

43. *Ibid.*, 53. *See also* Mutz, *Hearing the Other Side*, ch. 2.

44. Berelson, Lazarsfeld, and McPhee, *Voting*, 73–74, 88–101.

challenge existing beliefs. Moreover, when people who feel unsure of their political beliefs or opinions want help in thinking them through, they generally turn to people they trust, and these trusted leaders or friends tend to be "others like themselves"[45] who are therefore likely to share, and in discussion to reinforce, the social group's dominant opinions and beliefs. Indeed, because people generally prefer socially reassuring contacts to socially dissonant ones, they are likely, when in a mood to talk politics, to seek out like-minded people.[46] In sum, according to Huckfeldt and Sprague, individuals "do purposefully attempt to construct informational networks corresponding to their own political preferences."[47]

Even when voters manage to encounter political ideas that differ from ones they already hold, powerful social forces tend to undermine their willingness to embrace those ideas. We do not live solely in a world of free and shifting ideological affiliations, as the metaphor of the marketplace of ideas or the First Amendment doctrine of expressive association might suggest. We also inhabit a world in which changes in a person's opinions or attitudes have "social repercussions"[48]—that is, in which embracing or rejecting the ideas that prevail within one's social group can have ramifications for how one lives within the group and relates to its members. Because people have strong reasons entirely independent of their political beliefs to remain in good standing with their social group, "[p]olitical discussion . . . becomes the vehicle through which dominant preferences within the larger community are transmitted to the individuals who are members of that community."[49] This process is "inherently conservative" and tends to "reproduce the existing distribution of opinion."[50] Indeed, social processes can be every bit as narrowing of view and as suppressive of dissenting opinions as cognitive biases:

> Democratic elections include a substantial element of social coercion. Electoral campaigns turn citizens' attention toward politics, and deviant

---

45. *Ibid.*, 109; *see also* Huckfeldt and Sprague, *Citizens, Politics, and Social Communication*, 118–19 (people tend to choose political discussion partners from the same general social and economic class).

46. Huckfeldt and Sprague, *Citizens, Politics, and Social Communication*, 149–55.

47. *Ibid.*, 143.

48. Katz and Lazarsfeld, *Personal Influence*, 66.

49. Huckfeldt and Sprague, *Citizens, Politics, and Social Communication*, 160.

50. *Ibid.*, 53.

> preferences are brought into correspondence with their political surroundings. The election campaign serves as a political stimulus setting into motion a social influence process, and this in turn imposes social order on the political chaos of individually held, idiosyncratic opinions.[51]

Under these circumstances, any attempt to persuade voters during a campaign to embrace a belief that they or their social group did not already hold prior to the campaign faces formidable obstacles. Thus, "disagreement is always on the verge of being eliminated, and the only individuals who are equipped to take on the full role of a participatory citizen are those imbedded within cozy cocoons of like-minded associates."[52]

Information-Processing Strategies

A third set of factors contributing to the stabilization of individual opinion arise from the ways in which voters process information. In today's society of instantaneous and ubiquitous communication, the main problem voters face is not typically a dearth of relevant information but an overabundance of it.[53] All this information is too much for any individual to work through,[54] requiring even the most responsible and dedicated of voters to develop coping strategies. Two are especially relevant here: the "on-line processing," or "running-tally" strategy for processing new information, and the strategy of remaining "rationally ignorant" of new information. Each strategy lends a kind of inertia to individual opinion that makes persuasion very unlikely in the short term, and each contributes to a paradoxical dynamic in which the most easily persuaded voters are the least likely to be reached.

In the classic model of democratic citizenship, an election campaign is a period during which voters absorb information, listen to arguments, deliberate privately and in groups, and then, at some point shortly before Election Day, make a decision about how to vote. Political psychologists call this

51. *Ibid.*, 96. *See also* Berelson, Lazarsfeld, and McPhee, *Voting*, 142–43 (campaign is "a period of reassertion of social discussion and thence of influence on the deviant political minorities in social groups"); Mutz, *Hearing the Other Side.*

52. Huckfeldt, Johnson, and Sprague, *Political Disagreement*, 6.

53. Jones, *Reconceiving Decision-Making in Democratic Politics*, 95.

54. Graber, *Processing Politics*, 15, 46.

a "memory-based model" because it contemplates that the voter continuously gathers information and tucks it away in memory, and that "the integration process is held in abeyance until an evaluation is called for (e.g., on election day)."[55] It is not, however, an especially plausible model for how people actually process a steady stream of new information. A better and more widely accepted model of information processing is the "on-line" model. According to this model, voters do not collect items of "raw" information in a value-neutral form and keep them handy until some point when they consider all the data at once to see what conclusion on balance it supports. Rather, voters collect information bit by bit, evaluating each new item as soon as they encounter it in what amounts to a kind of "running tally" on the subject in question.[56] That is, the voter at some point has some evaluative judgment of some object in the political universe—the Republican Party, for example.[57] The voter maintains that judgment, holding it stable but not attending to it in any way until some new piece of information about the Republican Party comes to the voter's attention.[58] At that point, the voter reconsiders his or her standing evaluation of the Party in light of the new information, adjusting it as necessary to give the new datum its appropriate weight, a process that the voter repeats upon collection of each new piece of information. It follows that unless the new information is dramatically different from whatever the voter has learned in the past, the voter's evaluation of the Republican Party is likely to be affected only marginally by each new item, and his or her judgment about the party will display over time what Page and Shapiro call a "central tendency of opinion."[59] And the longer the voter has observed the Republican Party, the greater the weight and likely consistency of this central tendency of opinion.

The on-line strategy offers a considerable advantage to the voter in cognitive efficiency. As Steenbergen and Lodge explain, once the voter has an on-line tally, he can rely on the tally itself without any need to recall all the many original judgments and considerations giving rise to the tally or to undertake

---

55. Steenbergen and Lodge, "Process Matters," 145.

56. *Ibid.*, 149.

57. Fiorina proposed just such a model of party evaluation as an artifact of his theory of retrospective voting. *See* Fiorina, "An Outline for a Model of Party Choice," 618; Fiorina, *Retrospective Voting in American National Elections*, 65–105.

58. Jones, *Reconceiving Decision-Making in Democratic Politics*, 67.

59. Page and Shapiro, *The Rational Public*, 16.

the more "cognitively taxing task" of "constructing a judgment from whatever evidence is available in memory."[60] In other words, on-line processing allows the voter, in essence, to know what he thinks without requiring him to recall why he thinks it. The voter thus gains the benefit of a well-informed opinion without the burden of remembering every detail that went into formulating it.

However, from the point of view of electoral democracy, the on-line processing strategy constitutes a potentially significant impediment to campaign-endogenous persuasion. The problem, of course, is that a running-tally method of opinion formation gives opinions a kind of inertia or staying power that they might not have if voters made judgments by weighing all the relevant data at once during the campaign. As a result, any individual's opinion can in most cases be moved only slightly on the basis of one or a few new pieces of information, no matter how positive or negative; a really significant change in a voter's evaluation of a party, a candidate, or a policy can in general result only from a lengthy and highly consistent stream of information that is inconsistent overall with the voter's existing provisional judgment.

Another, closely related information-processing strategy with implications for campaign persuasion is the strategy of "rational ignorance." In his influential work developing an economic theory of democracy, Anthony Downs hypothesized from purely theoretic premises that voters, contrary to the usual understanding of democratic citizenship, normally have strong incentives to avoid informing themselves during election campaigns.[61] Acquiring information sufficient to make an informed decision between candidates, Downs argued, can be costly in both time and money, and a rational voter will therefore make the investment in electoral information only when the expected benefits exceed the costs. According to Downs, voters will rarely undertake the costly burden of acquiring the necessary information because any difference in the degree to which they will personally benefit or suffer under one party or the other is likely to be trivial, and thus who wins the election is likely to be a matter of indifference to them.

Downs's prediction appears to be borne out by the evidence. Certainly voters tend to be ignorant of electorally relevant facts.[62] The question is what,

---

60. Steenbergen and Lodge, "Process Matters," 150.

61. Downs, *An Economic Theory of Democracy.*

62. Campbell et al., *The American Voter*; E. Smith, *The Unchanging American Voter*; Delli Carpini and Keeter, *What American Know About Politics and Why It Matters*; Page and Shapiro, *The Rational Public*, 4–9.

if anything, makes this behavior rational. Downs found it to be rational by assuming that voters are motivated primarily by economic self-interest, but recent research into information-processing strategies provides a more democratically attractive explanation. The concept of on-line processing provides a ready explanation for voters' factual ignorance, while both preserving the possibility that their ultimate judgments may be rational and accounting for why voters often cannot readily articulate the factual foundations of their opinions. Political scientists have also identified other information processing strategies that, they argue, allow voters to function at an acceptable level of rationality without learning or retaining large amounts of electoral information. Popkin argues that strategies such as party loyalty, shorthand evaluations of candidates' character and competence, and reliance on political symbols are all "information shortcuts" that permit voters to reach rational judgments from parsimonious data.[63]

While voter ignorance may be consistent with rational political judgments, either individually or collectively,[64] such ignorance seems to be bad news for campaign-endogenous persuasion: candidates and partisans cannot persuade voters whose attention they cannot command, especially when inattentiveness can be a rational and democratically defensible strategy. This problem has been usefully explored by John Zaller, who has noted an interesting paradox in the degree to which citizens are susceptible to electoral persuasion. Zaller begins from the premise that "[t]he greater a person's level of cognitive engagement with an issue, the more likely he or she is to be exposed to and comprehend—in a word, to receive—political messages concerning that issue."[65] This makes engaged and interested voters the easiest to reach with messages intended to persuade them. However, Zaller argues, "[p]eople tend to resist arguments that are inconsistent with

63. Popkin, *The Reasoning Voter*.

64. Popkin argues that individual voters are capable of reaching rational decisions despite their ignorance. Popkin, *The Reasoning Voter*. Page and Shapiro, in contrast, argue that it is not necessary for voters to make rational judgments individually because they are capable of doing so collectively because individual irrationalities and idiosyncracies tend to be mutually cancelling on the aggregate level. Page and Shapiro, *The Rational Public*. For a contrary view, Caplan, *The Myth of the Rational Voter*, which argues that the electorate is not collectively rational because the kinds of errors that voters make are systematic rather than mutually cancelling. Indeed, Caplan goes so far as to argue that individual voters operate in an environment in which they have incentives positively to indulge their irrational beliefs rather than to moderate them. *Ibid.*, 18.

65. Zaller, *The Nature and Origins of Mass Opinion*, 42.

their political predispositions, [and] the likelihood of resisting persuasive communications that are inconsistent with one's political predispositions rises with a person's level of political attentiveness."[66] It follows that the voters who are easiest to reach with persuasive messages are also the very people who are best-informed, and who therefore find it easiest to resist messages with which they disagree. Zaller's analysis, then, means that those who are not already firmly committed to a position, and are thus good candidates for persuasion, are the least likely to receive persuasive campaign messages, and those who are least likely to be persuaded by campaign messages are the most likely to receive them.[67]

The Tabulative Campaign

If, as the evidence abundantly suggests, it is extremely difficult—maybe close to impossible—to persuade any significant number of voters during the course of an election campaign to embrace opinions that they did not already hold when the campaign began—if, that is to say, public opinion is overwhelmingly campaign-exogenous—what, then, is the function of an election campaign? Political scientists have offered several answers, all pointing in more or less the same direction: the purpose of an election campaign is to ensure, insofar as possible, that the candidate exogenously preferred by a majority is in the end the one who actually wins the election.

Sometimes political scientists have couched this conclusion in terms of "activation"[68] or "mobilization."[69] These terms imply, correctly, that a significant

66. *Ibid.*, 44.

67. Zaller's analysis is consistent with the findings of Lazarsfeld, Berelson, and Gaudet, *The People's Choice*, 95: "In summary, then, the people who did most of the reading and listening not only read and heard most of their own partisan propaganda but were also most resistant to conversion because of their strong predispositions. And the people who were most open to conversion—the ones the campaign managers most wanted to reach—read and listened least." Lazarsfeld et al., termed this phenomenon "the bottleneck of conversion." *Ibid.* To be clear, Zaller does not claim that persuasion cannot occur; indeed, he thinks it happens frequently, but only under specific conditions: high salience, voter receptivity, and extensive and one-sided media communications. Zaller, *The Nature and Origins of Mass Opinion*; Zaller, "The Myth of Massive Media Impact Revived."

68. *E.g.*, Berelson, Lazarsfeld, and McPhee, *Voting*, 253: "An effect of the campaign was to draw out, or revive, or activate latent predispositions."

69. *E.g.*, Delli Carpini and Keeter, *What American Know About Politics and Why It Matters*, 227 (arguing that knowledge is mobilizing).

function of a campaign is not to persuade but to motivate those who are exogenously inclined to support a particular candidate actually to turn out at the polls and make their support count.[70] But these descriptions oversimplify to the extent that they suggest that a campaign is in some fundamental sense a competition of organizational ability rather than of political ideology. On the ground, organization undoubtedly plays a role in a successful election campaign, but it is in no sense an end in itself: organization is democratically justifiable only insofar as it improves the accuracy of electoral outcomes by ensuring that the final vote count expresses the wishes, as nearly as possible, of every voter who is not indifferent toward the candidates.

The better accounts of election campaigns instead emphasize their role in bringing electoral outcomes into alignment with exogenous public opinion. As usual, Lazarsfeld and Berelson made the point first. According to them, arguments made during election campaigns that appear to be calculated to persuade voters in fact serve "more as *indicators* than as *influences*. They *point out*, like signboards along the road, the way to turn in order to reach a destination which is already determined."[71] Such communications, in other words, identify for voters the way to reach their chosen ends. "Campaigning for votes," Lazarsfeld and Berelson continue, "is not writing on a public *tabula rasa*; it is showing men and women that their votes are a normal and logical and more or less inevitable expression of tendencies with which each has already aligned himself."[72]

More recently, Finkel has similarly argued that the main function of an election campaign is to bring the electorate's voting decisions into proper alignment with its precampaign political preferences. In Finkel's account, the campaign helps to orient those whose initial candidate selection differs from the one that their predispositions demonstrate they "should" prefer—that is, some voters initially choose the "wrong" candidate, and the campaign straightens them out so that they ultimately vote for the person they should have been supporting all along.[73] "Conversion," Finkel argues, thus does occur during campaigns, but it is conversion of a very limited sort, and the observed amount of conversion is likely to depend not on the extent to which candidates

70. Holbrook and McClurg, "The Mobilization of Core Supporters."

71. Lazarsfeld, Berelson, and Gaudet, *The People's Choice*, 83.

72. *Ibid.*, 83–84. To similar effect is Gelman and King, "Why Are American Presidential Election Campaign Polls so Variable when Votes Are so Predictable?"

73. Finkel, "Reexamining the 'Minimal Effects' Model in Recent Presidential Campaigns," 16.

persuade voters of new ideas, but much more simply on "the extent to which the electorate's initial dispositions and initial preferences are in accord with one another."[74] It follows, says Finkel, that a campaign-induced change in support for *candidates* does not reflect a change in *beliefs*, but quite the opposite: such changes reflect "predictable movement by the electorate toward casting votes in accordance with [predictive] underlying conditions and their accompanying predispositions."[75]

Another such account of what campaigns accomplish is provided by Holbrook's model of campaign equilibria. No campaign, Holbrook observes, begins at some abstract starting line in which each candidate has an equal chance to win the election; on the contrary, every campaign begins in a concrete political context in which each candidate should predictably enjoy a certain amount of exogenous voter support—an equilibrium.[76] But, says Holbrook, "candidate support at the beginning of the campaign is frequently out of equilibrium," meaning that "[o]ne of the important roles of the campaign is to help move public opinion toward the expected outcome. As events unfold and voters update their evaluations, public opinion gravitates toward the equilibrium level."[77]

All of this suggests not that campaigns are completely devoid of persuasion, but that there is precious little of it, and the bulk of the persuasion that does occur during campaigns is of a much more limited and unambitious kind than is contemplated by the social ideology of the democratic campaign or by the high First Amendment rhetoric of free campaign speech. In the real world, voters are not persuaded during a campaign to embrace, or even in most cases to contemplate, ideas that are unfamiliar or that challenge their existing beliefs. Voters know more or less what they think and what they want, and are not about to be moved during something so brief and slight as an election campaign. The main issue for the voter is much smaller and

---

74. *Ibid.*

75. *Ibid.*, 18.

76. Holbrook, *Do Campaigns Matter?*, 48.

77. *Ibid.*, 157. To similar effect, *see* J. Campbell, "Presidential Election Campaigns and Partisanship" (arguing that presidential campaigns tend mainly to reinvigorate latent partisan leanings, thereby bringing voters back to their basic predispositions). On the other hand, campaigns still may not do a very complete job at helping voters make the "correct" choice. Recent work by Lau and Redlawsk suggests that a substantial portion of voters may not end up casting a vote consistent with their underlying policy predispositions, although a sizable majority may do so in two-candidate races. Lau and Redlawsk, *How Voters Decide.*

more contained: Given my views, which candidate should I vote for? Which of these candidates will most reliably do what I think should be done?

For the great majority of voters, this is an easy question to answer. Campbell has put the point well:

> Why is the vote choice so simple for many voters? . . . Most American voters are . . . to one degree or another, liberals or conservatives and Democrats and Republicans. . . . If you are a conservative, how much do you really need to know to be sure that a Republican vote best reflects your point of view? If you are more inclined to see things from the liberal perspective, there is probably nothing you would learn from the campaign that could dissuade you from a Democratic vote. Similarly, if you are convinced that the in-party has done an excellent job in office, that the economy is humming along, and that all is right with the world, the campaign is not going to prevent you from returning that party to office. On the other hand, if you think that the in-party has fouled up the nation, nothing that is said during the campaign will prevent you from trying to "throw the bums out."[78]

For the minority of voters who do not so clearly know whom they will support, the campaign may well open the possibility of persuasion—but persuasion of what? At one end of the spectrum, the substance of persuasive efforts may be extremely limited and entirely factual: no, no, John Kerry, not George Bush, is the candidate who thinks we should secure the support of our major European allies before invading another country. Indeed, there is evidence to suggest that basic factual knowledge of the candidates' actual positions is a frequent subject of confusion among voters.[79] Fortunately, recent research suggests that although it is extremely difficult to persuade people to change their views on normative questions,[80] particularly where

---

78. J. Campbell, *The American Campaign*, 32–33.

79. For example, year after year, substantial minorities evidently do not know whether the Democratic or Republican parties is more conservative, or which party controls Congress. Delli Carpini and Keeter, *What American Know About Politics and Why It Matters*, 316. See Gelman and King, "Why Are American Presidential Election Campaign Polls So Variable When Votes Are So Predictable?," 433–35 (arguing that the answer to the question posed in the title is that voters acquire factual information during campaigns enabling them to know how to apply their personal "fundamental variables" to the vote decision).

80. Mendelberg, "The Deliberative Citizen," 160–61.

those questions are of high personal salience,[81] it is much easier to persuade people on questions of basic fact.[82] This makes campaigns potentially useful vehicles to guide voters to the candidates they wish to support by correcting any factual errors that might otherwise cause them to make a "mistake" at the polls.

In other cases, there may be some room for persuasion on a somewhat grander scale. For example, because voters may not necessarily know how to decide which set of actions and policies will best achieve the ends that they want elected officials to pursue, candidates may attempt to persuade voters to "make new connections between specific problems and specific offices"[83]—to persuade voters, that is to say, of the political salience of certain information and ideas. But this is about the most elaborate and complex degree of persuasion likely to occur with any kind of frequency during an election campaign, and the number of voters who will even be susceptible to this kind of persuasion, much less actually persuaded by campaign speech on these grounds, is likely to be small.[84]

The New Campaign Effects Findings

I turn finally to a newer body of social science research that its most enthusiastic proponents believe suggests significant promise for undermining the minimal effects thesis by showing that campaigns do in fact affect the decisions voters make about how to cast their votes.

Skeptics of the minimal effects hypothesis have long been fascinated by a simple question: if campaigns are really incapable of persuading voters, why

---

81. Trost and Kenrick, "Ego Involvement in the Minority Influence Paradigm."

82. Mendelberg, "The Deliberative Citizen," 160–61 ("the more the discussion takes up questions of truth and fact, and the less it deals with values, the more isolated it becomes from the social pressures that deliberative theory would regard with alarm, and the more rational and argument-driven it becomes, as deliberative theory would like"). This is not to say that values and facts cannot be intimately connected. Kahan and Kahan and Braman have recently argued that even routine factual commitments may be highly influenced by what they call "cultural commitments"—*i.e.*, culturally induced value judgments are prior to empirical beliefs, which after all are subject to interpretation. Kahan, "The Cognitively Illiberal State"; Kahan and Braman, "Cultural Cognition and Public Policy."

83. Popkin, *The Reasoning Voter*, 46.

84. For an examination of some of the social and symbolic functions of campaigns, see Hart, *Campaign Talk*.

do candidates and political professionals insist in each election cycle on spending millions upon millions of dollars on campaign communications? It is obvious, these skeptics argue, that the media portrayals that dominate political discourse in this country have an impact on what people think about political subjects. If we fail to detect such effects during campaigns, it can only be because our measurements are inaccurate, our methods sloppy, or our assumptions about what to look for require revision.[85]

In the last two decades, researchers studying mass political communication, especially televised political advertising, have begun to generate results consistent with the expectations of the minimal effects skeptics. These studies have shown that political communication can affect the voting decisions of those exposed to it and that the electorate does not simply and entirely shrug off political communications of the kind with which they are routinely bombarded during campaigns.

Researchers working in this area have turned up three related kinds of campaign effects: agenda-setting, framing, and priming. *Agenda-setting* refers to the capacity of certain political actors such as the mass media, politicians, or candidates, to bring an issue to public attention in the first place. Voters rarely have their own, independent sources of information about public affairs and must consequently rely on information provided by others to stay informed. In so doing, voters not only submit themselves to judgments made by others about the facts but also about which facts are important. Thus, according to the authors of one prominent study, the "agenda-setting hypothesis" holds that "those problems that receive prominent attention on the national news become the problems the viewing public regards as the nation's most important."[86]

The fact that an issue comes to public attention does not, however, carry implications for how it will be received. *Framing*, in contrast, deals squarely with the evaluative component of public political decision making. Facts and issues do not carry intrinsic moral or political content; such evaluations must be supplied by the voter through a process of interpretation. To frame an issue, then, is to present it in such as way as to influence the voter to reach one interpretation rather than another.[87] Framing therefore generally weaves

85. Zaller, "The Myth of Massive Media Impact Revived"; Bartels, "Message Received."

86. Iyengar and Kinder, *News That Matters*, 16 (italics omitted).

87. Chong, "Creating Common Frames of Reference on Political Issues"; Chong and Druckman, "Framing Theory."

facts into a consistent and easily understood narrative that increases the likelihood that voters will reach one evaluation of the facts rather than another. For example, framing an event as an example of injustice is more likely to prompt collective social action than framing the same event in more neutral terms;[88] during the 2000 presidential election, Republicans successfully framed factual errors made by Al Gore, the Democratic candidate, as revealing a tendency habitually to exaggerate, and so on.[89]

Like framing, *priming* also influences voters' ultimate evaluative judgments, but it operates more subtly. "[P]olitical evaluation," according to Donald Kinder, a leading researcher in the field, "is subject to the availability heuristic"[90]—voters, that is to say, generally decide what they think on political subjects (and presumably on any other subject) not by drawing deliberately and reflectively on everything they know, but by drawing selectively and to some degree reflexively on whatever information or associations tend to be most immediately and readily accessible.[91] Because people may be invited to make political judgments in many different circumstances, the information and associations most likely to come readily to mind may differ from circumstance to circumstance, from which it follows that the substantive judgments people make on the same topic may differ as well, depending upon the precise conditions in which they happen to render the judgment. As a result, researchers have found, influencing the circumstances in which political judgments are made—as by selectively directing a voter's attention to some matters rather than others in televised political ads—can influence the judgments that voters make on the merits of political issues or candidates. For example, voters exposed to a barrage of media stories about defense policy are more likely to base their evaluation of the President on his performance on defense, whereas voters exposed to stories about environmental policy are more likely to evaluate the President based on his performance on the environment.[92]

---

88. Gamson, *Talking Politics*.

89. Jamieson and Waldman, *The Press Effect*.

90. Kinder, "Communication and Opinion," 181.

91. Iyengar and Kinder, *News That Matters*, 4, 65.

92. Chong and Druckman, "Framing Theory," 114–15. These authors also argue that there is no real difference between framing and priming, properly understood, a conclusion that I find appealing, but I shall stick to the conventional distinctions here. In any case, it is clear that the same communication can simultaneously exemplify agenda-setting, framing, and priming. A series of campaign ads criticizing President Bush's handling of global

Some political scientists have argued that demonstrations of agenda-setting, framing, and priming effects require a reevaluation of the minimal effects thesis. "It is safe to say now," argue Goldstein and Ridout, "that campaigns in general do matter."[93] "[M]inimal effects," claims Kinder, "have given way to a family of real effects: agenda setting, priming, framing, and even, looking in the right places, ample persuasion"[94] The question for present purposes, however, is not whether agenda-setting, framing, and priming affect how people vote, but whether a demonstration of these effects amounts to a demonstration of *persuasion*, and if it does, how closely these particular kinds of persuasion approach the social, historical, and legal ideal of persuasion that is deep, deliberative, and rational. In my view, this work does not demonstrate anything remotely approaching widespread, meaningful persuasion during campaigns, and suggestions to the contrary rest on either an overly enthusiastic assessment of the significance of the findings or a misunderstanding of causation that mistakenly attributes changes in political outcomes to exercises of political agency.

To begin, even a quick review of some of the literature on agenda-setting, framing, and priming reveals numerous reasons counseling against an overly hasty abandonment of the minimal effects thesis. First, and perhaps most obviously, nothing in this work has undermined in any way the ability of election forecasters to make predictions with impressive accuracy based on campaign-exogenous factors. If framing and priming occur now, they have been occurring forever, and modelers seem to be in no hurry to delay or alter their forecasts so as to account for the content of ads aired during campaigns. If there is an effect, then, it is presumably either very small and felt only at the margins, or if larger, is bidirectional and thus self-cancelling. Certainly, it is striking how even the greatest enthusiasts of this body of work qualify their findings as likely having relevance only in close races,[95] a rarity in American politics below the presidential level. Second, much of the work

---

warming, for example, might simultaneously place the issue of global warming on the political agenda; frame his performance in a negative light; and prime voters to evaluate the President on this dimension of his performance.

93. Goldstein and Ridout, "Measuring the Effects of Televised Political Advertising in the United States," 223.

94. Kinder, "Communication and Opinion," 189. *See also* Iyengar and Simon, "New Perspectives and Evidence on Political Communication and Campaign Effects."

95. Kinder, *Communication and Opinion*, 187; Goldstein and Ridout, "Measuring the Effects of Televised Political Advertising in the United States," 210.

in this area has taken place in the laboratory rather than in the field, making generalizations to the real world of politics extremely hazardous. Third, the effect of framing and priming is likely of short duration—one study found it faded within ten days[96]—suggesting that voters' normal predispositions quickly reassert themselves, stabilizing not only their opinions but their voting decisions. Fourth, framing effects are frequently offset or moderated by environmental factors such as exposure to counter-frames, subsequent discussion in heterogeneous groups, or individual expertise.[97]

Even more important, however, studies of agenda-setting, framing, and priming do not in fact argue that these effects change voters' actual political *beliefs*. These studies demonstrate only that political actors and the media are capable of influencing voters' decisions on what to think *about*—not what to *think*[98]—and that they operate largely on a subrational rather than self-consciously deliberative level. Furthermore, even if we were inclined, plausibly in my view, to treat influencing how citizens direct their attention as a kind of persuasion, albeit a kind of persuasion that lies far from the ideal, it is clear that the potential range of the relevant persuasive effect is extremely limited. Specifically, the potential range of persuasion is limited by the opinions and predispositions that voters already possess *before* they are exposed to agenda-setting, framing, and priming effects. As Ansolabehere and Iyengar explain:

> Candidates can direct the voters' attention to an issue only if the voters are predisposed to care about that issue to begin with. . . . Candidates succeed not by distracting voters, but by addressing the problems that individuals [already] believe to be important. . . . Through their advertising, candidates can exploit favorable electoral circumstances and they can solidify the support of their own partisans, but they cannot convert nonpartisans and members of the opposite party, and they cannot redirect the interests of most voters and change the substance of the election.[99]

96. Druckman and Nelson, "Framing and Deliberation," 741.

97. Druckman, "Political Preference Formation."

98. Iyengar and Kinder, *News That Matters*, 2.

99. Ansolabehere and Iyengar, *Going Negative*, 88–89.

Or as Chong similarly observes, "it is implausible [to think] that political elites can arbitrarily designate any dimension to guide public discussion of an issue."[100] Not even the most sophisticated techniques of agenda-setting, framing, and priming, in other words, can enable candidates to bring into the campaign and successfully to exploit issues that voters are not predisposed to think are politically important. "Hillary Clinton—a low-born commoner," for example, will not be the basis for a successful campaign by the Monarchist Party. Every appeal must in the first instance lie somewhere on the public's conceptual map of politics—a map the bounds of which are defined overwhelmingly by beliefs and preferences formed by voters exogenously to the campaign.

To be successful during a campaign, appeals based on agenda-setting, framing, and priming must have something to appeal to, and laying the groundwork for such appeals necessarily occurs outside of and before the campaign in which the appeal is made. Agenda-setting, framing, and priming techniques are not bootstraps: they cannot exploit a tendency while simultaneously supplying the very tendency they seek to exploit. In short, demonstrations of agenda-setting, framing, and priming effects do not in any way disturb the central finding of decades of political science research: public political opinion is enormously stable, and very little that happens during a campaign is likely to budge it.

This is not to say, however, that agenda-setting, framing, and priming effects have no significance for electoral outcomes. They are significant, but their significance lies elsewhere, bringing me to the second mistake of the new campaign effects enthusiasts. The importance for political outcomes of the power to set the agenda has long been understood,[101] and it is the basis for important work in social choice theory, such as Arrow's Theorem, that is often said to throw into question the coherence of the core democratic concept of popular sovereignty.[102] The main idea, common in the public choice literature, is that the way in which choices are presented to voters—for example, the sequence in which choices are offered or the number of choices

---

100. Chong, "Creating Common Frames of Reference on Political Issues," 221–22. To similar effect, *see, e.g.*, Sears, "Symbolic Politics," 146; Iyengar and Kinder, *News That Matters*, 97; Iyengar, *Is Anyone Responsible?*, 126; Neuman, Just and Crigler, *Common Knowledge*, 76–77.

101. Schattschneider, *The Semi-Sovereign People*.

102. *E.g.*, Riker, *Liberalism against Populism*.

among which voters are permitted to choose—can have a decisive impact on the final result. This impact does not occur, however, because anything about the way in which choices are presented persuades or otherwise alters voters' opinions. On the contrary, the power of this argument lies precisely in its demonstration that variations in the *procedures* applied to a *fixed* set of preferences can yield dramatically different results. Manipulation of the agenda, moreover, can have this effect even when voters are perfectly rational and behaving ideally in every way. Changes in outcomes here have nothing to do with voter behavior and everything to do with the way elites succeed in presenting choices to voters.

Like agenda-setting, framing and priming also are techniques by which an electorate's preferences can potentially be manipulated, but it is unnecessary to resort to the concept of persuasion to explain this effect. By rearranging the way in which evaluative judgments are presented to voters, framing and priming can affect those judgments even if voters' preferences remain entirely fixed. Changing the way voters apply existing, fixed preferences to the judgments they are asked to make is fully sufficient to produce the "campaign effects"—namely, changes in voting intentions—that political scientists working in this field have observed.

Now, this is an unsettling problem, to be sure. If I can induce (prime) you to vote for Bush by talking about military policy prior to asking you to vote, but can just as easily induce (prime) you to vote for Kerry by talking about environmental policy instead, in what sense can you really be said to rule yourself? That is why, as Bryan Garsten has recently pointed out, liberalism has long been suspicious of rhetoric, which it tends to see as "a form of rule."[103] On the other hand, this is a problem that is endemic across the length and breadth of democratic practice: procedural choices have consequences. If we use a first-past-the-post electoral system we get one result; if we use proportional representation, or cumulative voting, or limited voting, or approval voting, we get another. If we elect at large we get one result; if we use districts we get another. If we draw the district boundary here we get one result, if we draw it somewhere else, another. If we vote on Tuesday, the results fall this way; if on Saturday, that way. Nothing in these procedural choices affect voters' beliefs; all that is affected is the way in which beliefs are measured and aggregated.

---

103. Garsten, *Saving Persuasion*, 6.

What all this means—and all that it means—is simply that we must be careful when we choose democratic procedures. We cannot, of course, prevent the choice of procedure from influencing substantive outcomes. We can, however, and we should, think carefully about what kinds of inputs we would prefer our democratic outcomes to reflect, and when possible lay a thumb on the scale by choosing procedures that are more rather than less likely to reflect the kinds of considerations to which we prefer to submit. For example, states generally ban electioneering within 100 feet of the polls to minimize the ability of candidates to prime voters as they proceed to cast their ballots.[104] Some states provide neutrally worded voter information guides to ensure that all voters receive the same basic factual information on all sides of an issue, reducing candidate control over framing effects. And so on.

Agenda-setting, framing, and priming effects thus raise questions for how we understand campaigns, but the questions they raise are procedural and pragmatic; they do not, alas, offer any grounds for thinking that voters somehow really do behave during campaigns in ways that approach the social ideal. And thus I end with the contention with which I began: the empirical social science research demonstrates that in any given citizen's life the deliberatively reflective alteration of political opinion is unusual and infrequent; that the norm is for political opinion to form early, to evolve very gradually, and to be largely immune from significant revision; and that campaigns play at best a minor role in the formation of public political opinion. Even on the most sympathetic view, then, the typical election campaign is far from the forum of vibrant, open, persuasive discourse contemplated by social convention and by judicial rhetoric.

The question is: should we care?

---

104. Gardner, "Neutralizing the Incompetent Voter."

FOUR

Democratic Theory and the Thin Election Campaign

TO THIS POINT, THE ARGUMENT has proceeded as follows. The basic premise of this book is that a stark disjunction exists between the lofty American aspirations for election campaigns and the desultory condition of the campaigns we actually have. Chapter 1 traced the evolution of the contemporary conception of campaigns as forums for reasoned persuasion and enlightenment on the pressing issues of the day, showing how it developed from very different antecedents. The law is often assigned some blame for the poor state of contemporary campaigns, or at least is looked to frequently as a vehicle by which the quality of campaigns might be usefully reformed. Chapter 2 accordingly examined the legal structure of campaigns and asked whether existing legal institutions are well-suited to produce the kind of campaigns to which we aspire. I concluded that our legal institutions are not well-suited to produce campaigns rich in the political discourse of persuasion, but in fact are structured so as to encourage just the opposite: thin campaigns better suited to the tabulation of exogenously held public opinion than to the deliberative, campaign-endogenous reconsideration and reformulation of public opinion.

This conclusion raised the question of whether the law might feasibly be reformed to produce better, more deliberative campaigns. In Chapter 3, I addressed that question by examining the social science literature of political opinion formation. I concluded, based on this review, that the prospects for achieving thicker, more satisfyingly deliberative campaigns, whether through legal reforms or otherwise, appear dim mainly on account of the way in which human beings acquire political knowledge. The cognitive strategies people commonly employ to acquire political information and the ensuing stability of their political beliefs pose significant obstacles to the successful inducement of voters, during the short period of an electoral campaign, to embrace opinions they did not previously hold. As a result, we must contemplate the possibility that we ought not expect more of our campaigns than what they apparently already aim to do: accurately tabulate public opinion as it stands roughly at the campaign's inception.

Such a conclusion, however, does not sit particularly well, for it seems grossly inconsistent with our conceptions of democracy itself. If all the speeches, appeals, debates, advertisements, news stories, editorials, and conversations that constitute campaign politics are not about the changing of hearts and minds—if the great swirl of campaign discourse does not, in the end, consist of citizens persuading other citizens about how we collectively ought to act—then in what sense can we be said truly to govern ourselves? Even the most minimal theories of democracy view elections as the indispensable means by which a polity holds its rulers accountable. But if campaigns do not and, for the most part, cannot result in the changing of minds, how can the electorate possibly hold its leaders to account? Surely a healthy, meaningfully discursive campaign is a critical stage in any process of democratic self-governance.

In this Chapter, I look to democratic theory for answers to these questions. I shall argue that, surprisingly, a deliberatively thick campaign of reasoned persuasion is not, according to any commonly accepted democratic theory, an essential requirement of a well-functioning democracy. Many theories of democracy, to be sure, demand a citizenry that is attentive, informed, reflective, reasonable, or deliberative, but in none of these theories is it absolutely required that such behavior be exhibited during *campaigns*. In most theories, so long as citizens discharge their democratic duties at some point—for example, *between* elections, in the ordinary course of daily life—the quality of democracy and the achievement of its aims are unlikely to be impaired.

In the next Chapter, I shall discuss why, if democratic theory is in fact largely indifferent to the deliberative thickness of campaigns, so many critics of contemporary American politics think that the thinness and superficiality of the typical modern campaign signifies a potentially catastrophic failure of democracy. But first, I must make good on my theoretical claim.

Democratic Theory

Before turning to the analysis, I need to say a few preliminary words about what is involved in turning for guidance to democratic theory. The field of democratic theory has in the last few decades enjoyed a period of impressive fertility, with the result that there are now almost as many different theories of democracy as there are democratic theorists. Nevertheless, specialists appear to have settled on a conceptual organization of the field into two broad categories of theories: deliberative and aggregative.[1] Deliberative theories, as the name suggests, emphasize the importance of meaningful deliberation by members of the polity to the formulation of a public will. Aggregative theories, in contrast, understand the public will not as the product of collective reflection and deliberation, but merely as the sum, or aggregation, of individually held private opinions.[2]

Although this is a sensible way to divide the kingdom of democratic theory for many purposes, and indeed I discuss below several theories of democracy that fall paradigmatically within each of these categories, it is not the best way to slice the subject for the purposes I pursue here. The central problems in democratic theory to which the deliberative-aggregative categorization responds concern, first, how to think about the concept of a democratic public will, and second, how such a will ought to be translated into official policy. These are problems, in other words, that revolve around the practice of representation in a mass democracy.

The problem I am mainly concerned with here, however, is slightly different and focuses more closely on the civic obligations of democratic citizens, a question more directly relevant to how the particular institution of the electoral campaign ought to be structured. Consequently, I prefer to think of the various democratic theories discussed below as arrayed along a different spectrum, from liberal to communitarian. Liberal theories of democracy tend to treat citizens as isolated, self-generating atoms[3] and therefore make rather few formal demands of citizens. Communitarian theories, in contrast, view citizens as interdependent members of a shared community and tend to make more significant demands on citizens which are justified as necessary for the collective good.[4]

The two inquiries—representation and civic obligation—are of course closely related. Whether a well-functioning system of democratic representation requires citizens to formulate their collective will through deliberation or aggregation has obvious consequences for the civic obligations of

1. *E.g.*, Shapiro, *The State of Democratic Theory*, ch. 1; Cohen, "Democracy and Liberty," 185–86; Young, *Inclusion and Democracy*, 18–26.

2. As Shapiro puts it, aggregative theorists "regard preferences as given and concern themselves with how best to tot them up." Shapiro, *The State of Democratic Theory*, 3.

3. *E.g.*, Barber, *Strong Democracy*, ch. 4; Young, *Inclusion and Democracy*, 22.

4. Barber, *Strong Democracy*; Sandel, *Liberalism and the Limits of Justice*.

citizens at various points in the political process. Nonetheless, thinking about democratic theories along a liberal-communitarian continuum has, for present purposes, two advantages. First, this theoretical cleavage has fairly direct ramifications for what an election campaign ought to be. The more citizens are required to do to make democracy function properly, the more elaborate campaigns must be to permit citizens successfully to discharge their civic obligations. Second, invoking liberalism directly allows me to consider theories of democracy that, although largely discarded by working democratic theorists as archaic, are still very much alive in the realm of American constitutional law and theory, tied as they are to an eighteenth-century document. This is useful here, since this book is in the end primarily an inquiry into the condition of the constitutional law of election campaigns.

One additional preliminary observation about democratic theory is in order. Although the significance of *elections* for democracy is a common point of emphasis in many theoretical accounts of democracy, election *campaigns* are surprisingly undertheorized. As a result, much of the analysis below relies on inferences from well-established general principles rather than specific accounts of the role of campaigns in democratic processes given by theorists who have directly treated the issue.

Liberal Democratic Theory: Protective Democracy

As the preceding chapters have made clear, American election campaigns are, or at least are nearly universally perceived to be, thin, superficial, and nondeliberative—or if you prefer the language of popular media criticism, "degraded," "content-free," and "Oprahfied."[5] The problem I shall address in the balance of this chapter is whether, according to any established theory of democracy, this state of affairs is incompatible with the proper functioning of a democratic state—whether, that is to say, any theory of democracy demands that election campaigns consistently be thick, meaningful, deliberative, dignified, full of content, and un-Oprahfied (which I take to mean "more like 'The News Hour with Jim Lehrer'"). As has been true throughout the book, I shall mean by election campaigns that period, largely though not entirely formalized in law, during which officially recognized candidates for

5. Greenfield, "Winning Respect"; Rich, "The Next Infomercials"; Will, "The Uselessness of Debates."

public office compete for the nomination of a political party or for election, and during which candidates, voters, the media, and other interested observers communicate with one another to evaluate the claims of candidates that they ought to be nominated or elected.

I begin with a venerable form of liberal democracy that I will call, following David Held and C.B. Macpherson, "protective democracy."[6] Protective democracy is rooted in the Lockean idea, transmitted to Americans during the colonial and founding periods and enshrined explicitly in the Declaration of Independence, that individuals have certain inalienable rights[7] and that these rights can be better protected jointly, in a society living under the consensual rule of a government, than individually in a state of nature.[8] The collective transfer of power to a government, however, even consensually, always entails some risk: governments are run by people, and people can abuse their powers. The principal form of abuse of power with which protective democracy concerns itself is the tyrannical invasion of the people's rights.[9] On this theory, then, the *telos* of democratic self-governance is popular self-protection against governmental tyranny. As Held puts it, "[p]rotective democracy emphasized the centrality of democratic institutions to safeguard the governed from tyranny of all kinds and from oppression by the state in particular."[10]

From the point of view of institutional implementation, protective democracy is a rather coarse theory: it does not seem to entail with great specificity any highly particularized set of institutional arrangements.[11] Nevertheless, to the extent it is a theory of democracy it by definition requires elections, and where there are elections there must be some kind of campaigns. So the question is: What kind of campaigns are consistent with the premises of protective democracy, and more specifically, does a properly functioning system of protective democracy inherently require campaigns that are thick and deliberative rather than thin and superficial? Or to put the matter

---

6. Held, *Models of Democracy*; C.B. Macpherson, *The Life and Times of Liberal Democracy.*

7. Declaration of Independence, ¶ 2.

8. *See, e.g.*, Locke, *Second Treatise*, §§ 4, 87, 89, 95–99.

9. This concern is evident throughout the writings of the founders, particularly in the work of Madison. *See especially*, Madison et al., *The Federalist Papers*, Nos. 10, 46–51.

10. Held, *Models of Democracy*, 43.

11. Some have argued that a workable theory of protective democracy may require at least some degree of separation of powers. *See* Held, *Models of Democracy*, 55–61. Certainly Madison thought so. Madison et al., *The Federalist Papers*, Nos. 47–51.

more colloquially, what must responsible citizens and candidates living in a protective democracy talk about during electoral campaigns?

If the *raison d'être* of protective democracy is the protection of liberty from governmental tyranny, it seems to follow that citizens must engage the electoral process with certain understandings and conceptions. They must have some understanding of what their liberties are. They must have some set of beliefs about what kinds of governmental actions would invade those liberties or would raise an unacceptable risk of such an invasion. If they are successfully to translate these beliefs into political action, they must be able to relate their beliefs to the specific candidates before them. Voters in a protective democracy must therefore have some idea of the policy commitments of the candidates so they can know which candidate supports policies that are the least threatening to popular liberty. They might also wish to know something about the various candidates' character traits so as to reach some assessment of how likely the candidates would be, if elected, to resist the temptation to misuse official power.[12]

Based on this very brief sketch, we might be able to imagine, broadly speaking, two different kinds of campaign conversations that might occur in a protective democracy. The thicker and more deliberative of the conversations would engage the public in deep discussions of the scope and content of their protected liberties. At a slightly less deep though still deliberatively thick level, it might ask them to contemplate whether specific public policies proposed by the candidates are sufficiently conducive to the protection of public liberties, or if such policies restrict liberty to some degree, whether the restrictions are adequately justified by countervailing considerations. Thus, a deliberatively thick campaign in the present political context might engage citizens on questions like these: Do we have a right to be free from unwanted government surveillance? Does such a right prevent the government from monitoring the content of our telephone conversations? Does it shield from

12. I am assuming here that the ends of protective democracy are best achieved through informed and self-conscious action of the citizenry, an assumption I believe to be consistent with the most common assumptions of classical liberal theory. For example, seventeenth- and eighteenth-century political thought often emphasized various kinds of individual competence—knowledge, intelligence, leisure time for reflection, and so on—as criteria for political participation. It seems inconsistent with the main thrust of this body of thought to suggest that the ends of protective democracy can be adequately achieved through the uninformed or unreflective action of the electorate. This idea, however, did emerge as a later variant, and is discussed in the next section under the heading of liberal pluralist theories.

government view the identity of those whom we call and who call us? Does it prevent the government from subjecting us to televised surveillance on public streets? How far can invasions of these rights be justified by a fear of terrorism? Is it compatible with public safety to require the government to obtain a warrant before engaging in surveillance of citizens? To what degree must criminal prosecutions of alleged terrorists and enemies be public? And so on.

It is also possible to imagine a thinner, less deliberative kind of public conversation. Such a conversation might engage voters on questions like these: What, precisely, are the present policy commitments of the Republican and Democratic parties? What are the precise policy commitments of the candidates? Where do they in fact stand on warrantless wiretapping, indefinite detention of enemy combatants, and the placement of cameras in public places? Can the candidates be trusted with power? Have they done anything in the past that might suggest they are unworthy of the public trust? Have they shown themselves to be the kind of people who are able to resist, or on the contrary are likely to give in to, the temptations of money and power? And so on.

This brings us to the heart of the matter: Does anything in the theory of protective democracy require voters to have the first kind of conversation *during the campaign*? Suppose we grant that the theory of protective democracy ideally requires all responsible citizens to have beliefs concerning all of these questions and that these beliefs should ideally be formed through diligent study, reflection, and conversation with other voters. Is it impossible for the purposes of protective democracy to be well-served if voters, during the campaign, have only the second, thinner kind of conversation? It seems fairly clear that the answer is no—that the ends of protective democracy can be adequately served by a campaign discourse that is, all things considered, rather thin. The reason is that even if protective democracy requires citizens to have beliefs concerning the deepest questions of liberty and public policy, it does not require them to formulate those beliefs at any particular time. More specifically, nothing in protective democracy requires them to formulate views on these subjects during a campaign for public office—between, for example, April and November of an election year. So long as citizens hold at the inception of a campaign defensible beliefs about the content of their liberties and the kinds of public policies that, and the character traits of public officials who, might threaten those liberties, nothing in protective democracy seems to require voters to do anything in a campaign more substantively taxing than to decide which of the candidates better meets the criteria for holding office to which they already subscribe. This does not, of course, mean that protective democracy might not require citizens periodically to rethink their views; perhaps they must do so to remain appropriately vigilant against new and emerging threats to public liberty. But, again, nothing in the theory seems to require that even such periodic rethinkings occur during campaign season, as opposed to any other times.

This conclusion comports well with an obvious fact about the timing of public political conversations about pressing issues: such conversations tend to occur whenever some event happens to bring an issue to public attention. The American public has had numerous opportunities to engage the kinds of deep issues of liberty and public policy alluded to earlier. Questions about government surveillance, for example, were raised by revelations in the media that President Bush had authorized the National Security Agency to spy on Americans inside the United States without first obtaining warrants, a story that broke in late 2005, more than a year after the previous presidential election.[13] Questions about the treatment of enemy detainees and suspects were raised by the Abu Ghraib scandal and by reports concerning the detention of terror suspects held at Guantanamo Bay, stories that unfolded between mid-2002 and mid-2004.[14]

These events were covered extensively in the media and engaged the public at the time they occurred as much as any event can possibly command public attention. Presumably, those citizens who follow public affairs in the way demanded by protective democracy had every opportunity to reflect deeply at those times on fundamental questions of the scope of liberty and the threats to liberty posed by the relevant policies. Protective democracy furnishes no *a priori* reason to think that citizens who reflectively engaged these issues at the time they arose bear some obligation to rethink them just because a campaign officially begins. Indeed, what primarily renders these issues *electorally* relevant under a theory of protective democracy is not the inception of a campaign, but the fact that policy decisions made by an incumbent administration in the ordinary course of business put the issues on the political map. In fact, it seems more likely that issues will

13. Risen and Lichtblau, "Bush Lets U.S. Spy on Callers without Courts."

14. Liptak, Lewis, and Weiser. "After Sept. 11, a Legal Battle On the Limits of Civil Liberty"; Van Natta, "Questioning Terror Suspects in a Dark and Surreal World"; Shanker and Steinberg, "Bush Voices 'Disgust' at Abuse of Iraqi Prisoners."

become publicly salient between elections than during campaign seasons because incumbents can be expected to do everything they can to prevent contentious public issues from erupting during the campaign period, when they risk spinning out of official control.

Finally, we might even go a step further and ask whether it might be possible for protective democracy to be adequately served even if the campaign involves virtually no public conversation at all. This might not always or even often be the case, but surely it could be the case in some circumstances. Where, for example, the candidates are already well-known to the public, party commitments are stable, party discipline is strong, and there is general public consensus on the most important electorally salient questions of liberty and public policy, a campaign consisting of little more than signs, bumper stickers, and reminders to turn out to vote might be entirely adequate to accomplish the end of protective democracy—the collective protection, through electoral processes, of individual liberty.

Liberal Democratic Theory: Economic and Pluralist Democracy

When we move from classical liberal theory to its more contemporary variants, any possible requirement that campaigns be deliberatively thick and characterized by reasoned persuasion evaporates almost entirely. Like their classical antecedents, contemporary liberal democratic theories generally treat citizens as "sovereign artificers," to use Goodin's phrase,[15] which is to say such theories take citizens to be independent and autonomous actors who come to politics already in possession of exogenously formed personalities and preferences. Contemporary liberal democratic theories generally differ from their antecedents such as protective democracy, however, in their more expansive conception of the ends that voters may legitimately pursue through politics. In modern theories, citizens are not confined to pursuing some finite set of morally acceptable ends dictated by natural law; instead, individuals are free to define their own ends and interests and to pursue those interests in the political arena. Thus freed from objectivist constraints, citizens in these theories are fully expected

15. Goodin, *Reflective Democracy*, 25 ff.

to have different tastes, leading them to embrace different ends and to formulate and pursue the satisfaction of different preferences—such theories contemplate, that is, a social pluralism that will be expressed in politics.

Democratic politics, on this view, therefore becomes a forum in which individuals, alone or in groups, compete to elect officials who will adopt policies that satisfy their preferences. Politics, in other words, is reconceived as a marketplace in which candidate-sellers and voter-buyers negotiate to make themselves better off by exchanging policy promises for votes. As Joseph Schumpeter famously summed up this view, "the democratic method is that institutional arrangement for arriving at political decisions in which individuals acquire the power to decide by means of a competitive struggle for the people's vote."[16] Moreover, like economic theories of commercial markets, pluralist and economic theories of democratic markets hold that the very process of competition for the satisfaction of individual preferences produces the common good, defined as the maximization of collective welfare or utility.[17] Such theories are therefore paradigmatically aggregative: the purpose of democracy on these accounts is to determine the political preferences of each individual and "tot them up."[18]

It is quite clear from their premises that economic and pluralist theories of democracy do not require deliberatively thick campaigns, and indeed they seem not merely to contemplate but positively to invite campaigns of just the opposite sort. If citizens are individualistic atoms who form their desires and acquire their interests outside of electoral politics, then politics is by hypothesis an arena in which desires and interests are to be asserted rather than formed. As an institution of politics, a campaign therefore need not concern itself with deeper and more personal questions of voters' underlying beliefs and preferences. The role of the ideal voter, on this model, is simply to enter politics with a set of demands. The role of the ideal candidate, in turn, is to listen to those demands and offer policies that will lead to their satisfaction. A successful match leads to a "sale" in the form of a vote. A campaign, on this view, is a transaction of exchange that requires not deliberation or reflection but bargaining,

16. Schumpeter, *Capitalism, Socialism, and Democracy*, 269.

17. *E.g.*, Downs, *An Economic Theory of Democracy*; Buchanan and Tullock, *The Calculus of Consent*; Beitz, *Political Equality*, 31.

18. Shapiro, *The State of Democratic Theory*.

a mode of interchange generally thought to be antithetical to meaningful deliberation and persuasion.[19]

This is not to say, of course, that campaigns could not in practice offer a thicker kind of political discourse. Economic theories of democracy require citizens to know essentially two kinds of things: first, their own interests and preferences; and second, which of the candidates is most likely successfully to advance those interests and preferences. Again, we might therefore imagine campaign conversations of varying thickness in which voters, on a pluralist account of democracy, might usefully engage. At its thickest, such a conversation might engage voters in reflecting upon and ultimately identifying where their self-interest truly lies. What do I really want? How do I know? How does anyone know what he or she really wants? What is truly in my self-interest and what is only seemingly so? Do my long-term and short-term interests coincide, and if they do not, how shall I resolve the conflict? These are of course among the most basic and important questions any human being can ask.

A somewhat thinner but still deliberatively thick conversation might focus instead on the kinds of public policies capable of promoting voters' self-identified interests and preferences. Suppose many voters hold a preference for living a long, healthy life. Campaign discourse might then focus on identifying which public health policies will best promote that goal. Socialized medicine or a privatized health care market? Public subsidies for research or a vigorously enforced system of private patent protection? And so on.

A much thinner campaign, in contrast, might bracket some or all of these questions as exogenous to electoral politics and focus more closely on how citizens ought to exercise their power in the political marketplace to achieve what they already know they want. Campaign discourse might then focus on a much narrower and more factual question: Which of the candidates in fact supports the policies that I believe advance my interests most effectively? I know that I want to live a long and healthy life, and I believe that free markets promote public goods most successfully, all things considered. Which of the candidates is in fact the most dedicated to a fully privatized health care market? Which candidate most strongly supports private property rights as an incentive to medical innovation? And so on.

---

19. Habermas, *Between Facts and Norms*; Manin, *Principles of Representative Government*; Richardson, *Democratic Autonomy*; *but see* Goodin, *Reflective Democracy*, ch. 4.

While not even the thickest of these potential campaign conversations is ruled out by economic theories of democracy, such theories nevertheless predict on their own assumptions that citizens often rationally need not, and therefore will not, participate *at all* in even the thinnest kinds of campaign discourse. Three factors account for this prediction: the cost of acquiring relevant electoral information; the nature of rational behavior in the face of uncertainty; and the low probability that any individual's vote will affect the outcome of an election.

First, information relevant to electoral decision making can be costly to acquire, to work through, and to digest. Time spent on these activities carries opportunity costs, and the more thorough and complex the voter's deliberation the greater the costs.

Second, questions about where any individual's true interests lie, which public policies will in fact best promote those interests, and the actual likely impact of policy proposals advanced by the candidates cannot be answered with scientific precision. This inherent uncertainty diminishes any potential payoff to the voter to be derived from putting in the time and effort to gather already costly information that might help answer the relevant questions. Downs describes the voter's calculus in the following terms:

> In the real world, uncertainty and lack of information prevent even the most intelligent and well-informed voter from behaving in precisely the fashion [that classical liberal theories of democracy require]. Since he cannot be certain what his present utility income from government is, or what it would be if an opposition party were in power, he can only make estimates of both. He will base them upon those few areas of government activity where the difference between parties is great enough to impress him. When the total difference in utility flows is large enough so that he is no longer indifferent about which party is in office, his *party differential threshold* has been crossed. Until then, he remains indifferent about which party is in power, even if one would give him a higher utility income than the other. The existence of thresholds raises the probability that the expected party differential will be zero, i.e., that abstention will occur.[20]

In other words, the cost of acquiring information and the inevitable uncertainty associated with its use means that voters often will rationally

20. Downs, *An Economic Theory of Democracy*, 45–46.

find it in their own best interest to abstain from politics altogether. That is, they will not find either voting or collecting the information necessary to cast an informed vote to be a cost-effective use of their time. This means, of course, that they will have no reason to engage in campaign discourse or reflection.

Third, modern mass democracies are large, and a great many people are usually eligible to vote in most elections. Because of the size of the electorate, the likelihood that any single vote will influence the outcome is vanishingly small. This too influences the cost-benefit calculus in a way that, on the assumptions of economic theories of democracy, gives voters a reason rationally to abstain from voting, and consequently to abstain from taking the preparatory steps of engaging and participating in the campaign.[21]

Finally, even if this analysis is overly pessimistic, and citizens will frequently have cost-effective reasons to deliberate on deep questions of the nature of their private interests and the kinds of policies that will best advance those interests, nothing in economic or pluralist theories of democracy requires that such deliberation occur during a campaign. There is no reason, on the assumptions of these theories, why voters could not deliberate just as beneficially between election seasons. Indeed, economic theories predict that voters will engage in such deliberation precisely when it becomes cost-effective to do so. That moment might occur during a campaign if the cost of deliberation falls then, which is certainly possible due to the somewhat greater availability of political information during campaigns. However, the cost of deliberating does not depend solely on the cost of acquiring and digesting the electorally relevant information; it also depends on the relevant opportunity costs, and those costs depend on all the many activities of a privately lived life, few of which seem especially likely to unfold in a rhythm that happens to coincide with the rhythm of the political seasons.

In sum, on the assumptions of economic and pluralist theories of democracy, there is no reason to think that a thin and superficial campaign is a sign of ill health in a democratic polity, and indeed such theories offer many reasons to think that a shallow campaign is in fact evidence that democratic citizens are behaving reasonably.

---

21. There is empirical evidence to suggest that this is more than a speculative deduction from theoretical premises. One of the more common explanations given by non-voters for their abstention is their belief that their participation and voting will make no difference in who is elected or what policies government pursues. *See, e.g.*, Doppelt and Shearer, *Nonvoters: America's No-Shows.*

Communitarian Democratic Theory: Developmental and Participationist Democracy

If the leading liberal theories of democracy do not require campaigns of any particular deliberative thickness, what about democratic theories of a more communitarian cast? Such theories generally understand democracy as a more overtly collective process and conceive of citizens as embedded members of a genuine community. Because campaigns are, or at least can be, moments of collective communal engagement, communitarian theories of democracy might therefore attach greater significance than do their liberal counterparts to the ways in which campaigns are conducted. In this section and the next, I show that, although this intuition is borne out to some degree, not even communitarian theories of democracy impose any strict requirement that campaigns be deliberatively thick. Rather, the importance of campaigns under communitarian theories of democracy is contingent, and depends on the nature of a polity's political life, understood as an integrated whole.

I begin with another venerable theory often termed, aptly, "developmental democracy."[22] Liberal theories of democracy, as we have seen, hold by and large that the ultimate justification for democracy lies in its capacity to enable citizens freely to pursue their private ends. Theories of developmental democracy, in contrast, hold that democracy is justified not primarily by its effect on the world, but by its effect on the citizenry. Active participation in a democratic polity, on this view, creates informed, politically aware, and public-spirited citizens who, as a result of participating jointly in the public enterprise of collective self-governance, enjoy meaningful membership in a genuine community. In Mill's formulation, democracy therefore "promotes a better and higher form of national character, than any other polity whatsoever."[23]

Closely allied to developmental theories of democracy is a family of participationist theories, many developed in a critical spirit,[24] which hold

---

22. Held, *Models of Democracy*; Macpherson, *The Life and Times of Liberal Democracy*.

23. Mill, *Considerations on Representative Government*, 245.

24. *See especially* Benello and Roussopoulos, *The Case For Participatory Democracy*; Pennock and Chapman, *Nomos XVI: Participation in Politics*; Pateman, *Participation and Democratic Theory*. Sympathetic accounts can be found in Barber, *Strong Democracy*; Mansbridge, *Beyond Adversary Democracy*; Brest, "Further Beyond the Republican Revival."

that the machinery of government must be radically opened to popular participation and control, primarily by distributing meaningful power downward toward decentralized local bodies small enough to allow individual citizens to experience self-governance in a direct, authentic, and meaningful way.[25] On this view, direct participation in self-governance is part of what it means to be a citizen:

> to be a citizen *is* to participate in a certain conscious fashion that presumes awareness of and engagement in activity with others. This consciousness alters attitudes and lends to participation that sense of the *we* . . . associated with community. To participate *is* to create a community that governs itself, and to create a self-governing community *is* to participate.[26]

What all these theories have in common are the beliefs, first, that the main value of democracy lies in its power to construct citizens who possess, both individually and collectively, certain desirable skills and character traits; and second, that the feature of democracy most directly responsible for cultivating these benefits is the opportunities it offers citizens to participate actively in the processes of governance.[27]

On these assumptions, it seems possible that developmental and participationist theories of democracy might assign to election campaigns a potentially important or at least a useful role in the construction of proper democratic citizens. Campaign activism, to take a somewhat extreme case, might offer many valuable lessons in democratic citizenship. Campaign activists—those who work directly and energetically rather than indirectly and passively for the election of candidates—must, for example, decide which principles and candidates are worthy of their support, something that requires at least some study of and reflection on issues of public concern. Activists must learn how to organize and deploy the talents of

---

25. *See, e.g.*, the suggestions in Barber, *Strong Democracy*, and Dahl, *After the Revolution?*

26. Barber, *Strong Democracy*, 155.

27. Although developmental and participationist theories stress the effect of democracy on the citizenry, they clearly do not intend thereby to displace entirely liberal conceptions of the *telos* of democratic governance. The purpose of governance and democratic politics, in other words, can't be *solely* to cultivate the benefits of participation; they clearly serve some substantive purposes as well. Citizenship must be for something other than its own cultivation. Macpherson, *The Life and Times of Liberal Democracy*, 47.

many individuals to achieve a shared goal. They must decide how best to communicate to other voters reasons why the candidate they support deserves to be nominated or elected, and must engage and attempt to persuade other voters to their point of view. They must of course vote, and they generally must take action to facilitate voting by other supporters. Most important, perhaps, they must in full public view take ownership of their beliefs and their actions, something that would surely inculcate one of the dispositions of democratic citizens upon which Mill placed the highest value: the ability and inclination to "stand up for" one's "rights and interests."[28]

Even the kind of considerably less active participation in election campaigns that most citizens might feasibly be expected to undertake could conceivably help them cultivate the skills of competent democratic citizens—provided those campaigns achieve at least some reasonable degree of deliberative thickness. Sitting on the couch and channel surfing through attack ads is not an activity likely to inculcate the virtues of democratic citizenship. However, attending actively to public affairs, diligently collecting and digesting information about the issues and the candidates, reflecting seriously about one's political beliefs, and testing and refining those beliefs in conversations with friends, neighbors, and coworkers might well help develop the active engagement, vigilance, and capacity for self-governance that democracy, on the assumptions of developmental theories, is capable of instilling. Discussion of public affairs with others in the context of a vigorously contested campaign with genuine consequences for the public welfare might in addition contribute to constituting the kind of community of citizens toward which participationist theories ultimately aim.

If deliberatively thick campaigns, then, are potentially capable in at least some circumstances of promoting the ends of developmental and participationist theories of democracy, does it follow from such theories that a well-functioning democracy *must* have campaigns that attain some threshold of deliberative thickness, and that the absence of such campaigns constitutes a failure of democracy to which we must attend? The answer is almost certainly no.

First, even if highly active involvement in election campaigns might serve developmental goals, theorists of deliberative and participationist democracy generally agree that the kinds of participation offered by campaigns are distinctly inferior to other forms of participation that democratic states are

---

28. Mill, *Considerations on Representative Government*, 245.

capable of providing. Specifically, such theorists seem to agree that the quintessential experience of democratic citizenship is not participating in a collective decision about who shall govern us—an election—but governance itself—the experience of actually wielding official power in behalf of, and for the benefit of, one's fellow citizens. This idea, very likely rooted in the Aristotelian belief that democratic citizenship consists of ruling and being ruled in turn,[29] is advanced strongly by Mill, who argues:

> the ideally best form of government is that in which the sovereignty, or supreme controlling power in the last resort, is vested in the entire aggregate of the community; every citizen not only having a voice in the exercise of that ultimate sovereignty, but being, at least occasionally, called on to take an actual part in the government, by the *personal* discharge of some public function, local or general.[30]

Thus, for Mill, as for Aristotle, the virtues of democratic citizenship are best cultivated not by campaigning and electing, but by periodically holding office of some kind.[31]

Indeed, some developmental and participationist theorists go even further and dispute the capacity of campaigns—even deliberatively thick ones—to help construct a democratic citizenry. Barber argues categorically that the modern institution of representative democracy, no matter how it is practiced, is by definition not only incapable of promoting an adequate kind of democratic citizenship, but in fact stunts the development of citizens' capacities. Representative government, Barber contends, "steals from individuals the ultimate responsibility for their values, beliefs, and actions," and "delegates and thus alienates political will at the cost of genuine self-government and autonomy." For Barber, citizens are not free unless they are "directly responsible through common deliberation, common decision, and common action for the policies that determine their common lives."[32] Democracy, on this view, must be direct, and where the scale of society

---

29. Aristotle, *Politics*, 41–42, 105, 112, 315.

30. Mill, *Considerations on Representative Government*, 244 (emphasis added).

31. *See* Manin, *The Principles of Representative Government*, describing the frequent use in ancient Athens of lot and rotation in office. In the contemporary context, it is often said that jury service discharges this function.

32. Barber, *Strong Democracy*, 145–46.

precludes feasible institutions of direct democracy, Barber contends, direct democracy must be simulated to the greatest extent possible through the creation of institutions such as neighborhood assemblies, televised town meetings, a national initiative and referendum process, and other innovative procedures.[33]

Even on assumptions more optimistic than Barber's about the theoretical capacity of election campaigns to inculcate democratic citizenship, it must be conceded that representative democracy as it is practiced in the United States throws up significant structural obstacles to the achievement of developmental and participationist goals. This is because what counts in these theories is not merely participation, but participation that is efficacious, or which at least holds out the prospect of efficacy. Again, Mill puts the point clearly and directly. In explaining why democracy is preferable to monarchical rule even by a superhumanly wise and virtuous monarch, Mill argues that such rule, no matter how good substantively, would nevertheless deaden the capacities of the citizenry. "A person must have a very unusual taste for intellectual exercise in and for itself," Mill observes, "who will put himself to the trouble of thought when it is to have no outward effect, or qualify himself for functions which he has no chance of being allowed to exercise." Humans will exert and, in exerting, improve themselves, only if there is "the prospect of some practical use to be made" of the fruits of their exertions.[34]

It follows from this reasoning that many, perhaps most American election campaigns are unlikely to present citizens with meaningful opportunities to develop democratic skills and virtues. Engaging in campaign activity holds out the prospect of efficacy only if the candidates one supports—and by extension the policy commitments to which one subscribes—have some realistic chance of prevailing. Yet most American elections are not competitive. In the 2002 congressional elections, for example, three-fourths of all incumbents won their districts by more than 20 percentage points, and only four incumbents were defeated nationwide. Out of 435 congressional races across the nation, only 38 were even minimally competitive.[35] At the state level, parties frequently do not even bother to put forward candidates, much less mount campaigns, in many districts because the likelihood that their

33. *Ibid.*, ch. 10.

34. Mill, *Considerations on Representative Government*, 239.

35. Pildes, "The Constitution and Political Competition," 254.

candidates will prevail is so remote as to make any effort futile. In the Wisconsin state house elections of 2004, in which all 99 seats were up for grabs, 43 seats—nearly half—were uncontested by a major party challenger. In the 56 contested races, 23 were won by a landslide (more than 60 percent) and only 16 were even minimally competitive.[36]

In uncompetitive districts like these, a substantial minority of the citizenry has no reason to think that any degree of campaigning, no matter how vigorous and sincere, stands any realistic chance of bearing fruit, while the majority knows perfectly well that its preferred candidate will win regardless of the quality of the campaign. As a result, no one in the district has the slightest reason to engage the campaign process with anything approaching the intensity and vigor that might conceivably produce the kinds of personal and social benefits to which developmental and participationist theories of democracy aspire. These are defects, moreover, that do not admit of any easy institutional cure, for it is impossible to design a system of democratic legislative representation that employs single-member, winner-take-all districts yet simultaneously ensures vigorous, hard-fought partisan contests in every district.[37]

If representative democracy as it is currently practiced in the United States falls so short of developmental and participationist ideals, it is tempting to conclude that these theories do not require deliberatively thicker election campaigns so much as truly radical reforms to American democratic institutions. It is surely no accident that Mill was also an avid supporter of proportional representation, an electoral system that is in principle capable of engaging a larger proportion of the electorate than winner-take-all districting due to its far greater capacity to permit direct legislative representation of political minorities.[38] Yet even instituting proportional representation in legislative elections would not alleviate the developmental

36. Gardner, "What Is 'Fair' Partisan Representation," 556 n.5.

37. The reasons for this are too complex to get into here, but in brief, it is because (1) single-member plurality electoral methods tend to produce a two-party system; (2) two-partyism leads to an electorate bifurcated into two groups of partisans, and (3) only in extraordinary circumstances will it be possible to draw geographical districts so as to contain within each district a number of supporters of each party sufficiently equal to ensure vigorous competition in every district. *See* Duverger, *Political Parties*; Gardner, "What Is 'Fair' Partisan Representation," 569–70.

38. Mill, *Considerations on Representative Government*, 34.

and participationist deficiencies of participation in electoral campaigns compared to other forms of more direct participation in governance.

In the end, then, it is probably most accurate to say that developmental and participationist theories tolerate representative democracy despite its minimal capacity even under the best of circumstances to construct good democratic citizens, but require that democratic states provide their citizens with other, more meaningful opportunities to participate that will benefit them considerably more. Such opportunities might include strong and participatory local self-government, filling offices by lot, workplace democracy, citizen participation in regulatory decision making, neighborhood advisory councils, and many other possibilities.[39] Or to put the point another way, any developmental burden borne by campaigns is highly contingent on the degree to which a democratic institutional arrangement offers citizens opportunities to participate in a more meaningful way than campaigns are capable of offering. Increasing the deliberative thickness of election campaigns can thus make at best only marginal improvements in the ability of democratic institutions to achieve developmental and participationist ends.

Communitarian Democratic Theory: Deliberative Democracy

If none of the democratic theories reviewed so far is particularly offended by thin and superficial electoral campaigns, we might surely expect, finally, to find some support in contemporary theories of deliberative democracy for the proposition that democracy simply cannot flourish without campaigns of significantly better quality. Yet, surprisingly, not even theories of deliberative democracy, which by their own terms demand meaningful, collective, public deliberation, require that such deliberation occur during campaigns or that the public deliberate deeply on the subject of the relative merits of competing candidates for office. Like all of the theories we have examined, deliberative democracy requires only that meaningful public deliberation about pressing issues of public concern occur at some times and in some forums, and those times and forums need not coincide with opportunities

39. *See, e.g.*, the many suggestions made in Barber, *Strong Democracy*; Pateman, *Participation and Democratic Theory*; Mansbridge, *Beyond Adversary Democracy*; Pennock and Chapman, *Nomos XVI: Participation in Politics*; Benello and Roussopoulos, *The Case for Participatory Democracy*.

available during formal campaigns for public office. Paradoxically, theories of deliberative democracy generally concern themselves far less with the formal electoral process than do aggregative theories, which treat fair elections as essential to democratic legitimacy yet explicitly disavow any need for a deliberatively thick electoral politics.

Like their liberal counterparts, theories of deliberative democracy begin with the concept of popular sovereignty—the idea that what the government does should be determined by what the people want it to do: "The fundamental idea of democratic, political legitimacy is that the authorization to exercise state power must arise from the *collective decisions* of the equal members of a society who are governed by that power."[40]

Where deliberative democracy parts company from liberal democratic theories and takes a decidedly communitarian turn is in its conceptions of what counts as a democratically relevant popular will and how such a will is formed. Theories of deliberative democracy explicitly reject the foundational tenet of pluralism that a meaningful and legitimately binding public will can be identified by aggregating the isolated private wills of individual citizens.[41] Deliberative theories are especially skeptical of will-aggregation procedures that make no attempt to distinguish between private wills that are hasty, uninformed, ill-considered, or based excessively on private self-interest from those that are reflective, reasonable, and public-regarding. Taking face-to-face deliberation among political equals as the paradigm of collective self-governance,[42] theories of deliberative democracy contend that an expression of the public will can legitimately bind those who are subject to it only insofar as it is reasoned, well-informed, and formulated after mutual consultation and discussion that is inclusive, respectful, and aimed at achieving mutually satisfactory agreement among society's members—when it is, in a word, deliberative.[43]

Consistent with this view, and quite unlike economic and pluralist theories of democracy, deliberative theories do not conceive of political beliefs and interests as exogenously determined preferences that citizens

40. Cohen, "Democracy and Liberty," 185.

41. Dryzek, *Deliberative Democracy and Beyond*, 1; Shapiro, *The State of Democratic Theory*, ch. 1; Goodin, *Reflective Democracy*, ch. 8; Young, *Inclusion and Democracy*, 18.

42. Fishkin, *The Voice of the People*.

43. Habermas, *Between Facts and Norms*; Cohen, "Deliberation and Democratic Legitimacy"; Young, *Democracy and Inclusion*.

bring with them into the political arena. Instead, deliberative theories understand preferences to be formed endogenously, in the crucible of politics itself, through the give and take of discussion with other citizens of different views.[44] Deliberation is thus doubly important in these theories: it is not only the forum in which citizens forge agreement on what to do, but also the very means by which they legitimately bind themselves to what they have collectively decided. Deliberation in these theories is thus a kind of self-moving mover.

Because of the immense importance that theories of deliberative democracy attach to political deliberation, they tend to impose demanding conditions on what kind of deliberation can count as sufficiently democratic. In most theories, processes of deliberation must be inclusive so that deliberators may consider the greatest variety of viewpoints, a practice said both to improve the quality of decision making and to ensure that all who will be bound by democratic decisions have a voice in making them.[45] Deliberation also must occur pursuant to fair procedures that guarantee equality so that deliberations are not inappropriately dominated by the powerful.[46]

The heaviest burden, however, falls on citizens, at least when they are engaged self-consciously in politics, for theories of deliberative democracy typically require citizens to approach their deliberations with an almost heroic degree of sincerity, openness, impartiality, tolerance, persistence, and enthusiasm. Citizens engaged in democratic deliberation must, for example, treat each other with mutual respect and civility.[47] They must work sincerely and cooperatively toward determining the truth.[48] They must remain open-minded and receptive toward views and perspectives expressed by others.[49]

---

44. Shapiro, *The State of Democratic Theory*; Cohen, "Deliberation and Democratic Legitimacy"; Young, *Democracy and Inclusion.*

45. Habermas, *Between Facts and Norms*; Young, *Justice and the Politics of Difference*; Young, *Democracy and Inclusion.*

46. Young, *Inclusion and Democracy*; Richardson, *Democratic Autonomy*; Cohen, "Deliberation and Democratic Legitimacy."

47. Rawls, *The Idea of Public Reason Revisited*; Guttmann and Thompson, *Democracy and Disagreement*; Richardson, *Democratic Autonomy.*

48. Estlund, "Beyond Fairness and Deliberation"; Gaus, "Reason, Justification, and Consensus"; Cohen, "Deliberation and Democratic Legitimacy."

49. Young, *Inclusion and Democracy*; Guttmann and Thompson, *Democracy and Disagreement*; Richardson, *Democratic Autonomy*; Melissa Williams, *Voice, Trust and Memory.*

They should focus in their deliberation on higher-order problems of ends rather than merely instrumental problems of means.[50] They must support any argument or position they advance with reasons, and in justifying their positions must confine themselves to invoking "public reasons," meaning reasons that all other reasonable citizens might in principle accept, a category typically said to exclude justifications based on religious dogma or personal self-interest.[51] And they must strive in deliberation to transcend disagreement by persuading others, rather than attempting to finesse disagreement through strategic bargaining,[52] or even worse to override disagreement through raw exercises of the power of numerical superiority.[53]

Deliberative democracy, then, clearly contemplates the construction of a democratic, public will through a process of deep and meaningful collective deliberation. The question for present purposes, however, is one of timing: do deliberative theories of democracy demand that the deliberative public will be formed during election campaigns? If so, then there can be little question but that most contemporary campaigns fall well short of the deliberative ideal. Campaign discourse is more often shrill and negative than civil and respectful. Voters and candidates more often dig in their heels than open their minds, more often ignore contrary views and information than contemplate them reflectively, more often attend to the narrow interests of their own small groups or regions than the overall welfare of the general public. Campaigns traffic less in persuasion than in mobilization, more in the power of numbers than the power of ideas. Critics of the contemporary election campaign seem to apply a standard straight out of deliberative democratic theory.

Surprisingly, then, theories of deliberative democracy have little to say about the kind of public discourse that ought to occur when candidates for public office campaign for election. This is not because deliberative theories would somehow object to a deliberatively thick campaign discourse, but because elections and their attendant campaigns play an insignificant role in fulfilling the political aspirations of deliberative theories of democracy.

50. Richardson, *Democratic Autonomy*.

51. Cohen, "Democracy and Liberty"; Rawls, *The Idea of Public Reason Revisited*.

52. Sunstein, *Democracy and the Problem of Free Speech*, 72; Christiano, *The Rule of the Many*, 117; Manin, *The Principles of Representative Government*, 198–201.

53. Young, *Inclusion and Democracy*; Manin, *The Principles of Representative Government*; Richardson, *Democracy Autonomy*; Cohen, "Deliberation and Democratic Legitimacy."

Deliberative democracy is not a theory about election campaigns because it is not at bottom a theory of legislative representation.[54] Indeed, for theories of deliberative democracy the presence of a representative legislature is typically something of an embarrassment—a pragmatically necessary inconvenience that serves only to complicate the achievement of what deliberative theories seek: concordance of the reflective popular will and the content of binding law.

Inspired by a normative preference for the kind of face-to-face deliberation among citizens that may occur within institutions of direct democracy,[55] theories of deliberative democracy hold that the principal condition legitimating the exercise of state power is that the *laws* that bind a polity issue from a public will formed discursively under appropriate conditions of equality. Except in rare instances of directly democratic legislation such as initiatives and referenda, however, an election in the modern mass democracy does not issue in laws but in representatives. This simple fact poses a host of problems for theories of deliberative democracy.

First, it is not at all clear that the kind of deliberation in which citizens are required to engage for the purpose of selecting a representative will very often satisfy the requirements that deliberative democracy imposes on the nature and content of public deliberation. To its proponents, the main attraction of deliberative democracy is that, unlike other democratic theories, it does not view citizens as having ends exogenous to politics: in deliberative democracy, collective, mutually respectful democratic deliberation is the forum in which citizens form their ends in the first place. This means, of course, that the kind of deliberation to which theories of deliberative democracy aspire—and which is therefore sufficient to legitimate the exercise of state power—is deliberation about collective ends.[56] Yet elected representatives are by definition a kind of instrumentality that polities use to advance their aims, and the decision about which representative to elect is therefore to some degree intrinsically a decision about a choice of means. Because means and ends are

---

54. One exception is Christiano, who insists that campaigns ought to be deliberative so as to permit citizens to use them as a forum to choose and clarify their ends, but his conception of implementation tends to collapse his approach into a kind of familiar and conventional responsible-party-model minimalism in which serious deliberation can hardly be expected. Christiano, *The Rule of the Many*.

55. Nino, *The Constitution of Deliberative Democracy*, 146–47.

56. Richardson, *Democratic Autonomy*; Barber, *Strong Democracy*; Christiano, *The Rule of the Many*.

often interrelated, it is of course possible that a collective decision about which person to choose as a representative will require at least some background consideration of the ends to which the representative is a means, but it is equally possible that framing the public discussion as a choice among candidates will force it into a thin, instrumental mode in which voters will find it unnecessary to discuss or even to contemplate their deeper conceptions of collective ends. If Mary is more competent than Pam, a voter might rationally think, it makes no difference what ends we have—Mary will implement them better in any case.

Another reason why electoral discourse is unlikely to satisfy the demands of deliberative democracy, at least in most jurisdictions in the United States, is because it is unlikely to be sufficiently inclusive. Theories of deliberative democracy generally require deliberation to be inclusive for two reasons. First, the more inclusive the deliberation, the greater the epistemic benefits to the deliberators and the greater the likelihood of reaching valid decisions about the common good.[57] Second, in most versions of deliberative democracy citizens are legitimately bound only by decisions that are the product of their own deliberation, and to be entitled to this binding effect decisions must proceed from public deliberation in which all who are to be bound participate.[58]

In most American jurisdictions, however, legislative elections occur in districts that are considerably smaller than the polity itself, and therefore by definition uninclusive. Elections to Congress, for example, take place in districts containing about two-tenths of 1 percent of the represented population. Even city council elections typically divide the represented polity into, say, five or more district groupings. Each district might, of course, contain a sufficient diversity of people and interests to approximate the diversity of the larger body, but of course this is virtually never the case in the real world. Even if it were the case, deliberation among different samples of the population is not the same as deliberation by the entire collectivity; even if one knew how to slice the polity to make all subgroups precisely equivalent in all relevant dimensions, there is no reason to suppose that each subgroup would

---

57. Bohman, *Public Deliberation*; Habermas, *Between Facts and Norms*; Dryzek, *Discursive Democracy*; Estlund, "Beyond Fairness and Deliberation"; Cohen, "Reflections on Habermas on Democracy."

58. Cohen, "Deliberation and Democratic Legitimacy"; Bohman, *Public Deliberation*; Habermas, *Between Facts and Norms*.

deliberate itself to precisely the same agreements and conclusions as every other subgroup.[59]

To handle these problems, we might be tempted to transfer the locus of significant deliberation from the citizenry to the legislature. A legislature, after all, is small enough to engage in genuinely face-to-face deliberation, must frequently make choices about ultimate policy ends, and, if properly constituted, may be more inclusive than any of the election districts from which its members are selected. Unfortunately, delegating democratic deliberation to a legislature poses a different and in some ways more difficult problem for deliberative democracy. The exercise of state power, it will be recalled, is legitimate in theories of deliberative democracy when the laws binding a polity issue from the discursively formed public will. Legislative activity, however, interrupts the vital connection between the public will and legislation because it interposes a different will—the will of the legislature—between the public and the laws that bind it.

If a deliberative democracy is to make any significant use of a representative legislature, then, some method must be worked out to ensure the congruence of the legislative will with the discursively formed public will that is the source of its legitimate authority. Yet this is easier said than done. First, it may be impossible to ensure such congruence because there may be no way of knowing the public will. If the reason we rely on a legislature in the first place is that a democratically adequate deliberative will cannot be formed—if the public is too large or is not properly organized to deliberate collectively and thus suffers from a Deweyan kind of incompetence as a public[60]—then we cannot know whether the legislature is acting consistent with such a will.

Even if we were inclined to think that elections can serve as a rough way for the public to control the legislative will, a problem arises immediately following the election when the legislature begins to deliberate. By hypothesis in theories of deliberative democracy, the value of deliberation lies precisely in its capacity to *change* even the most deeply held views and opinions of the deliberators. Consequently, even a legislature that, when seated, represents accurately the well-considered, reflective views of a deliberative public will begin to alter its collective views, and thus to diverge from the public

59. Goodin, *Reflective Democracy.*

60. Dewey, *The Public and Its Problems.*

will, the moment legislators begin to deliberate.[61] Such a divergence, on deliberative democratic assumptions, ought to tend relatively quickly to undermine the legitimacy of the laws the legislature enacts.

If elections are likely to serve neither as reliable forums for the discursive formation of a democratically meaningful public will, nor as mechanisms for ensuring congruence between the legislative will and a public will formed by other means, how then can deliberative democracy on its own assumptions assure the legitimacy of state power? Theories of deliberative democracy tend to respond to this problem in the only way they can: by grossly downgrading the importance of elections and electoral campaigns. As a result, most of the really important action in deliberative democracy tends to take place outside of electoral institutions altogether.

Most deliberative theorists argue quite explicitly that the democratically relevant deliberative public will is not formulated suddenly, in any single event such as an election campaign, but through a slow, decentralized, disaggregated process that occurs in many places at many times. Habermas, for example, contemplates a two-stage process[62] in which the deep, legitimating public will takes shape in "an open and inclusive network of overlapping, subcultural publics having fluid temporal, social, and substantive boundaries [that] together . . . form a 'wild' complex that resists organization as a whole."[63] Only after its formulation in this chaotic arena does the public will eventually make its way into the formal setting of institutionalized democratic politics.[64] Theorists who have considered more specifically what kinds of institutions are capable of contributing to this disaggregated process of public will-formation sometimes mention political parties, social movements, local neighborhoods, the workplace, coffeehouses, newspapers, and radio call-in shows.[65] With the exception of political parties, none of these is linked in any formal way to electoral processes, and can be expected to perform any functions that contribute to formation of the public will continuously, regardless of election cycles.

61. Goodin, *Reflective Democracy*; Guttmann and Thompson, *Democracy and Disagreement*, 32.

62. *See* Cohen, "Reflections on Habermas and Democracy," 389.

63. Habermas, *Between Facts and Norms*, 307.

64. Habermas, *Between Facts and Norms*, chs. 4, 7.

65. Cohen, "Deliberation and Democratic Legitimacy," 31; Benhabib, "Liberal Dialogue Versus a Critical Theory of Discursive Legitimation," 73; Barber, *Strong Democracy*, ch. 10; Richardson, *Democratic Autonomy*, 93, 184.

Similarly, deliberative democracy theorists deemphasize the role of elections in disciplining elected officials by envisioning mechanisms that steer elected officials toward compliance with the public will as they go about their business—by definition, between elections. Guttmann and Thompson approach the problem by expanding the traditional notion of what counts as legislative representation. "Deliberative democracy," they contend, "does not specify a single form of representation. It searches for modes of representation that support the give-and-take of serious and *sustained* moral argument within legislative bodies, between legislators and the citizens, and among citizens themselves."[66] Guttmann and Thompson thus understand deliberative democracy to require "an ongoing process. Deliberation continues through stages, as officials present their proposals, citizens respond, officials revise, citizens react, and the stages recur," a process they call "the reiteration of deliberation."[67] An election, on this view, is merely one point—and a not very significant point, at that—in an *ongoing* conversation between and among the public and elected officials about what ought to be done. The more important moments in this conversation occur not so much when candidates propose themselves for office as when officials propose specific policies and actions for actual implementation. These proposals then serve, much more efficiently and precisely than do election campaigns, to focus public attention and discussion on exactly what deliberative democracy conceives to be the really important question for public deliberation: what ought we to do? The public will, then, guides the legislative will mainly through ongoing *policy* consultation, not through episodic electoral disciplining. As John Dryzek has forthrightly observed, "[d]owngrading the centrality of voting would involve a substantial ontological shift in our basic conceptualization of democracy."[68] Yet it is precisely the shift that a successful theory of deliberative democracy requires.

---

66. Guttmann and Thompson, *Democracy and Disagreement*, 13 (emphasis added).

67. *Ibid.*, 143. Habermas conceives of a roughly analogous process in which a public will forms in an anarchic and uncontrollable informal sphere, is then given expression in procedurally formalized fora resulting eventually in state legislative and administrative actions, and then thereby recirculated into the informal sphere for contemplation and possible revision. Habermas, *Between Facts and Norms*, chs. 4, 7.

68. Dryzek, *Deliberative Democracy and Beyond*, 47. In fact, what may really be required is a revision of our thinking about representation in particular. In a thoughtful article, Michael Saward has argued persuasively that democratic theory often errs in conceiving of representation as a static relationship of correspondence when it is in fact, he argues, a performative relationship in which the representativeness of the representative is (or may be) constantly in play. Saward, "The Representative Claim."

The low status of elections and electoral campaigns in theories of deliberative democracy is nowhere more starkly revealed than in the work of those who focus on the practical implementation of deliberative democracy. Most of the work in the field has been theoretical, but some scholars and activists have begun to turn increasingly to the question of how a regime of deliberative democracy might be implemented in the real world. This work overwhelmingly ignores election campaigns as a potential forum for thick deliberation, bypassing it altogether in favor of emphasizing ways in which citizens might deliberatively exert direct influence on policy decisions made by governments that have already, so to speak, been installed. Certainly the most prominent example is the work of James Fishkin, who has developed what he calls the "deliberative poll." In these polls, random samples of citizens are briefed on issues of public concern and then deliberate among themselves in facilitated sessions to arrive at informed, deliberative opinions regarding the best ways to deal with the problems they have discussed.[69] When the output of these "deliberative juries" has actually been used outside experimental settings, it has typically been used to provide policy advice to official decision makers. Deliberative juries are almost never convened for the purpose of deliberating in the setting of an electoral campaign. Their function is not to help citizens figure out how best to use their votes, but to help government figure out how best to make specific policy decisions.

Similarly, in a recent book Ethan Leib argues for the creation of a permanent fourth branch of government that would consist of randomly selected subgroups of citizens who would, in a deliberatively rigorous way, actually set policy and make law.[70] Leib proposes, in other words, not that a functionally deliberating public should have a role in the electoral process, but that it should have a role in governance itself. Archon Fung's recent work on implementing deliberative democracy also focuses not on improving the deliberative credentials of public electoral decision making but on how citizen deliberation can be incorporated into ongoing governmental processes of making and administering policy. Much of his work has examined efforts to incorporate neighborhood-level public deliberation into decision making by local school and police agencies.[71] When those who work at implementing

---

69. Fishkin, *The Voice of the People*.

70. Ethan Leib, *Deliberative Democracy in America*, ch. 1.

71. Archon Fung, *Empowered Participation*.

deliberative democracy talk enthusiastically about successful models, they talk about participatory budgeting in Porte Alegre, Brazil, or deliberative urban planning in Perth, Australia;[72] they rarely talk about enhancing the deliberative quality of electoral campaigns.[73]

The most significant exception to this pattern is Ackerman and Fishkin's recent book, *Deliberation Day*, in which the authors propose a national holiday, dedicated to public deliberation, to be held two weeks before Election Day in presidential election years.[74] On this holiday, presidential candidates debate each other on national television, whereupon the citizenry divides itself up into small deliberative groups. The work of these groups is then funneled into larger bodies, resulting in facilitated discussions between citizen assemblies and local party officials.[75] This arrangement, Ackerman and Fishkin argue, "by informing and engaging the citizenry, will transform public opinion,"[76] inducing responsive changes in position by candidates and officials, enforced by the discipline of popular elections.

Suppose Deliberation Day is a feasible way to improve the quality of electoral discourse. Is it necessary for Deliberation Day to be held during the campaign season? Probably not. Indeed, the goals of Deliberation Day might be better promoted by holding it between elections, before any candidates have emerged. By scheduling public deliberation to occur as late as they do, Ackerman and Fishkin may exploit the benefits of more focused public attention and higher public motivation, but they also import all the disadvantages associated with public consumption of late-stage campaign events. As indicated in Chapter 2, party selection procedures, ballot access laws, and campaign finance regulations will already have drastically narrowed the

---

72. de Sousa Santos, "Participatory Budgeting in Porto Alegre"; Hartz-Karp, "A Case Study in Deliberative Democracy."

73. Gastil and Levine, *The Deliberation Democracy Handbook*, purports to be a comprehensive guide to the ground-level implementation of deliberative democracy. Yet of nineteen chapters, only two (Chapters 4 and 18) deal at all with deliberation in the context of an election, and even these involve only very minimal changes from existing electoral procedures, such as having citizens instead of journalists ask questions of candidates at formal debates. In one example, such questions were put to candidates by students too young to vote. The most comprehensive work on implementing deliberative democracy, in other words, has almost nothing to say about how elections could be made more deliberative.

74. Ackerman and Fishkin, *Deliberation Day*, 3. They also propose a parallel Congress Day holiday dedicated to deliberation during congressional election years. *Ibid.*, 22. Gastil has made a similar proposal. Gastil, *By Popular Demand*, chs. 7–9.

75. Ackerman and Fishkin, *Deliberation Day*, ch. 2.

76. *Ibid.*, 40.

scope of views represented by the candidates to those that already command the broadest public support before Deliberation Day even gets underway.[77] And by the time Deliberation Day rolls around, the public may well have been exposed to a numbing deluge of low-quality discourse that might damage citizens' ability to deliberate impartially, open-mindedly, and cooperatively.[78]

But let us return to the original question: Are theories of deliberative democracy offended by poor-quality, deliberatively thin election campaigns? The answer seems to be that they are not. Theories of deliberative democracy certainly would never object to the appearance of a deliberatively thick campaign discourse, but they neither expect nor require it. For the most part, such theories hold that the kind of deliberation necessary to legitimate state power occurs mainly outside of electoral institutions, which they tend to view with considerable skepticism. Of course, if the necessary deliberation is not occurring elsewhere, theories of deliberative democracy might look to campaigns as a possible venue for deliberation. But, at best, the degree to which theories of deliberative democracy require that meaningful deliberation occur during campaigns depends heavily on the availability of other, better opportunities for citizens to deliberate. Moreover, theories of deliberative democracy tend to suggest strongly that in any society worthy of the label "democratic," most of this deliberation will necessarily occur in a legally protected, informal public sphere rather than within the formal institutions of the electoral process.

Conclusions

For liberal theories, then, the theoretical importance of campaigns is limited mainly to providing an opportunity for the exchange and collection of information sufficient to make an informed decision, but if this information has been collected and reflected upon between elections, there is no theoretical requirement of campaigns of any particular thickness. For more communitarian theories, campaigns may serve theoretically valuable functions, but the significance of campaigns varies inversely with the availability of alternative avenues for participation and deliberation. In sum, none of the

77. *See also* Flanders, "Deliberative Dilemmas."

78. Gastil's proposal would deal with this problem by using a mix of advisory, legislative prioritization, and candidate evaluation juries. Gastil, *By Popular Demand.*

established theories of democracy prescribes with any particular urgency that election campaigns be deliberatively thick occasions in which citizens engage one another in deep contemplation of collective ends. Conversely, the thinness and superficiality of our current campaigns is not, from the perspective of democratic theory, strong evidence of a sickness in the body politic. We can apparently continue to go on as we have and still count ourselves a democratically self-governing society.

This conclusion raises some interesting questions. What, exactly, are critics of American election campaigns complaining about, and why? It seems obvious that they believe a defining feature of democracy to be reasoned and deliberative election campaigns. Surely this is an attractive model, but what is the source of its attraction? What is the ideal to which the critics would have us aspire? In the concluding chapter, I propose some answers to these questions.

FIVE

The Tabulative Campaign

LET US RETURN TO WHERE WE BEGAN—the Campaign Critique. Numerous critics from all over the political spectrum find American election campaigns to be degraded and inadequate. Mainly what they complain about is the inability, or perhaps downright refusal, of political actors to live up to standards of electoral behavior that emerged at the beginning of the last century. Candidates and parties, according to this commonplace critique, make no real attempt to persuade others to their views. Campaign discourse is thin, uninformative, and superficial. On the rare occasions when candidates really do try to persuade voters on the merits of important issues, voters fail to open themselves to being persuaded. In short—and this seems to be the nub of the complaint—public political opinion is insufficiently campaign-endogenous. Everyone is trying to win elections, but hardly anyone is trying to win the right way: by campaigning to convince others sincerely to their point of view.

But what makes the Campaign Critique a valid criticism of the American electoral process? If, as we saw in the last chapter, democratic theory does not so require, why, precisely, *should* public political opinion be formed during a campaign rather than before it? What's wrong with a campaign that merely mobilizes voters for the purpose of permitting a democratic polity simply to discover, as best it can, what its citizens collectively happen to think? Why must a good campaign also *change* citizens' beliefs? What, at the end of the day, is wrong with what citizens *already* believe before the campaign starts, and why can't those beliefs serve as the foundation for democratically legitimate electoral decision making?

The first part of this chapter takes up these questions. I shall suggest that the persistent contemporary longing for campaign-endogenous public opinion is rooted in a kind of elite frustration with the slow pace of political and social change, and I shall argue that the real source of this frustration lies less in behavior attributable to individual political actors than in a brute social fact, rooted in the structure of democratic political communication: the powerful majoritarian bias of public political opinion. Having identified the problem, the chapter then goes on to ask whether and by what means it might be possible to make our election campaigns what their critics evidently would prefer them to be: recurring occasions for the (modest) destabilization of majoritarian public opinion. I conclude that the prospects for doing so are dim and that those measures which might most contribute to the successful destabilization of public opinion raise troubling issues of liberty and autonomy for democratic citizens.

The chapter then reverses field to undertake a more respectful examination of the tabulative campaign. In this section, I review some of the implications for constitutional doctrine and legal policy that might flow from an officially sanctioned public embrace of campaigns that are merely tabulative rather than persuasive. I also discuss briefly how we might think about election law if we lower our expectations to strive only to ensure nothing more than that campaign-exogenous public opinion is tabulated as accurately as possible. This chapter concludes with a discussion about what the abandonment of our aspirations for thickly deliberative campaigns might mean for those portions of the law that structure political communication occurring outside the formal electoral process.

The Demand for Campaign-Endogenous Public Opinion

What grounds might exist to justify the core belief of the Campaign Critique that public opinion should be campaign-endogenous—that it is insufficient merely for elections accurately to tabulate campaign-exogenous public opinion, and that citizens have some obligation to engage in a specific kind of political labor not (or not only) between elections but during the campaign itself? Clearly, the Critique not only elevates election campaigns to a place of unique importance in a democracy, but deems them of such great importance that no substitute is possible. On this view, democratic participation and deliberation between elections, no matter how thick and productive of the values of citizenship, simply is not sufficient; democratically relevant participation and deliberation is by definition participation and deliberation that occurs during campaigns regardless of whether it might also occur at other times.

One reason that democratic theory affords the Campaign Critique little support is that the Critique stakes out an uncomfortable and in some ways self-contradictory position. Like liberalism, and particularly Schumpeterian minimalism, which it in some ways resembles, the Critique stresses elections as the major and defining event of democratic self-rule. Unlike liberalism, however, the Critique seems to reject the legitimacy of public opinion when it is formed exogenously to the campaign—the very kind of public opinion that is a staple of liberal democratic theories.

At the same time, the Critique's demand for campaign-endogenous public opinion seems to express approval for the communitarian belief in the social and political significance of individual participation and deliberative, collective decision making. Yet unlike communitarian theories, the Campaign Critique rejects the contention that democracy can be satisfied when high-quality participation and deliberation take place outside the electoral arena. In this respect, the Critique is actually *more* demanding than deliberative democracy, itself a theory that makes extremely high demands of citizens. According to the Critique, even if democratic participation and deliberation occur outside the electoral setting, they also, and perhaps primarily, must occur during campaigns. On this view, public opinion formed during campaigns is apparently understood to be of a different and superior quality than public opinion formed at other times, and this superiority in turn gives rise to an obligation among citizens to do whatever is necessary to arrive at their opinions during the campaign phase of the electoral process. But why? Here I consider two possible explanations, one grounded in a conception of citizenship and the other in a conception of elections.

The Cincinnatus Model of Citizenship

One possible explanation for this position is that the Critique implicitly adopts a bimodal conception of liberal citizenship, one that might be called the Cincinnatus model. A patrician of the ancient Roman Republic who had been reduced by family misfortune to the economic circumstances of a poor farmer, Cincinnatus was twice appointed by the Senate during periods of great crisis to serve temporarily as Dictator. On each occasion, Cincinnatus agreed to leave his farm only with the greatest reluctance, after being prevailed upon by appeals to his sense of civic duty. Upon successfully completing the tasks for which he had been appointed Dictator, he immediately resigned this all-powerful post to return to his plow and the simple life of a private citizen.[1] The story of Cincinnatus held great resonance for the

1. Livy, *The Early History of Rome*, 3:18–29, 4:14–16, pp. 204–16, 285–87.

American founders, who viewed Cincinnatus as the ideal republican citizen. A simple man of nevertheless great talent and virtue who preferred the pleasures of private life to the burdens of public service, Cincinnatus left his farm when duty so demanded, exercised power with great competence, and then immediately returned to private life upon successfully discharging his civic obligations. George Washington is said to have self-consciously modeled his public persona on Cincinnatus, a comparison well-understood and much approved by the American public.[2]

This model has obvious relevance to the conditions of modern American democratic citizenship. Regardless of one's theoretical commitments, it is a social fact that most citizens of modern mass democracies attend mainly to their private affairs between elections, and in a sense emerge from their farms, often reluctantly, during campaign season to perform the civic obligation of informing themselves and then voting. While nothing in this model forbids citizens to attend closely to private affairs between elections, it contemplates that most will not do so, leaving politics between elections largely to elected officials and a small number of self-appointed political activists.

Citizens who do in fact live this kind of bimodal life might plausibly be said to bear a heavier burden during campaign season than citizens who attend to politics year-round. All citizens, to be sure, must make good quality decisions, but those who do not attend to politics at other times are at a disadvantage in this enterprise. Because they have been disengaged from politics, they must now attend closely, and make up their minds during the campaign, because the information they are receiving will by definition be new to them, and because public circumstances will almost surely have changed since they last emerged from behind their plows. On this model, then, we are thinly liberal democrats most of the time (though always with the option to be more), but we must temporarily take up the communitarian mantle—or at least become as politically engaged as though we were communitarians—every two or four years.[3]

---

2. *E.g.*, Brookhiser, *Founding Father*, 101–02.

3. The Jeffersonian version of the Cincinnatus story goes even further. In this version, working the farm between elections is not merely a social fact, but a normatively desirable feature of republican life. For Jeffersonian agrarian romantics, life on the farm would have recharged the spirit, inculcated and reinforced civic virtue, and inoculated citizens against the corruption that every exposure to politics might have risked. Jefferson, *Notes on Virginia*, 280.

But if this is in fact the model of democratic citizenship on which the Campaign Critique implicitly relies, it is an unrealistic and, in the end, normatively unattractive model. While there is no denying the democratic romance and uplift of the story of Cincinnatus, it is a highly implausible tale. No one steps off his farm after years of isolation from public life, takes complete command of the military and civilian government apparatus of a powerful state, and successfully manages a national crisis that has overwhelmed the capabilities of experienced elected officials and professionals.[4] One suspects that Cincinnatus was in fact extremely well informed and politically active, if behind the scenes, before the delegation from Rome showed up at his door, and that his appointment as Dictator was well vetted with all the significant political players.

More to the point, however, is that the bimodal conception of citizenship implicitly approved by this model—a model of citizenship as political isolation punctuated by brief periods of intense engagement—is both unsustainable and undesirable. First, democratic citizenship requires certain skills—listening, reasoning, judging, and so on—and these skills demand cultivation and frequent use to keep them well-honed.[5] Democratic decisions made episodically, after lengthy periods in which the skills of citizenship go unused, would therefore not likely be good ones. Second, democracy requires citizens to be vigilant between elections as well as during them, so a complete withdrawal from politics between elections poses serious dangers. Indeed, public liberty and the public good are far more at risk between elections, when democratically approved officials actually exercise power, than during elections, when those officials' records come under systematic public scrutiny.

Third and most important, the Cincinnatus model presupposes an unrealistically sharp distinction between private and public affairs. Citizens' private, everyday lives cannot be separated neatly from their collective lives—that is, from public affairs.[6] No one is totally isolated from politics. Citizens inevitably

---

4. The story nevertheless still resonates for some sectors of the American public. It is the basis, for example, of claims to office by successful business executives, such as Ross Perot, who claim that their lack of governing experience is an asset. Occasionally the public will actually elect someone of this description—a Jesse Ventura or Arnold Schwarzenegger, say—but rarely or never in times of severe crisis. Sometimes the public is also willing to confer office on a celebrity as a kind of gift, *see* Gardner, "Giving the Gift of Public Office," but again not in times of crisis.

5. Aristotle, *Politics*; Mill, *Considerations on Representative Government.*

6. Shapiro, "Optimal Deliberation?," 129–30.

develop and cultivate political knowledge between elections, either deliberately by attending self-consciously to public affairs, or inadvertently through discussion and action with others, and there is no good reason to think that knowledge acquired in this way would be insufficient to formulate political opinions outside of the formal campaign period.[7] Moreover, attempting to confine political learning and judgment to the brief period of a campaign would place an excessive and unsustainable burden on voters. The amount of information necessary to make sound decisions is simply too great to gather and process if attended to exclusively during campaign season. Virtually all campaign communication presupposes a base of citizen knowledge and judgment that has been cultivated in advance of the campaign.[8]

Electoral Exceptionalism

If the characteristics of modern democratic citizenship do not provide a satisfactory basis for insisting that political opinion be formed during campaigns, another possible ground might lie in the nature of election campaigns themselves. Suppose we concede that much of the information-gathering, reflection, and reasoning necessary to the formulation of sound, well-informed political opinion occurs between elections, in the course of an ordinary, privately lived life. Still, might there be something so unique and consequential about election campaigns that they simply *must* serve as the forum in which public opinion is, to some very significant degree, ultimately formulated (rather than merely tabulated)? Is there any reason to think that opinions formed during campaigns are somehow better and more democratically valid than opinions formed at other times?[9]

---

7. Fleischacker, "Insignificant Communities."

8. Some mild empirical support for this intuition appears in Claasen and Highton, "Does Policy Debate Reduce Information Effects in Public Opinion?"

9. Dennis Thompson has argued that campaigns must be understood to play a uniquely important role in democratic political processes and that the uniqueness of their function justifies heavier regulation during campaigns of processes, such as political speech, that are continuous both during and between campaigns. But Thompson does not rest this claim on a contention that political opinions formed during campaigns are in any way superior to those formed at other times. Indeed, Thompson explicitly acknowledges "the difficulty of separating electoral from nonelectoral politics." Thompson, "Election Time," 61. Instead, Thompson maintains, the reason for treating elections as distinct from ordinary politics "is not that campaign activity is more influential or more important, but that it is more final." Thompson, "Making Campaigns Safe for Democracy," 1054.

One possibility, based on a kind of sociological realism, may be rejected immediately. On this view, sometimes advanced in the political science literature, voters are simply more motivated and attentive during campaigns,[10] from which one might be inclined to conclude that they will make better decisions during this period. The problem with this argument is that it is circular: it is true only if the political is defined to mean the electoral. It is certainly the case that voters are more motivated to attend to an *election* as the election approaches, but this says nothing about their motivation and attention toward the acquisition and processing of political knowledge that may ultimately prove useful in making decisions once election time rolls around. Citizens who are disposed to attend to public affairs at election time presumably are motivated to attend to public affairs frequently, if episodically, on all kinds of occasions besides the arrival of campaign season—namely, whenever some event occurs that captures their attention and prompts their engagement and reflection. Indeed, it seems less plausible to expect voters to pay attention to political issues during the somewhat forced and artificial context of a campaign than when those issues press themselves upon the public consciousness in the form of actually occurring and therefore fully contextualized events.

A more promising approach might be to ask not whether voters are different during campaigns, but whether the political environment itself differs during the formal campaign period in some way that significantly assists electoral decision making. For example, information that is salient to voting decisions might be more readily accessible during campaigns than between elections. Voters might encounter more arguments and conversation of direct electoral relevance, from a wider variety of sources, during campaigns than at other times. If so, then a campaign might be, not by theory but by contingent social practice, a kind of designated forum in which citizens agree to pay attention and to make up their minds. This does not of course mean that voters are incapable of formulating sound political opinions before the inception of a campaign. It might mean, however, that political opinions held or arrived at between elections ought at least to be held in suspension as provisional until checked and, if appropriate, ratified during the campaign. Voting, on this account, should therefore enact a kind of representation by citizens that they have performed an important civic duty consisting of

10. Huckfeldt and Sprague, *Citizens, Politics, and Social Communication*, 96; Lazersfeld, Berelson, and Gaudet, *The People's Choice*, ch. 8.

reviewing their standing beliefs and preferences against information made available to them during the campaign. Every voter, in other words, ought to be a late-deciding uncommitted, or at most a late-deciding, provisional leaner. The point, in any case, is for voters to review their opinions, causing them to commit late rather than early.[11]

But why should voters be under a duty to confirm their strong initial leanings through time-consuming cross-verification of their beliefs against information that may happen to become available during a campaign? What if they have confidence in the opinions they hold at the inception of the campaign? What if those opinions are well-considered and mature? What if a voter justifiably believes that virtually nothing a candidate could say would cause a change in the voter's positions on the issues most likely to be salient during an upcoming campaign?

Indeed, if we examine this view further, it begins to seem more than a little paternalistic. Here, it seems to say—not there, in the ordinary experiences of your daily life, but here, in the campaign environment—are the arguments and the information that you *should* consider as actively and deliberatively as possible, as well as the setting in which you should consider them. Whatever you have come to believe in the experiences of the life you live between elections must be treated as provisional and suspect. You consequently must confirm—and if you cannot confirm, you must alter—your beliefs after active engagement during a formal electoral campaign before you may responsibly rely on those beliefs to decide how to cast your vote.

But does this make sense? Is the set of information and arguments available during a campaign so far superior—so much richer, so much better reasoned—than the information and arguments available between elections, or available during the most recent campaign for the same office two or four years ago, that a voter's failure to engage the material currently available during the present campaign casts real doubt on the reasonableness and integrity of his or her voting decision? I think not. Indeed, this possibility seems to me so dubious that I want to suggest an altogether different explanation for the belief that political opinion ideally must be formulated during campaigns.

---

11. We will set aside for purposes of this discussion the fact that late deciders tend to be among the least informed, least interested, and least motivated voters—precisely the kind of behavior that critics of our campaigns presumably would not wish to encourage or reward. *See, e.g.*, Lazarsfeld, Berelson, and Gaudet, *The People's Choice*, chs. 6–10; Converse, "Information Flow and the Stability of Partisan Attitudes"; Delli Carpini and Keeter, *What Americans Know about Politics and Why It Matters*, 172–73.

The Majoritarian Bias of Public Opinion

One of the most powerful findings of the social science research reviewed in Chapter 3 is the stability of political opinion. Numerous cognitive, social, and structural biases cause citizens and voters to avoid encountering information contrary to their current beliefs, to ignore it when they encounter it, and to misinterpret it when they attend to it in a way that reinforces rather than challenges their existing beliefs. On an individual level, this makes political opinion to a great extent self-reinforcing: whatever a voter believes now is likely to be what he or she continues to believe, even after exposure to new or contrary information and ideas.

At the collective level, the self-reinforcing aspect of currently held political opinion is even more pronounced. In a democracy, the political opinion that counts is the opinion of the majority. But just because it is a majority, the opinions it holds will be more widely held, more widely disseminated, more widely known, and more frequently recognized than opinions held by minorities. Defenders of the majority view will be by definition more numerous; information in support of their positions will be more readily available. All citizens will therefore be more likely to encounter, understand, and process information and arguments supporting majority political opinion than information and arguments supporting any other point of view. In the short run, this dynamic produces an exceedingly strong majoritarian bias in the direction of public political opinion. That is, collective political opinion is much more likely to converge on what a majority already believes than it is to deviate from the majority view; majority opinion is far more likely to intensify and entrench itself than it is to weaken and surrender the field to its competitors.[12]

To say that public political opinion has a majoritarian bias, however, is to say also that public opinion is biased in favor of the status quo. Because a

---

12. This phenomenon was demonstrated in several ways in Chapter 3 but for a truly stunning example see Huckfeldt et al., "Ambiguity, Distorted Messages, and Nested Environmental Effects on Political Communication." The authors argue in this study that political communication is in general inherently ambiguous, and that ambiguous signals are routinely interpreted by observers to be consistent with majority opinion. As a result, "individuals quite frequently and incorrectly infer majority opinion with respect to other individuals who are, in fact, members of the minority," and that this gives rise to "an overall political bias that favors the continued dominance of majority opinion." *Ibid.*, 1026. Or, as some of the same authors put it elsewhere, "political minorities operate under pronounced disadvantages in democratic politics." Huckfeldt, Johnson, and Sprague, *Political Disagreement*, 115.

well-functioning democracy is, or at least ought to be, responsive in some degree to the wishes of the majority, the policies it chooses should ideally reflect the substance of majority opinion. But if the majoritarian bias of public opinion causes it to reinforce and entrench itself, then the policies that a democratic polity supports are also likely, at least in the short term, to command increasing rather than decreasing support, a phenomenon that makes political change extremely difficult. As Cass Sunstein has observed, we suffer from a "tyranny of the status quo."[13]

I want to suggest that it is this phenomenon—the deeply entrenched, structural, majoritarian bias of public opinion—to which proponents of the Campaign Critique are ultimately responding. The contention that our campaigns are poor when public political opinion is not actually formulated during the campaign itself may simply reflect a kind of elite frustration with the slow pace of political and social change, a pace caused in no small part by the majoritarian and status quo biases of public political opinion. What, after all, is likely to result from an election in which public political opinion is formed exogenously to the campaign, and the election therefore merely tabulates preexisting public opinion? Obviously, such an election is likely to do little more than ratify the status quo. By the same token, what such a campaign fails to do is to summon forth a genuinely transformative politics in which meaningful change is laid on the table for reflective, mature contemplation.

To overcome the deep, self-reinforcing biases of public opinion, critics seem to sense, some external event must provide a shock to the system; if public opinion is to change, it must first be destabilized. That, the Campaign Critique suggests, is what campaigns ought to be for.[14] Far from merely tabulating existing public opinion, the purpose of a campaign should be to provide a mildly destabilizing shock to entrenched, majoritarian political opinion so that it can reformulate around a new center of gravity, one defined by information and arguments disseminated by political actors during the campaign itself. The prescription for accomplishing this shock is simple: citizens must work hard to detach themselves intellectually and emotionally from what they already think they know and believe. All beliefs must therefore be deemed provisional and must be checked and rechecked against any newly available information and arguments.

---

13. Cass Sunstein, *Republic.com*, 190.

14. It bears mentioning that like-minded reformers at one time thought that destabilizing majoritarian, status quo institutions was what judicial review was for.

This self-detachment, critics seems to believe, is the gate to the citadel of entrenched majoritarian opinion through which alternative ideas may just possibly enter. Proponents of the Campaign Critique therefore prescribe more campaign-endogenous opinion formation because they want voters to put into play their deep dispositions and long-held opinions. This is the only way to give any possible chance of success to views *not* held by the majority. What views might these be? Perhaps they are the views of elites, or highly specialized experts, or dissidents. To some degree, they may be the views of minorities, whether on the left or the right, who believe that they have unredeemed claims of justice against the majority.[15] To the extent that campaigns should be a time when voters listen to people whom they do not ordinarily encounter or to whose views they do not ordinarily attend, an election, on this view, should be a time for needed changes of course, not ratification of the existing course. Elections, that is, should be disruptive to slow, evolutionary development of public opinion; they should be opportunities for political revolution, not evolution. That they are not, I am inclined to think, is what so frustrates critics of our politics.

Campaigns as Destabilizing Events

At this point, we begin to approach a great contradiction at the heart of modern liberal democratic thought. On one hand, the principal purpose of representative democracy surely is to place power into the hands of majorities precisely so that they can have their way; that is what distinguishes it from the monarchical and aristocratic forms of government it replaced. On the other hand, unrestrained majority rule can be disastrous for minorities,[16] particularly if the majority is stable and thus, for practical purposes, permanent and therefore unaccountable.[17] Consequently, societies with democratic aspirations have for more than two centuries attempted simultaneously both to empower majorities and to restrain them.

Many of the best-known mechanisms that have been devised to restrain democratic majorities, including such constitutional devices as bills of rights,

15. Young, *Inclusion and Democracy*; Dryzek, *Deliberative Democracy and Beyond*; Unger, *False Necessity*.

16. Madison et al., *The Federalist Papers*, No. 10.

17. Guinier, *Tyranny of the Majority*.

judicial review, separation of powers, and federalism, seek to inhibit majorities from misbehaving after they have been handed the reins of power. Such devices perform, so to speak, a kind of aftermarket retrofitting designed to render fit for use a product—majority rule—that is not completely suitable right out of the box. Other mechanisms, however, are calculated to manufacture majorities in such a way that majorities pose no serious dangers to begin with, thereby reducing, even if not entirely eliminating, the need for effective after-the-fact restraints. The large republic according to Madison falls into this category,[18] as do efforts to improve democratic decision making through education or the cultivation of civic virtue.[19] The deliberative democracy project itself is perhaps best conceived as a program to improve citizens' capacity and willingness to treat minorities more respectfully and empathetically so that majorities pose less of a threat to minority welfare.[20]

Similarly, the idea that election campaigns should destabilize majoritarian opinion may be understood as falling into the latter category of protective devices. It is a way of rendering majorities less dangerous by rendering them less permanent. The danger posed by extremely stable or permanent majorities has been made forcefully by Lani Guinier in the context of American racial politics:

> [T]he claim that majority rule is legitimate rests on two main assumptions that do not hold where racial prejudice pervades the majority: (1) that majorities are fluid rather than fixed; and (2) that minorities will be able to become part of the governing coalition in the future. Only by making these assumptions, which essentially means that the majority will rule in public-regarding fashion (that is, the winners will virtually represent the interests of the losers), is it possible to argue that winner-take-all majority rule is fair.[21]

But one need not conjure up something so ugly as irrational majoritarian hatreds and biases to find value in the idea of elections as a mechanism for destabilizing majority opinion. The majority may be mistaken about

18. Madison et al., *The Federalist Papers*, No. 10.

19. Brown, *The Strength of a People*.

20. *E.g.*, Goodin, *Reflective Democracy*; Young, *Inclusion and Democracy*; Gardner, "Shut Up and Vote"; Knops, "Delivering Deliberation's Emancipatory Potential."

21. Guinier, *The Tyranny of the Majority*, 103.

many things. It may overvalue or undervalue certain collective ends, causing it to make poor decisions regarding tradeoffs or to misallocate resources. It may have longstanding preferences for specific policies that fail to attain effectively its acknowledged shared ends, or that fail to do so as effectively as alternative policies, or that have collateral consequences too severe to justify retaining the policies.[22] The majority, in other words, may hold beliefs that are bad, or irrational, or counterproductive, and it could in principle be induced to see and correct its errors were public political opinion genuinely campaign-endogenous.

To repeat: these are perennial questions for democratic states. To what degree should democracy concern itself with creating an efficient route to effective majority power, and to what degree should it concern itself with imposing constraints on the effective use of power handed to a majority? I do not propose, however, to enter into this debate. Instead, I shall presume for purposes of discussion that making public opinion more campaign-endogenous could serve a valuable public purpose. This will allow us to pose a different, less frequently asked question: If election campaigns are not now forums for the endogenous formation of public political opinion, could they be retooled to serve that function, and if so by what means? If we believe that election campaigns should be mechanisms for the regular destabilization of public opinion, how could we accomplish that goal?

Methods of Destabilizing Political Opinion

The social science findings, of course, suggest that majoritarian political opinion is so stable and self-reinforcing that it would be very, very difficult to dislodge, but let us set these dismal tidings aside for now. What could we do, what reforms might we institute, to convert campaigns into venues in which citizens primarily form, or regularly reform, their political opinions?

We may begin by excluding some cures that are obviously worse than the disease. We could, for example, deprive people entirely of all political information except during campaigns. That would surely force them to formulate their political opinions during campaign season, but requiring citizens to remain ignorant of political information most of the time poses severe civic

22. Bryan Caplan, *The Myth of the Rational Voter*.

dangers that need hardly be rehearsed; not for nothing is public ignorance the preferred policy of autocrats everywhere.

If we must leave citizens to form political views year-round, then the goal must be to destabilize those views during the campaign. How might this be accomplished? If the main mechanism by which citizens defend their views against destabilization is simply ignoring contrary views, then the strongest dose of medicine would be to structure campaigns in such a way that it is impossible for most citizens to ignore information, arguments, and viewpoints with which they do not already fully agree. A campaign, then, must become a forum not just for pleasant, voluntary, reinforcing encounters with the like-minded, but also for unwanted, destabilizing, and perhaps unpleasant encounters with those who hold different or even contrary views.

Citizens might be forced into these unwanted encounters by one of two methods: compelled exposure to contrary ideas, and compelled association with those who hold them.

Compelled Exposure

In some of his recent work on democratic deliberation, Cass Sunstein has endorsed the idea that citizens ought to be exposed to ideas that they would not ordinarily choose to encounter or engage.[23] It must be said at the outset that Sunstein's reasons for advocating unwanted exposure to ideas differ from those presently under discussion. Here we are concerned with the possibility that the majority's avoidance of exposure to and engagement with ideas it opposes might cause it to adhere excessively rigidly and unreflectively to its existing beliefs. Sunstein, in contrast, is more concerned with the possibility that group self-insulation from contrary views will facilitate a fragmentation of public opinion, causing it to become both more polarized and more extreme. For Sunstein, the important consideration is that isolated subgroups at risk of descending into extremism receive unwanted exposure to moderating, majoritarian views. For the present inquiry, in contrast, the important consideration is that a moderate and complacent majority receive unwanted exposure to dissenting views held by political minorities.

In any case, the aspect of Sunstein's analysis of greatest direct interest is a collection of specific proposals he makes to increase the likelihood that people

---

23. Sunstein, *Republic.com*; Sunstein, *Why Societies Need Dissent.*

will encounter "points of view that they have not selected."[24] These include the creation of internet-based "deliberative domains" for discussion by people of diverse views; public subsidies for fora that meet criteria of deliberativeness and inclusiveness; and rules requiring popular or highly partisan Web sites to include links to sites where visitors could obtain alternative views.[25]

The most striking feature of Sunstein's proposals is that they are all voluntary: those unaccustomed to having their existing views challenged would need first to decide that they ought to broaden their horizons, and then take affirmative steps to gain access to contrary information and ideas by deliberately visiting a Web site or some other forum and attending closely to its content. This is not a solution likely to destabilize the current practice of self-insulation even for those who are willing to open themselves to contrary views, much less for those who are not. Yet Sunstein distances himself firmly from measures that would involve actual compulsion: "Only tyrannies," he says emphatically, "force people to read or to watch."[26]

Yet even if it is true, as it surely is, that only tyrannies of the *Clockwork Orange* variety physically compel people to watch or to read approved messages, it is certainly possible to imagine measures that might, without resorting to physical compulsion, nevertheless more effectively induce citizens to endure exposure to unwanted ideas than Sunstein's purely voluntary and largely self-initiated ones. The logical method for doing so—indeed, the logical method for getting people to do anything that they would prefer not to do—is to raise the cost of avoidance. Private actors do this all the time. If you want to see the movie, you have to sit through the commercials first. If you want to download the video, you have to watch the ads. In both cases, you are perfectly free to avoid the unwanted messages, but only at the cost of forfeiting the opportunity to receive the communications you actually desire.

---

24. Sunstein, *Republic.com*, 169.

25. *Ibid.*, 169–90.

26. *Ibid.*, 11. *See also ibid.*, 112 (disclaiming that "people should be required to see things that do not interest them") and 113 (government should not "feel free to move preferences and beliefs in what it considers to be desirable directions"). *See also* Goodin, *Reflective Democracy*, 162. However, in a recent paper with Vermeule, Sunstein comes closer to recommending measures that go further than merely making available contrary and unwanted information. To disrupt the tendency of dialogue among members of like-minded, isolated, extremist groups, Sunstein and Vermeule recommend that "[g]overnment agents (and their allies) might enter chat rooms, online social networks, or even real-space groups and attempt to undermine percolating conspiracy theories by raising doubts about their factual premises, causal logic or implications for political action." Sunstein and Vermeule, "Conspiracy Theories," 22.

Even government engages frequently in this kind of behavior. For example, government often posts or requires others to post all sorts of notices and warnings, or to make required announcements or disclaimers. Such notices might concern product safety, say, or airport security. Typically, these notices, warnings, and disclaimers are required to be made or displayed in just such a way as to be extremely difficult to avoid—that is their point. Warning labels or workplace safety rules must be posted where they will be seen; announcements about airport security must be made so that they will be heard. Even consumers who genuinely wish to remain totally uninformed about automotive safety, for example, will find it difficult to refer to the owner's manual for their new car without encountering, and thereby possibly absorbing, numerous unwanted tips and warnings.[27]

None of these measures literally forces anyone to endure unwanted messages or ideas. There are obvious ways to avoid seeing or hearing them, and if an unwanted message happens to slip past one's defenses, one can always do one's best to ignore it, or if it is too late to ignore a message, to forget it. Yet surely most people absorb at least some of the content of these generally unwanted communications. Can anyone who has been in an American airport since September 11, 2001 not know that he should not leave his bags unattended? The reason why most people do not take heroic measures to shut out such communications is that doing so is somewhat costly, at least in comparison to the generally brief and relatively minor discomfort associated with enduring an unwanted advertisement or public service announcement. As a result, we sit through them even if we would rather not.

It is possible to imagine similar tactics being applied to unwanted political speech during the course of a formal campaign. Those who want some benefit must first receive a message. Of course, something like this already happens all the time: in the course of going about our daily business we may unexpectedly encounter political messages, advertisements, or even the occasional street rally. But these are often costlessly avoided or ignored—drop the flyer in the trash, turn the page of the newspaper, cross the street, and so on—and stronger measures may be available.

---

27. Of course, it is even more common for government to take actions designed to protect citizens from unwanted speech. Legal doctrines of trespass, nuisance, and content-neutral restrictions on the time, place and manner of speech all enlist government in the enterprise of insulating citizens from speech they do not wish to hear. *See* Zick, "Speech and Spatial Tactics."

Suppose that no telephone call you place during campaign season will be completed until you have listened to a randomly selected, 15-second issue spot produced by a candidate who is running for office in your telephone service area, or by a political advocacy organization promoting its agenda. Suppose that you cannot connect to any Web site of the Republican Party or its candidates without first sitting through a short advertisement for the Democratic Party, and vice versa. Or, between August and November of election years, advocacy messages could be posted prominently, on a random or rotating basis, in all government office buildings, or on billboards. Radio and television stations could be required to carry political messages. All web browsing sessions might be interrupted briefly, but regularly, by issue advocacy spots. Indeed, the Web's capacity to track user characteristics and preferences, already well-honed by commercial data-miners, could doubtless be used to determine with some precision every user's political preferences. This would permit issue advocacy spots to be directed toward individual users in a way that will virtually guarantee that each Web user will receive only communications contrary to his or her standing political beliefs.

None of these devices would literally coerce anyone to endure unwanted political speech. You may avert your eyes, turn off the television, leave the government building, terminate your Web browsing session, and so on. Yet it seems relatively clear that few would avoid the exposure by forgoing the benefits they seek because the value of placing a phone call, watching television, browsing the Web, and applying for a driver's license or unemployment benefits is comparatively large, and the cost of enduring the unwanted speech is, for many users, comparatively small.[28]

On the other hand, all of these proposals are vulnerable to at least two potentially serious objections. First, although these measures do not involve physical coercion, they nevertheless intrude to some degree upon the liberty and personal autonomy of democratic citizens by restricting their freedom to choose how to conduct their daily lives, at least in the couple of months immediately preceding an election. Government, of course, invades our personal autonomy constantly by requiring or prohibiting all manner of behavior, but this kind of intrusion is more serious than most because it does not so much regulate our behavior as it does our attention. Admittedly, there is no

28. *See* Lichtman, "How the Law Responds to Self-Help," arguing that the existence of a captive audience may be understood as an opportunity to expose citizens efficiently to views that they might not ordinarily encounter, making speech to such an audience a favored rather than disfavored form of speech for purposes of the First Amendment.

clean division between government regulation of behavior and attention—my obligation to pay taxes, for example, requires me to devote many hours of my attention to a particular activity to which I would prefer not to attend, while simultaneously diverting my attention from other activities that I greatly prefer.

Still, there is a difference between the government taking action to augment and improve my options for attending to political matters, as Sunstein recommends, and taking action essentially to conscript my attention to political subjects at moments when I would otherwise choose, perhaps quite earnestly and passionately, to direct it to other matters. No one has made this point more forcefully and eloquently than Charles Black:

> What is perfectly clear is that the claim to freedom from unwanted speech rests on grounds of high policy and on convictions of human dignity closely similar to if not identical with those classically brought forward in support of speech in the usual sense. Forced listening destroys and denies, practically and symbolically, that unfettered interplay and competition among ideas which is the assumed ambient of the communication freedoms. It contradicts, moreover, what some would regard as a deeper though not often spoken ground for letting people say freely what they choose—respect, namely, for each man as a person. . . . A society which uses toward its members the wanton contempt of treating their *listening* to words as a *thing* . . . cannot long hold fast to a contradictory respect for their *utterance* of words as something inviolably close to the center of man as man.[29]

To deprive citizens, in other words, of some degree of autonomous control over their own political thinking is to undermine the very kind of autonomous citizenship that democratic society both presupposes and ought to cultivate. Compelled exposure to unwanted speech is thus, on this view, a serious betrayal of democratic ideals.[30]

---

29. Black, "He Cannot Choose but Hear," 967–68.

30. In a recent decision, the Supreme Court has recognized obliquely that the First Amendment is not designed to displace entrenched, majoritarian political opinion, but to give it effect: "The reason one-party rule is entrenched [in some places] may be (and usually is) that voters approve of the positions and candidates that the party regularly puts forward. It is no function of the First Amendment to require revision of those positions or candidates." New York State Board of Elections v. Lopez Torres, 128 S.Ct. 791,801 (2008).

Second, even if the objections from autonomy might be overcome, any attempt to exploit the attention of a captive audience is likely to suffer from serious problems of inefficacy. Even when they cannot avoid an unwanted stimulus, most people can, with some degree of success, actively take countermeasures to minimize their attention to it: they may avert their eyes, lower the volume, mentally tune out, think about what to make for dinner, and so on. And these conscious strategies of course supplement all the unconscious ones—the attention filters, cognitive biases, and creative misinterpretation strategies—that we have already encountered. Thus, whatever the cost to liberty and autonomy that programs of compelled exposure to contrary ideas may impose, they might very likely do so for little or no significant benefit.

A different way to promote citizens' exposure to ideas with which they may not fully agree, and one more consistent with liberal qualms about invading individual autonomy, is to make use of positive rather than negative incentives—to give people good but still voluntary reasons to want to expand their exposure to political ideas. One promising possibility may be to adopt electoral systems such as instant runoff voting (IRV) or the single-transferable vote (STV), a form of proportional representation, that require voters to rank candidates for the same office instead of casting only a single vote for a single candidate in each race. Electoral systems that ask voters to rank candidates require voters to learn more information about more of the candidates so that they can make informed second and third choices. Where such systems are used, voters may thus be expected to attend more closely to the campaign speech of candidates who are not their preferred choices so as to exercise their electoral duties in a responsible way.

Empirical evidence beginning to come in from the handful of American jurisdictions that have recently adopted IRV[31] suggests an additional benefit that might also enhance voter attention to a greater breadth of campaign communication: IRV seems to discourage negative campaigning, often identified as a factor contributing to voter disengagement.[32] Because IRV gives candidates an incentive to campaign for the second-place votes of voters

---

31. At this writing, these jurisdictions are San Francisco; Burlington, Vermont; Takoma Park, Maryland; and Cary, North Carolina. Louisiana, South Carolina, and Arkansas use IRV for overseas and military voters. *See* www.fairvote.com.

32. Ansolabehere and Iyengar, *Going Negative*. The degree to which negative campaigning actually alienates or demobilizes voters is, however, somewhat contested in the political science literature. Compare Brooks and Geer, "Beyond Negativity"; Sigelman and Kugler, "Why Is Research on the Effects of Negative Campaigning So Inconclusive?"

outside their main base of support, candidates are less likely to risk alienating supporters of their opponents by campaigning against those opponents in strongly negative terms.[33] Thus, positive-incentive mechanisms such as IRV might not only give voters affirmative reasons to pay attention to a greater range of political opinion, but might also remove an existing disincentive for them to do so, all without any direct or serious diminution of citizens' political autonomy.

Compelled Association

Another mechanism by which majoritarian political opinion might in theory be destabilized is compelled association. This is potentially a much more powerful tool than merely compelling exposure to contrary ideas. Compelling someone to endure an unwanted exposure to an idea with which he or she disagrees is generally a one-time, anonymous transaction, making it relatively easy to ignore. Compelling someone to associate with another person who holds such views, on the other hand, may involve long-term, repeated, face-to-face encounters that may be much harder to ignore, and indeed may occur in situations where personal bonds or the pursuit of shared goals may create a fruitful environment for honest, constructive engagement and dialogue. Such encounters, in other words, may occur in circumstances favorable to the message actually getting through.

In her study of the role of the workplace in fostering democratic skills and bonds, Cynthia Estlund found that "the instrumental and even the hierarchical dimensions of workplace relations help to bring individuals together across lines of social division that they would not otherwise choose to cross, and to make those potentially conflict-ridden interactions relatively constructive."[34] As a result, Estlund reports, "conversations among co-workers are more likely to cross lines of social division, such as racial, ethnic, or cultural identity" than they are in any other grouping, including the family and networks of freely chosen friends.[35] These characteristics, Estlund concludes, make the workplace a significant resource for cultivating the skills and values of

33. Murphy, "New Runoff System in San Francisco Has the Rival Candidates Cooperating"; Hill, "How Ed Jew Got Elected."

34. Estlund, *Working Together*, 14.

35. *Ibid.*, 120.

democratic citizenship despite the lack of democracy that usually prevails within the workplace itself. A similar understanding of the benefits of compelled association underlies the Supreme Court's decision in *Brown v. Board of Education* requiring integration of public schools. Merely forcing children of different races to associate would, the Court clearly hoped, break down false and noxious beliefs about race and forge democratically valuable bonds across an important social divide, thereby weakening it.

If compelled association at school or work is capable of destabilizing socially profound divisions of race and class, some form of compelled association might also be able to destabilize entrenched barriers of political opinion of the kind that divide a stable, self-reinforcing majority from the many minority groups that hold dissenting views. Yet the same characteristics that make compelled association a powerful tool for breaking down barriers of belief also make it a much more intrusive measure than compelled exposure in impairing the ability of individuals autonomously to construct their own lives. Of course, the intrusiveness of compelled association does not by itself place the practice beyond the bounds of what government may sometimes do. Jury service, military service during a draft, and racial and gender integration in the workplace are all commonplace forms of compelled association. All represent, however, relatively narrow, carefully targeted disruptions of voluntary associational patterns undertaken for extremely compelling public purposes.

American constitutional law generally takes a strong stand against compelled association except as a remedy for very serious forms of deeply disfavored discrimination.[36] In a line of cases stretching back half a century, the Supreme Court has held that the First Amendment protects a right of expressive association that confers upon private organizations nearly complete control over their membership, including the right to exclude unwanted participants.[37] The main justification for these rulings is that an organization devoted primarily to the contemplation or cultivation of ideas, whether in politics or otherwise, must be able to exercise control over its membership if it is to remain free successfully to pursue the objectives for which it

36. *E.g.*, Smith v. Allwright, 321 U.S. 649 (1944); Terry v. Adams, 345 U.S. 461 (1953); Roberts v. U.S. Jaycees, 468 U.S. 609 (1984); New York State Club Association, Inc. v. City of New York, 487 U.S. 1 (1988).

37. NAACP v. Alabama, 357 U.S. 449 (1958); NAACP v. Button, 371 U.S. 415 (1963); Tashjian v. Republican Party of Connecticut, 479 U.S. 208, 214 (1986); California Democratic Party v. Jones, 530 U.S. 567 (2000).

was organized.[38] The reasoning of the cases stands in considerable tension with any justification for compelled association rooted in the value of exposure to unwanted ideas. In a somewhat more recent line of cases, the Supreme Court has ruled that constitutionally protected principles of due process also invest individuals with a right to control their intimate, personal associations—to choose their friends, life partners, and other close associates.[39] These cases, too, might pose a serious obstacle to using compelled association to destabilize public opinion.[40]

Even if legal obstacles could be overcome, it is not at all clear that association could be compelled in a way that effectively destabilizes majoritarian political opinion. First, it is hard to see how forced association in the political setting could be sufficiently broad-based to make much of a difference. Certainly the most obvious possibility would be to prevent political parties from excluding members who do not share their ideological commitments. Unfortunately, this is an arrangement that is predicted not to destabilize but more deeply to entrench majoritarian opinion by forcing all parties to the political center. That is precisely the justification given by political reformers who have promoted the use of open or blanket primaries—primary elections in which voting for a party's official candidate is not limited to party members, but is instead open to other groups of voters or even to all voters indiscriminately. In these kinds of primary elections, the deliberate inclusion of voters who are *not* committed, like-minded members of the party is said to result in the selection of party candidates who are less extreme in their views,

---

38. Hurley v. Irish-American Gay, Lesbian and Bisexual Group, 515 U.S. 557 (1995); Boy Scouts of American v. Dale, 530 U.S. 640 (2000).

39. Griswold v. Connecticut, 381 U.S. 479 (1965); Moore v. City of East Cleveland, 431 U.S. 494 (1977); Roberts v. U.S. Jaycees, 468 U.S. 609 (1984); Lawrence v. Texas, 539 U.S. 558 (2003).

40. Virtually all scholarly consideration of compelled association revolves around the propriety and justifications for permitting or prohibiting forms of exclusion by private groups that are in some sense discriminatory, i.e., when exclusion is undertaken for reasons (race or gender, for example) that do not comport with prevailing social conceptions of human equality and dignity. *See, e.g.*, Rosenblum, *Membership and Morals*; Kateb, "The Value of Association." Almost no one has analyzed compelled association as a tool for social engineering in circumstances where those excluded are not seeking inclusion to redress a claimed dignitary injury, but rather for the purposes of advancing their own ideological goals. I assume that the almost universal silence on this subject suggests that no one seriously thinks that forcing inclusion for these reasons would strike a justifiable balance between the virtues and vices of selectivity in private association. The few authors to have touched on the subject seem to be highly skeptical. *E.g.*, Alexander, "What Is Freedom of Association"; Shiffrin, "What Is Really Wrong with Compelled Association?"

closer to the political center, more appealing to a broader cross-section of the electorate, and thus more electable.[41]

Voting in party primaries, moreover, is far from the kind of compelled, face-to-face association that might in principle be capable of producing genuinely destabilizing communicative exchanges. For Democrats or Republicans, liberals or conservatives, libertarians or communitarians to destabilize one another's views, they will need to have occasions to engage one another in meaningful personal conversation, opportunities that are scarce within the highly decentralized structure of the twenty-first-century political party. Furthermore, political opinion is most often and most reliably transmitted through interactions with family and coworkers.[42] To inject unwanted political conversation into the places where it is really formed would thus require a degree of intrusion into daily associational choices that would be for most people not merely intolerable but unthinkable. Just try to enforce a law permitting Rush Limbaugh or Bill Clinton to invite himself to dinner at any home in the nation.

This discussion has been suggestive rather than conclusive, but here is what I think it suggests. Compelled exposure to ideas and compelled association *during the course of an election campaign* are not likely to be useful tools for destabilizing majoritarian political opinion. You can no more force a campaign to be an occasion for voters deeply and meaningfully to reexamine their longstanding political beliefs than you can force a romantic, candlelit dinner to be an occasion for falling in love, or a camping trip with your teenage children to be an occasion for family bonding and reconciliation. The price of making the attempt, moreover, may well be high, possibly in absolute terms but almost certainly in comparison to the likely benefit. Forcing people to endure exposure to unwanted ideas or to associate with those who espouse them interferes at least to some degree with their liberty and autonomy, and the objects of this social engineering may well resent the intrusion, reducing the likelihood that they will profit from it. The particular kind of intrusion involved also is worrisome for it meddles with, and therefore has some potential to undermine, the kind of autonomy that at least

41. Gerber and Morton, "Primary Election Systems and Representation"; California Democratic Party v. Jones, 530 U.S. 567 (2000).

42. *E.g.*, Jennings and Niemi, *The Political Character of Adolescence;* Jennings and Niemi, *Generations and Politics*; McPhee, Ferguson, and Smith, "A Theory of Informal Social Influence"; Huckfeldt and Sprague, *Citizens, Politics, and Social Communication.*

some prominent theories of democracy require citizens to cultivate and possess.

For anyone committed to the belief that campaigns ideally should be occasions for the systematic destabilization of majoritarian public opinion, these are sure to be depressing conclusions, for they leave us with only the usual array of voluntary methods—principally exhortation and education—by which to induce citizens to reexamine their beliefs during campaign season, and these methods have hardly been successful up to now. Indeed, I would go a step further. The ultimate lesson to be drawn, it seems to me, is that there is no shortcut to altering majoritarian political opinion. True, if all citizens were to take the occasion of a campaign to engage in a fundamental reexamination of their standing beliefs, majoritarian political opinion might well change rapidly, and rapid change of this sort might well be to the good. But this hope, unfortunately, represents the lazy man's path to political revolution. The truth seems to be that if you want to change what the majority believes, you must do it the hard way: by talking long enough and loudly enough and persuasively enough to convince a majority to your point of view. This is difficult and expensive, and it can take a long, long time.[43] This point has important ramifications for our political institutions, and I shall return to it at the end of this chapter.

Doctrinal and Policy Implications of the Tabulative Campaign

Let us turn, then, in a different direction. Suppose we take a more sympathetic view of the tabulative campaign, the kind that is not especially deliberative,

43. This way of looking at the problem of majoritarianism puts in a slightly different light the frequently expressed belief that democracy is possible only in very small polities. The usual explanation for this proposition is that democracy requires face-to-face deliberation among citizens, something that is possible only when the citizenry is small in number. Yet this has never been a very satisfying explanation because, among other reasons, it is not clear that even in ancient Athens, the great paradigm of small-polity democracy, there was a great deal of face-to-face deliberation among citizens. Manin, *Principles of Representative Government.* Perhaps a better explanation for why democracies need to be small is that majoritarian opinion can be successfully destabilized only when the polity is relatively small. Destabilization does not necessarily require face-to-face persuasion, but it does require a polity small enough to allow dissenters to reach a large enough proportion of the majority to make the enterprise of deliberately changing majority opinion a realistic possibility.

that neither causes nor results in any great reexamination or transformation of public opinion, that merely takes the opinions of citizens as it finds them and counts them up. In its historical context, after all, a tabulative campaign represents a significant political achievement: it is the principal device by which a democratic polity achieves a measure of self-transparency; it is the way in which a society may come to know itself by learning something, however thin or minimal, about what it collectively thinks.[44] Collective self-knowledge, even of a limited sort, is a political condition that compares quite favorably to the collective self-opacity of a populace living under autocracy. The lack of popular self-knowledge not only permits autocratic governments to claim without fear of effective contradiction to possess the confidence and support of the populace, but greatly inhibits the ability of individuals to organize for lack of information about what issues concern their fellow citizens. This leaves the state to deal with a disaggregated collection of individuals, a much easier task than dealing with a civil society that supports some degree of citizen organization.

Suppose, then, that we aimed in our laws no higher than institutionalizing an accurate, well-run tabulative campaign. What implications for legal doctrine and policy would this have? In general, downgrading our legal aspirations in this way tends to lead simultaneously in two opposing directions. On one hand, shifting to a tabulative model of campaigns would obviate most of the major criticisms, reviewed in Chapter 2, that might be made of our principal electoral regulations and the constitutional doctrines under which they are evaluated. Those criticisms, it will be recalled, derive their force from a judgment that the major legal doctrines structuring the campaign arena improperly thwart the possibility that campaigns will be deeply deliberative. Once that objection is removed, however, these legal doctrines can be understood to make positive contributions to the achievement of successful campaigns, albeit campaigns that are tabulative rather than deliberative.

At the same time, lowering our aspirations for campaigns also opens constitutional space for much more extensive and indeed highly intrusive regulation of the campaign process. Were we to jettison the idea that campaigns, by constitutional command, must be important forums for meaningful political debate and persuasion, extensive regulatory oversight of the campaign arena could no longer be seen as deeply threatening to core democratic values.

---

44. Publicity is often said to be a key feature of democracy. Nelson, *On Justifying Democracy*, ch. 6; Posner, *Law, Pragmatism, and Democracy*, 108.

Indeed, such regulation might then be understood as advancing the very important democratic value of tabulating public opinion as accurately as possible. On this model, we might no more object to intrusive regulation of the campaign phase of elections than we object to intrusive regulation of the way ballots are cast and counted. Much, surely, is permitted if all government seeks to do is to assure the accurate recording of a public will that is, by hypothesis, formed exogenously to the procedure used to record it.

Ballot Access

Restrictive ballot access laws are often criticized for excluding minor parties and independent candidates from meaningful participation in elections.[45] This narrows the scope of campaign debate and discussion to ideas advanced by the major parties and their candidates, which are by definition ideas that are already embraced before the campaign by enormous numbers of voters. The narrowing of the terms of campaign discourse to ideas that already command significant political followings in turn operates, as we saw in Chapter 2, drastically to reduce the possibility that a campaign might serve as a forum for serious contemplation and debate of ideas that are new, controversial, or otherwise outside the great currents of existing political thought.

Yet the narrowing effect on political debate of restrictive ballot access laws is a concern that clearly presupposes the campaign-endogenous formulation of public political opinion. If, however, the regulatory structure of campaign law is meant to create tabulative rather than deliberative campaigns, and the main purpose of a campaign is simply to identify and tabulate the campaign-exogenous preferences of the majority as they exist at the inception of the campaign, then little is lost by declining to take steps to expose voters during the campaign to ideas they do not already embrace. The goal of the campaign, after all, is to find out what people already think, not to encourage them to reexamine, expand, or alter what they think. In these circumstances, we can afford to be a good deal less concerned about the

45. *E.g.*, Hasen, "Do the Parties or the People Own the Electoral Process?," 840; Issacharoff and Pildes, "Politics as Markets," 683-87; Winger, "The Supreme Court and the Burial of Ballot Access"; Anderson, Berger, and Robson, "Presidential Elections—The Right to Vote and Access to the Ballot."

exclusion of minor parties and independents *from campaigns* so long as they have a fair opportunity to persuade voters of their views between elections, in the course of everyday politics.[46]

If this last condition is satisfied (a point to which I shall return shortly), then the restrictiveness of ballot access laws ought to cause us no great concern. From the point of view of constitutional doctrine, a tabulative conception of campaigns would provide a justification for courts to apply a relatively relaxed level of scrutiny to ballot access laws, and to defer generously to legislative judgments about how best to structure ballots so as to produce clear electoral majorities.

At the same time, conceiving of campaigns as primarily tabulative might also plausibly be taken to counsel in favor of loosening restrictions on ballot access as a matter of sound policy, if not constitutional imperative. Critics of the two-party system often complain that it does not permit a full expression of the range of opinion to be found in the electorate; voters with viewpoints that are complex or that lie outside the main currents of public opinion often must shoehorn their beliefs into one or two highly constraining choices.[47] If so, then easy ballot access for minor parties and independent candidates might permit a more accurate recording of public opinion in its diversity. And to the extent that a line on the ballot serves as a platform from which such candidates may campaign for the votes of the (exogenously) like-minded, low barriers to ballot access might permit campaigns to serve more effectively as devices to mobilize a broader segment of the electorate, increasing turnout.

To be sure, creating ballots that permit the expression of a wider variety of views—and encourage the emergence of candidates to express them—does not solve the problem of what to do with those views after they have been voted. Rules still must be established to determine how votes translate into results, and in that process opinions expressed during the campaign and at the ballot box inevitably will be lost by the time a legislature is actually assembled. That is why multipartyism often goes hand in hand with a preference for proportional over winner-take-all electoral systems. Thus, a strong

46. There is some evidence that this occurs: a nearly 75-year decline in voting for third parties may well be attributable to cooptation by major parties of issues pressed by minor parties. Hirano and Snyder, "The Decline of Third-Party Voting in the United States." Presumably, much of this cooptation occurs between elections.

47. *E.g.*, Amy, *Real Choice/New Voices*, ch. 1; Cox, *Making Votes Count*.

concern for tabulative accuracy might, on this view, be served best by a move toward proportional or semiproportional forms of representation.[48]

Campaign Finance

Both critics and defenders of regulated campaign spending and contributions have generally been maddeningly vague about what they understand to be the actual relationship between money and votes. Everyone seems to agree on the obvious—that having more money allows candidates to "reach" more voters.[49] But what happens once the candidate "reaches" the voter? What is the effect on the voter of having been "reached"? Does being reached mean being persuaded? Motivated? Informed, and if so, of what? These are not trivial distinctions because the problem of campaign resource inequality looks very different when campaigns are understood as tabulative rather than deliberative.

The usual complaint about unequal campaign resources is that the side with greater resources has an advantage. When public political opinion is conceived as campaign-endogenous, and campaigns are therefore understood as deliberative, such an advantage seems unfair because it gives the side with greater resources more extensive opportunities to persuade voters to its point of view. As a result, critics maintain, whenever candidates have significantly unequal resources with which to campaign a real danger arises that elections will turn not on the merits of the candidates' ideas but on the wealth of their supporters.[50]

---

48. For an overview, see Gardner, "Madison's Hope," 95–104. The problems involved in translating the diversity of views in the electorate into ultimate *policy* choices is even more complex than the related problem of translating such views into electoral results. *See, e.g.*, Powell, *Elections as Instruments of Democracy*.

49. *E.g.*, Sullivan, "Political Money and Freedom of Speech," 685 (restrictions on campaign spending would "impair politicians' ... ability to reach large masses of the electorate"); Smith, *Unfree Speech*, 43 (politicians must spend money "[t]o reach ... potential voters"), 50 (problem of restricted spending is not that the high spender buys an election, but that the low spender spends "too little to reach the mass of voters").

50. *E.g.*, Rawls, *Political Liberalism*, 360–61; Thompson, *Just Elections*, 112–14; Sunstein, *Democracy and the Problem of Free Speech*, 99; Strauss, "What is the Goal of Campaign Finance Reform?"; Briffault, "Public Funding and Democratic Elections"; Wright, "Politics and the Constitution," 1004; Morton and Cameron, "Elections and the Theory of Campaign Contributions," 81.

If, however, public opinion is understood as campaign-exogenous, and campaigns as tabulative, inequality of campaign resources looks much more benign. Now, by hypothesis, campaign resources are spent not to persuade voters, but merely to mobilize existing supporters by transforming campaign-exogenous voter preferences into actual votes. Candidates who take exogenously popular positions, and thus have more supporters, will of course require more resources to mobilize those supporters, and consequently there is nothing sinister about the leading candidate having a greater ability than his or her less popular rivals to transform support into cash, cash into mobilization effort, and mobilization effort into votes. In a tabulative campaign, the main goal is accuracy, and if the costs of mobilization are roughly similar for all voters regardless of their views, then the most accurate results will be obtained when candidates command resources in direct proportion to their campaign-exogenous public support.[51]

Even in a tabulative campaign, of course, resources can be maldistributed when candidates command resources proportionately greater than their campaign-exogenous public support for no reason other than that they happen to have access to large sums of money. However, the harm of such maldistribution is likely to be less when campaigns are tabulative than when they are deliberative, at least if we make the plausible assumption that mobilization is cheaper than persuasion—that it costs less to mobilize a supporter than to create one.[52] Under these circumstances, candidates can make far more effective use of a disproportionate "excess" of money if their goal is persuasion than if it is mobilization, from which it follows that, to the extent campaigns are seen as tabulative rather than deliberative, the urgency of equalizing campaign spending is reduced.[53]

---

51. Conservative critics of campaign finance reform have been making a similar argument for years, although on the very different presupposition that campaign speech is persuasive. *See, e.g.*, BeVier, "Money and Politics"; Smith, *Unfree Speech*, 42–43, 73–76.

52. This assumption seems justified if for no other reason than voters who have been persuaded still also have to be mobilized. *See* Holbrook and McClurg, "The Mobilization of Core Supporters," 691. The cost of mobilization may be low indeed, perhaps a few dollars per voter. *See* Gerber and Green, "The Effect of a Nonpartisan Get-Out-the-Vote Drive."

53. There is some empirical evidence of diminishing marginal returns to campaign spending. *See, e.g.*, Jacobson, "The Effects of Campaign Spending on Congressional Elections"; Green and Krasno, "Salvation of the Spendthrift Incumbent: Reestimating the Effects of Campaign Spending in House Elections"; Stratmann, "Contribution Limits and the Effectiveness of Campaign Spending."

On the other hand, committing to a conception of campaigns as tabulative rather than deliberative also cuts the other way, by counseling constitutional tolerance for regulation, even perhaps highly intrusive regulation, aimed at improving or ensuring the accuracy with which public opinion is tabulated. As shown in Chapter 2, at the heart of the Supreme Court's highly skeptical jurisprudence of campaign finance regulation lies the belief—infrequently honored, to be sure, but surely sincere nonetheless—that the purpose of an election campaign is to provide a forum for politically significant deliberation and persuasion. On that assumption, the Court quite naturally treats laws limiting political speech as raising profound constitutional questions.

If, however, we no longer indulge that assumption, and instead conceive of a campaign as little more than one phase of an essentially ministerial process of counting heads, the main justification for the Court's skepticism of campaign finance regulation falls away. Campaign speech no longer implicates the core democratic process of public opinion formation and instead implicates only lesser concerns attendant upon managing democratic processes. Here, the Court has long been lenient, frequently taking the position that the Constitution affords government considerable latitude to regulate electoral procedures: "as a practical matter," the Court has said, "there must be a substantial regulation of elections if they are to be fair and honest and if some sort of order, rather than chaos, is to accompany the democratic processes."[54]

From this point of view, the Constitution might therefore be understood to tolerate a good deal of campaign speech regulation provided it were aimed at promoting the tabulative accuracy of elections. Considerations of fairness and equality of inputs normally excluded by the Court as a justification for campaign regulation[55] might then be readmitted to the constitutional calculus if they can be shown to bear on the accuracy of electoral tabulation. That possibility is hardly farfetched. Candidates who lack resources proportional to their exogenous support among voters might be unable to mobilize their supporters, introducing inaccuracy into the final vote count. Candidates with resources exceeding what they need to mobilize their own supporters might use their cushion to launch negative attacks that demobilize supporters of their opponents. Even false or misleading campaign speech might be regulated on the theory that it may lead voters to cast votes at odds with their

54. Storer v. Brown, 415 U.S. 724, 730 (1974).

55. Buckley v. Valeo, 424 U.S. 1 (1976).

exogenously held political preferences, something that current doctrine emphatically rejects.[56]

On this model, campaign speech might be analogized less to core political speech aimed at inducing persuasion than to commercial speech aimed at inducing consumption. Like commercial speech—a category of speech afforded much more modest constitutional protection than political speech[57]—campaign speech might be understood, on a tabulative model, to aim primarily to match buyers with appropriate sellers in an electoral marketplace, and as a result to be an appropriate arena for regulatory action aimed at protecting the efficiency of marketplace sorting mechanisms. Another possible model for the tabulative campaign might be labor union elections, which may be extensively regulated to ensure that they occur under "laboratory conditions" in which an employer's superior power to distort election results may be restrained in the name of tabulative accuracy.[58]

In any event, the main point is that reconceptualizing campaigns as tabulative rather than deliberative lowers the stakes all around. Restrictive constitutional doctrines that prohibit significant regulation of campaign finance may introduce one kind of error into the process of tabulation, and extensive regulation of campaign finance might introduce a different kind of error. But in both cases, the errors may be seen as mild—not severe distortions of the autonomous formation of political opinion by democratic citizens so much as the ministerial kind of error that inevitably accompanies every aspect of the tabulation of public opinion.[59]

Party Association

I argued in Chapter 2 that the current First Amendment jurisprudence of strong party association rights undermines the likelihood that campaign speech will take place in circumstances facilitating persuasive exchange.

---

56. Monitor Patriot Co. v. Roy, 401 U.S. 265 (1971); New York Times v. Sullivan, 376 U.S. 254 (1964). *See generally*, Marshall, "False Campaign Speech."

57. Virginia State Board of Pharmacy v. Virginia Citizens Consumers Council, 425 U.S. 748 (1976); Central Hudson Gas & Electric Corp. v. Public Service Commission, 447 U.S. 557 (1980).

58. NLRB v. Gissel Packing Co., 395 U.S. 575 (1969). *See generally*, Gorman and Finkel, *Basic Text on Labor Law*, § 4.5.

59. Bush v. Gore, 531 U.S. 98 (2000).

This is because allowing parties to exclude those who do not share the dominant opinions of their membership effectuates a kind of ideological sorting that reduces the opportunities for political interaction and meaningful discourse among those of fundamentally different views.

If campaigns are meant to be deliberative, this arrangement may be worrisome because it impedes opportunities for meaningful discussion and persuasion. But if campaigns are merely tabulative, strong party association rights not only provide no cause for alarm but appear downright desirable. By facilitating the sorting of voters into large groupings of the roughly like-minded, strong party association rights might well improve the accuracy of elections by helping to ensure that voters actually cast their votes for those candidates who most closely conform to their campaign-exogenous ideological preferences. The more parties may carefully control their membership and their ideological composition and speech, the more likely they are to provide voters with clear and ideologically distinct choices, and the more likely it is that voters may rely with some confidence on party labels as simple cues to help them accurately vote their beliefs.[60] To say this is to say nothing more than what has already been established in Chapter 2: strong party association rights are consistent with the responsible party model, a model that presupposes the campaign-exogenous formation of individual and public political opinion.

The Lockup Critique

The idea that campaigns might be tabulative rather than deliberative also has implications for the influential critique of judicial oversight of the electoral process advanced recently by Professors Samuel Issacharoff and Richard Pildes. In a series of articles, Issacharoff and Pildes argue that the main principle guiding judicial construction of the Constitution in election law cases should be the preservation of meaningful electoral competition.[61]

---

60. *See, e.g.*, Campbell et al., *The American Voter*; Miller and Shanks, *The New American Voter;* Finkel, "Reexamining the 'Minimal Effects' Model in Recent Presidential Campaigns"; Hasen, "Entrenching the Duopoly"; Persily, "Toward a Functional Defense of Party Autonomy."

61. Issacharoff and Pildes, "Politics as Markets"; Pildes, "The Theory of Political Competition"; Issacharoff, "The Role of Government Regulation in the Political Process"; Issacharoff, "Gerrymandering and Political Cartels"; Pildes, "Foreword."

Analogizing to economic principles of antitrust, they maintain that courts should police electoral competitiveness by taking a presumptively critical view of electoral laws and practices that result in "partisan lockup,"[62] by which they mean laws and practices that entrench incumbent power-holders by insulating them from serious electoral challenge.

If election campaigns ought to be deliberative and destabilizing, the logic of this critique is straightforward: challengers should have a fair chance during the campaign to persuade the electorate of reasons to turn out incumbents, as well as a fair prospect that, should they succeed in persuading the electorate, legal obstacles will not unduly impede their ability to assume power. On this view, devices such as ballot exclusion and partisan gerrymandering are presumptively suspicious because they suppress the ability of challengers to reap the benefits of successful campaign persuasion of voters—in the former case by preventing challengers from collecting votes in the first instance, and in the latter case by preventing challengers from reaping the benefit of votes cast in their favor.[63]

The possibility that election campaigns might be purely tabulative, however, presents certain problems for the antientrenchment approach because it raises questions about what, precisely, election laws and practices might be guilty of entrenching. If the purpose of a campaign is not to destabilize, create, or reform majority public opinion but merely to identify and empower it, then any problem of "lockup" that arises may not be partisan, but simply majoritarian. To be sure, the use *by a minority* of legal tools to entrench itself in power raises especially serious and troubling problems when campaigns are tabulative rather than deliberative because, by hypothesis, campaign persuasion is no longer an available antidote, even in theory, to minoritarian attempts at self-insulation. But when electoral laws do nothing more than "entrench" the (stable and self-reinforcing) opinion of a campaign-exogenous majority, it becomes much more problematic to characterize such laws as entrenching "partisans" or "incumbents"; a partisan or incumbent who is supported by, and whose power is therefore derived from, a majority stands on a very different footing from one who

62. Issacharoff and Pildes, "Politics as Markets."

63. *See* Issacharoff and Pildes, "Politics as Markets," 683–87 (criticizing anticompetitive ballot access restrictions); Issacharoff, "Gerrymandering and Political Cartels" (criticizing partisan gerrymandering as anticompetitive); Pildes, "Foreword," 117 (criticizing ballot access restrictions), 55–83 (criticizing partisan gerrymandering).

lacks majority support.[64] Under these circumstances, Pildes and Issacharoff's concerns about unfair competition are still well taken, but can no longer be satisfied by a theory of *electoral* competition; instead, their goal of fair competition requires a theory of *political* competition, much more broadly conceived. While undoubtedly capable of justification, such an extension of their theory would be far from trivial.

Policy Implications

A social decision to embrace the tabulative campaign would have ramifications not only for constitutional doctrine but also for legislative policy at the subconstitutional level. Where deliberative campaigns are the goal, the main purpose of laws and policies that shape and regulate the campaign environment ought presumably to have something to do with producing widespread, meaningful opportunities for public deliberation on electorally salient issues. But in a democratic society that asks no more of its campaigns than that they tabulate campaign-exogenous public opinion, the main goal of election law and policy ought simply to be to count up public opinion as accurately as possible.

What it means for an election to count up public opinion "accurately" is in some respects a complex question. Democratic theorists have for at least 150 years argued over which electoral system most accurately measures the popular will.[65] Different electoral systems tend to be more or less sensitive to different kinds of inputs, however, so one's answer to the question of which electoral system most "accurately" measures public opinion necessarily depends a great deal on how one answers antecedent questions concerning the kinds of inputs that ought to count for purposes of collective

---

64. Granted, any legal regime that claims accurately to measure campaign-exogenous public opinion must confront difficult indeterminacy problems. *See, e.g.*, Benn and Peters, *Principles of Political Thought*, 397 ("The will of the people cannot be determined independently of the particular procedure employed, for it is not a natural will, nor is it a sum of similar wills of persons sharing common interests, but the result of going through a procedure which weighs some wills against others"). I set these aside here because they apply to all electoral regimes, and because they get at a problem that is distinct from the kind of entrenchment that concerns Pildes and Issacharoff.

65. Mill may have started the modern debate in 1861 when he came out strongly for proportional representation over the winner-take-all system that is to this day the norm in Britain and America. Mill, *Considerations on Representative Government*.

decision making.[66] We may set this controversy aside here, however, because every electoral system, no matter what normative choices about democratic inputs it represents, can be rendered more accurate by two kinds of measures: those that increase voter turnout; and those that help voters make electoral decisions that are more fully informed (along whatever dimension of information the electoral system happens to require).

Reform proposals to increase voter turnout are legion. Some of the most common proposals include easing voter registration requirements; better publicizing elections; changing the period during which voters may vote from a single weekday to the weekend, or extending it to several days or a week; making absentee voting easier; permitting voters to cast ballots by mail or electronically; increasing the number of polling places and locating them more conveniently; and subsidizing transportation to the polls for voters who lack easy access to polling places. A proposal to enter everyone who votes into a lottery with a substantial prize even made some headway recently in Arizona. Any of these reforms might make elections more tabulatively accurate accountings of public opinion by increasing turnout, thereby increasing the proportion of the electorate whose opinions the election actually canvasses.

Measures that make it easier for voters to collect information about the candidates and their positions would also make elections more accurate. Granted, precisely what kind of information would most effectively achieve this goal depends in part on antecedent judgments about the kind of decisions that a vote ought ideally to reflect. According to economic theories of democracy, all voters really need to know is their preferences, and such theories make no normative judgments about the quality of preferences; indeed, a basic premise of economic theories is that voter preferences are entirely subjective, and therefore cannot be evaluated by any objective, external standard. Deliberative theories of democracy, in contrast, distinguish mature, well-informed, and reflective preferences from those that are hasty, ill-informed, impulsive, or badly reasoned, and would give democratic weight only, or predominantly, to the former kind of preference.

---

66. For example, should absolute preferences be determinative, or should intensity of preference factor in? Should first-place choices count more heavily than lower ranked choices? Should the electoral system seek candidates who have the broadest support, even if it is relatively shallow, or should they seek candidates who have intense support, even if it is relatively concentrated? And so on. *See, e.g.*, Berg, *Democracy and the Majority Principle*, ch. 8; Kendall and Carey, "The 'Intensity' Problem and Democratic Theory."

Again, though, this controversy need not detain us here. Whatever they might require voters to do with information that comes into their possession, all theories of democracy hold that it is better, all other things equal, for voters to have more rather than less information on which to base their decisions. Moreover, although some theories of democracy make demands on citizens that can only be discharged through the contemplation of a wide array of information, all theories of democracy presuppose that voters will have access to a certain core of basic data. These data include the powers and responsibilities of the offices that the electorate is asked to fill; the names of the candidates competing for these offices; the party affiliations of the candidates; their qualifications and experience; their positions on relevant issues; perhaps the endorsements they have received; and so on. Consequently, measures that make this information more readily available to voters may improve the tabulative accuracy of elections by making it more likely that voters will accurately vote their own preferences, regardless of the precise standard against which those preferences ultimately may be judged.[67]

A commitment to tabulative campaigns, then, suggests that the quality of elections might be improved by taking steps to disseminate as widely as possible basic information about government offices and the candidates who seek election to those offices. Again, many such proposals have been advanced. They include improved civic education in the schools; advance dissemination of sample ballots; publication and distribution of voter information guides at public expense; mandatory broadcast by mass media of campaign advertisements and debates; publicly subsidized media forums dedicated to campaign issues; and many others. Any or all of these measures might improve the accuracy of electoral tabulation of public opinion by improving voters' ability to bring their actions in the electoral arena more accurately into conformity with their own political preferences, however and whenever those preferences might ultimately be formed.

The Locus of Democratic Politics

As we have repeatedly seen, a tabulative campaign is not primarily about forming or influencing public opinion; it is about counting heads. Such a

---

67. *See, e.g.*, Lazarsfeld and Berelson, *The People's Choice*, 83; Finkel, "Reexamining the Minimal Effects Model," 16, 18; Holbrook, *Do Campaigns Matter?*, 48, 157; Gelman and King, "Why Are American Presidential Election Campaign Polls So Variable When Votes Are So Predictable?"

campaign is therefore largely administrative, even ministerial, rather than political. This simple observation brings us at last to what are without a doubt the most important questions raised by the dominance of the tabulative campaign. First, if a campaign is not a forum for the forging or altering of public political opinion, can we plausibly be said to have a democratic politics at all? Second, if we have such a politics, where is it? Finally, if we have a democratic politics but it does not occur primarily during campaigns, how, if at all, can or should we regulate or otherwise influence it?

The fact that public political opinion is unlikely to be moved during campaigns does not by any means imply that the political opinions of voters are permanently fixed and incapable of change—that we lack, in other words, a meaningful democratic politics. We have, it seems to me, a fairly robust democratic politics, but it does not occur mainly during campaigns. It occurs instead at other times, indeed at all times and in all places where citizens' talk and behavior may have relevance for the formation of political opinions, which is to say, constantly, in the course of everyday life.[68] The main effect, then, of substituting tabulative for deliberative election campaigns is not to destroy or to diminish democratic politics, but rather to shift their locus from the tightly confined and comparatively well-regulated realm of the electoral to the dauntingly wider and far more unruly realm of the political.

To use a by now somewhat shopworn term, the democratic politics in which public political opinion is primarily forged occurs mainly in civil society—not, or at least not especially or disproportionately, in the officially circumscribed electoral arena itself.[69] Citizens obviously do attend to and absorb information and arguments that they will later use to fashion the political opinions that will guide their official electoral behavior, and they do so frequently, perhaps even continuously. But the venues in which they do so are to be found mainly among the organizations, associations, and personal relationships in

---

68. Zaller, for example, argues that a voter's "predispositions are at least in part a distillation of a person's lifetime experiences, including childhood socialization and direct involvement with the raw ingredients of policy issues, such as earning a living, paying taxes, racial discrimination, and so forth." Zaller, *The Nature and Origins of Mass Opinion*, 23. *See also* Page, *Who Deliberates?*, 6 (arguing that campaign information supplied by the media is "supplemented and amplified to varying degrees by personal experience and by conversations with friends, neighbors, and coworkers"); Popkin, *The Reasoning Voter*, 22 (advancing a "by-product theory of political information: the information that people acquire to negotiate their daily lives is later applied to their political judgments and choices").

69. As Dennis Thompson has recently suggested, "Campaigns should be considered more a part of government than a part of politics that influences government." Thompson, "Two Concepts of Corruption," 1055.

which they move in their private, "nonelectoral" capacities. Such venues might therefore very likely include churches, schools, workplaces, clubs, neighborhood organizations, business and trade associations, sporting groups, political parties, and of course the family.[70]

Political opinion also very likely is formed not just in these relatively "formal" organizational frameworks (if the term "formal" can properly be applied to any organization in civil society), but also in what Sam Fleishacker calls "insignificant" or "particle" communities. These are communities that exist neither for the sake of community itself, nor for the solidaristic achievement of some self-consciously adopted common goal, but that arise spontaneously "where people are doing quite different things, even where they do not directly pay attention to one another." Such communities might arise among people who are simply standing around talking, or playing pool, or "hav[ing] a quiet drink while listening vaguely to the ambient music and chatter, without the pressure of wondering whether or how all this fits into their higher-level ends."[71] The formation of political opinion, that is to say, occurs in the most diffuse settings imaginable. It occurs as often when people are not self-consciously trying to form such opinions as when they are, and people may frequently form political opinions, or at least arrive at beliefs around which their political opinions ultimately will coalesce, when they have no idea at all that it is happening.

Whatever may be said of academics, politicians have known this for a long time. According to a fairly common account of recent trends in American politics, the Republican Party owes its success over the last quarter-century to the self-conscious adoption of a strategy designed to influence political opinion where it is formed—not during elections and campaigns, but in the ordinary activities of daily life. Mark Smith argues in a recent book that Republicans reversed a long decline in their political fortunes that lasted from the New Deal through the mid-1970s by mounting a systematic and ultimately successful effort to change public opinion. This effort involved the establishment of think tanks, the commissioning of position research, the founding of conservative magazines and other media outlets, and a steady stream of public communication all aimed at persuading the American public to accept the premises of conservative positions on public issues.[72]

---

70. Rosenblum, *Membership and Morals*; Gutmann, *Freedom of Association.*

71. Fleischacker, "Insignificant Communities," 288, 293.

72. Smith, *The Right Talk.*

This effort eventually bore fruit with the election of Ronald Reagan in 1980, and Republicans have continued to press their strategy through a proliferation of interest groups, talk radio shows, television shows, Web sites, and even entire cable television networks dedicated unapologetically to the advocacy of conservative political positions. It seems clear that only in virtue of waging a long-term battle for public opinion *outside* the formal electoral arena were Republicans capable of making successful appeals for votes *within* campaigns.

The efficacy of this strategy seems lately to have dawned on some Democrats. Bill Clinton was occasionally accused after taking office of waging an "endless campaign,"[73] a charge he probably would not deny. In 2004, comedian Al Franken, now a Democratic senatorial candidate, was among the founders of Air America, a syndicated talk radio show intended to establish a liberal foothold in a medium now dominated by conservative voices. These are choices, evidently, to engage in ideological battle on the fields in which it actually can be effectively contested.

Problems of Public Opinion Formation Outside Campaigns

The foregoing analysis suggests that much of the campaign commentary devoted to identifying and criticizing problems in the way that public political opinion is formed has been misdirected. Concerns for the way in which a democratic public forms its political opinions are obviously valid and important, but they do not necessarily gain much traction by being directed toward election campaigns because that is not where the main action takes place. Instead, concerns about public political opinion are more usefully directed toward the venue in which such opinion is actually formed—in the great mass of communicative activity that occurs *outside* the electoral process, in civil society.

To reframe the issue in this way is unfortunately to open up a daunting Pandora's Box of potential problems. For all its complexity, the electoral arena is at least temporary and confined, and electorally relevant communication, which is typically aimed at the election or defeat of specific, officially declared candidates for office, can with at least some rough degree of success be

73. *E.g.*, Kelly, "Clinton May Carry the Campaign into Office."

identified and isolated for regulatory purposes.[74] Communication within civil society, on the other hand, is completely unconfined, either by time or by subject matter. It occurs in an environment that is, largely by design, essentially unregulated—a nearly laissez-faire marketplace of ideas. And it is virtually impossible to predict, or even to know, precisely what kinds of communication, on what subjects, in what contexts, will end up influencing the formation of opinions with overtly political content.

Although relocating the problems of political communication from the campaign arena to civil society may thus pose great difficulties for fashioning solutions, it does not make the problems of political discourse any the less significant. In fact, the communicative environment outside the electoral arena is plagued by potentially worrisome inequalities and structural problems that may have important ramifications for the way democratic politics unfolds once it enters the more circumscribed phase of the official campaign. These inequalities and structural problems are not for present purposes important for their own sake, or because of any kind of social injustice they may reflect (though these may of course be noteworthy for other reasons), but because of the possibility that they might be systematic in a way that entrenches predictable biases in the production of mass political opinion in the public sphere.

Consider inequality of access to communicative resources. Communication—not just for electoral purposes but for more broadly political ones—costs money. The forms of mass communication capable of reaching and influencing the widest audiences, such as movies and television are accessible only to the wealthiest individuals and corporations. DVDs and CDs are likewise costly to produce and require technical expertise. Advertising in newspapers and magazines and conducting mass mailings are also prohibitively expensive for all but a few. The Internet reduces the costs of distribution but not of production,[75] and is at present a haphazard

---

74. For example, the Federal Election Campaign Act defines an "expenditure" for regulatory purposes as "any purchase, payment, distribution, loan, advance, deposit, or gift of money or anything of value, made by any person for the purpose of influencing any election for Federal office." 2 U.S.C. § 431(9)(A)(1). The Bipartisan Campaign Reform Act defines "electioneering communication" as "any broadcast, cable, or satellite communication which—(I) refers to a clearly identified candidate for Federal office; (II) is made within [30 or 60 days of a relevant election]; and... is targeted to the relevant electorate." 2 U.S.C. § 434(f)(3)(A)(i). The precise boundaries of these categories are of course somewhat arbitrary, but much of the core electoral speech—at least the portion of it that is most likely to have an immediate impact on voters—can be identified without too much trouble.

75. Baker, *Media Concentration and Democracy*, 101.

method of reaching an intended audience, except for those able to pay for placement in targeted venues.

The high cost of communication coupled with the inequitable distribution of communicative resources means that information available in the most readily accessible regions of the public communicative sphere is likely to be biased in favor of the views of the rich. If the political views and preferences of the rich and the poor tend in the aggregate to differ on some issues, then the content of information and persuasive discourse generally available in the communicative sphere will be biased in favor of the substantive positions of the rich on those topics.

Even among those who have the resources to make use of mass media, inequality of actual access to media can have a skewing effect on the content of public political discourse. One of the more disturbing trends in the mass media sector is the increasing concentration of ownership of media outlets. We might expect that any particular media outlet will exhibit some bias in favor of the views of its owners, but this problem might be ameliorated if ownership of media is widely dispersed.[76] Yet control of mass media is anything but dispersed: according to Ben Bagdikian, only five companies own most of the nation's newspapers, magazines, book publishers, motion picture studios, and television and radio stations.[77]

A second kind of inequality that might bias the substance of political discourse outside the campaign arena is inequality of individual capacity. As some political theorists have pointed out, the ability to persuade through speech or other forms of communication is not equally distributed across the population. Even among people of equal motivation, some are more articulate, more eloquent, or more confident than others, making them more persuasive advocates for the positions they espouse.[78] Of course, no reasonable conception of equality could require that everyone possess precisely the same ability to speak persuasively. What is necessary is not that every person have an equal capacity to persuade, but that every viewpoint have capable spokespersons.[79] Unequal distribution of the capacity to persuade is therefore potentially worrisome only if deficits in persuasive ability occur

---

76. Baker, *Media Concentration and Democracy*, ch. 1.

77. Bagdikian, *The New Media Monopoly*, 3.

78. Sanders, "Against Deliberation"; Young, *Democracy and Inclusion*.

79. Meiklejohn, *Free Speech and Its Relation to Self-Government*, 25; Baker, *Media Concentration and Democracy*, 122.

disproportionately among certain groups, and those groups tend, on the whole, to embrace substantive views that differ from the views of groups that are better endowed in persuasiveness. That is the kind of maldistribution that has the potential unfairly to bias the substance of communication in the public sphere.

There is some reason to think that deficits in the capacity to communicate persuasively are found disproportionately among some of society's more vulnerable and disadvantaged groups, including the poor, the uneducated, racial minorities, women, and perhaps certain cultural groups that disfavor public political contestation.[80] If the views of such groups differ from the views of dominant groups, their views will not as readily secure a presence in public political discourse, and they will be less able to move public political opinion toward their positions.

Delli Carpeni and Keeter's 1996 study of the extent and distribution of Americans' knowledge of political facts suggests reasons for concern. Overall, the authors found, the distribution of political knowledge follows a "consistent pattern in which the same groups of citizens (whites, men, the more educated, the more generally politically interested and engaged) are relatively better informed about virtually all aspects of politics." Political ignorance, they correspondingly found, "is not randomly distributed but is most likely to be found among those who arguably have the most to gain from effective political participation: women, blacks, the poor, and the young."[81] A lack of good information alone is likely to be an impediment to effective communication and persuasion. More important in the long run, it is certainly plausible to suspect that the same mechanisms that cause these groups to be underendowed in information might also cause them to be underendowed in other tools of communicative persuasiveness, exacerbating any substantive biases against their views in the formation of public political opinion.

Inequality is not the only possible source of systematic bias in the public communicative sphere; bias also can arise from structural flaws in the production of information and civic discourse. In a recent book, C. Edwin Baker argues persuasively that media markets are riddled with structural imperfections that diminish the ability of the press to provide high-quality content in adequate quantities. For example, Baker argues, the mass media will tend to

---

80. Sanders, "Against Deliberation"; Young, *Democracy and Inclusion. See also* Goodin, *Reflective Democracy*, chs. 9–11.

81. Delli Carpeni and Keeter, *What Americans Know about Politics*, 176–77.

underproduce content because media products are public goods from which nonpaying consumers can be excluded only with some difficulty. The mass media's dependence on advertising revenue also creates a structural conflict of interest between advertisers and audiences. Because wealthy consumers are more valuable to advertisers, they will pay more for content that delivers a wealthy audience than for content that delivers a poor one, even if the poor audience is larger, causing media content to be biased in favor of the tastes of wealthier consumers. All other things being equal, advertisers also will pay more for a larger audience than a smaller one, creating a structural incentive for media to produce mainstream content with the broadest possible appeal. This bias in turn may squeeze out controversial or challenging content, contributing to a self-reinforcing cycle of majoritarian bias in the formation of public opinion.[82]

Other structural problems also may introduce various biases into public opinion formation. Cass Sunstein has warned of potentially harmful group deliberative dynamics that may cause opinion cascades and the polarization of group opinion.[83] We need not dwell on the details, however; my point is not to make the case for any particular policies or reforms but merely to flag an issue for contemplation. Here is the main point. The fact that our campaigns are primarily tabulative and majority-reinforcing rather than deliberative and majority-destabilizing means that we would be better off worrying less about the highly visible problems of public opinion that appear during campaigns, and worrying more about the much less visible but more important and insidious problems of public opinion that exist every day.

Attending, moreover, to the problems of public opinion formation in civil society further demonstrates the probable futility, certainly in the short term, of attempting to destabilize majoritarian public opinion by demanding that campaigns regularly perform that function. The burden is simply too great; election campaigns cannot plausibly be made the principal vehicle by which to engineer major reforms in democratic habits. Probably the best we can reasonably hope to do in campaigns and elections is to capture accurately the state of public political thought, warts and all, as it exists in the general public sphere, outside of the electoral arena. The good news, however, is that recognizing this limitation may free the reform impulse to redirect itself to the place where it may do the most good.

---

82. Baker, *Media, Markets, and Democracy.*

83. *E.g.*, Sunstein, "Deliberative Trouble."

Conclusion

I HAVE SUGGESTED IN THIS BOOK that the American public and its electoral laws have for over a century aspired to election campaigns that are rational and deliberative, even destabilizing and thus inherently progressive, but that we have managed to achieve instead campaigns that are not deliberative, that reinforce rather than enlighten majoritarian political opinion, and that in the end amount to little more than elaborate rituals for counting up and ratifying a public opinion that is largely settled before the campaign even gets underway. So what do we do? Is this condition of democracy inevitable and therefore intractable? Must we abandon our aspirations for better campaigns as hopeless? Should we reject attempts to reform the campaign process as misguided and useless, or even harmful? Although the book's argument provides grounds for a chastened and reflective review of our highest collective aspirations for democratic practice, nothing in it counsels that those aspirations need be abandoned.

First, I do not believe that accepting the inevitability, for the present and in the short or medium term, of the tabulative campaign is equivalent to an acceptance of campaigns that are, by public standards, poor quality. Our ideals for campaigns reflect our ideals for democratic discourse and practice generally, and there is nothing contradictory about applying our ideals to every venue in which they are implicated, even if we cannot in every venue fully realize them. The fact that my garage and basement are disorderly does not furnish an argument for permitting disorder in my living room and kitchen, and insisting on order in those sites but permitting it in others does not make me a hypocrite.

On the other hand, this book's argument does suggest that reform efforts aimed *solely* at elevating the democratic quality of campaigns are unlikely by themselves to have much success. The way candidates and especially voters behave during campaigns tends to reflect social norms that also guide their behavior at other times, and it is implausible to think that people who behave one way all the time will suddenly behave in another way simply because their calendar tells them they must. Certainly this is our experience of other recurring special occasions, such as Thanksgiving and Christmas, that conventionally demand a temporary change in behavior.

Nevertheless, while it is true that campaign practices mainly reflect prevailing social norms, this is the case only mainly, not completely. The relation between campaign and noncampaign political norms can be a two-way street. Just as year-round norms of political behavior can influence how we behave during campaign season, the opposite is also true: electoral practices can offer social lessons about democracy that may be absorbed, generalized, and relied upon outside of the formal electoral arena. Campaigns, in other words, have a teaching role—they help people learn how to be democratic citizens, and sometimes those lessons will spill over to other areas. This possibility furnishes a reasonable justification for continuing to seek beneficial reforms in the campaign arena, though it also should chasten our expectations for sweeping success.

At the same time, the book's argument provides ample justification for attempting to gain greater control over the campaign environment for a different reason: to improve the accuracy with which elections record public opinion. Most objections to official interference with campaign decisions made by private actors proceed from the premise that campaigns are vital forums for the formation of a democratically significant public will, and regulatory meddling with the formation of this will is therefore understood as raising acute dangers to popular self-rule. If, however, campaigns are reconceived as merely one phase of an elaborate public process for counting political opinions that citizens have formulated outside the campaign arena, such objections lose much of their force. Thus, we might plausibly demand of legislators that they give greater consideration to reforms that might lead to a more accurate tabulation of public opinion, and we might plausibly demand of courts that they treat such measures with a greater degree of deference than is presently the case.

Finally, the book's argument suggests, as I indicated in the last chapter, that we might be well-advised to shift priorities by worrying somewhat less than we do about problems of public opinion formation that appear during campaigns, and worrying somewhat more than we do about the problems and dynamics of public opinion formation in civil society. That is where inequalities and structural biases can do real damage, damage that is merely carried over into the electoral arena where it is extremely difficult to treat and control. It must be conceded that worrying usefully about public political habits outside the electoral arena is difficult because it requires making hard judgments about what kind of society we actually want. This is hard enough and painful enough in its own right, but it is only made more difficult by the fact that it is just the kind of public decision that can be biased and obstructed by existing inequalities and structural impediments.

Nevertheless, it is a discussion and an effort worth attempting. The less we attempt collectively to take charge of our own politics, the more we leave things to chance. Chance will inevitably cause our habits and collective opinions to change—nothing stays the same—but they will change primarily in response to lived experience, whatever it happens to be. Now, I have nothing against lived experience—it is the principal engine of human learning. Certainly the generations of Americans who lived through various society-wide shocks—the Revolution, the Civil War, the Great Depression, the civil rights movement, the 1960s—learned from those events, and what they learned changed their empirical beliefs and political opinions.

But another distinctive characteristic of human beings is their capacity to learn from the opinions, beliefs, and lived experiences of other human beings rather than learning exclusively from their own. In the well-known opening paragraph of *The Federalist*, Publius claims: "It has been frequently remarked that it seems to have been reserved to the people of this country, by their conduct and example, to decide the important question, whether societies of men are really capable or not of establishing good government from reflection and choice, or whether they are forever destined to depend for their political constitutions on accident and force."[1] The United States, on this view, is a kind of experiment in calculated living; it is an attempt, as far as humanly possible, to remove chance from among the forces that dictate the course of human existence. This is a noble aspiration, not to be abandoned. To hold otherwise would be to elevate surviving above living. Democracy recommends a way of life, not a strategy of survival. To the extent it is a good way of life, we should keep trying to get it right.

---

1. Madison et al., *The Federalist*, No. 1.

Bibliography

Ackerman, Bruce and James S. Fishkin. *Deliberation Day*. New Haven: Yale University Press, 2004.

Alexander, Larry. "What Is Freedom of Association, and What Is Its Denial?" *Social Philosophy and Policy*, 25(2008): 1–21.

Alford, John R., Carolyn L. Funk, and John R. Hibbing. "Are Political Orientations Genetically Transmitted?" *American Political Science Review*, 99(2005): 153–67.

Altschuler, Glenn C. and Stuart M. Blumin. *Rude Republic: Americans and Their Politics in the Nineteenth Century*. Princeton: Princeton University Press, 2000.

American Political Science Association, Committee on Political Parties. "Toward a More Responsible Two-Party System". *American Political Science Review*, 44(1950 Supp): 1–99.

Amy, Douglas J. *Real Choice/New Voices: The Case for Proportional Representation Elections in the United States*. New York: Columbia University Press, 1993.

Anderson, John B., Mitchell W. Berger, and Grace E. Robson. "Presidential Elections—The Right to Vote and Access to the Ballot". *Nova Law Review*, 29(2005): 571–634.

Ansolabehere, Stephen and Shanto Iyengar. *Going Negative: How Attack Ads Shrink and Polarize the Electorate*. New York: The Free Press, 1995.

Argersinger, Peter H. "'A Place on the Ballot': Fusion Politics and Antifusion Laws". *American Historical Review*, 85(1980): 287–306.

Aristotle. *Politics*. Edited, with an introduction by Ernest Barker. Oxford: Oxford University Press, 1978.

Bagdikian, Ben. *The New Media Monopoly*. Boston: Beacon Press, 2004.

Bagehot, Walter. *The English Constitution and Other Political Essays*. New York: D. Appleton & Co., 1902.

Baker, C. Edwin. *Media, Markets, and Democracy*. Cambridge: Cambridge University Press, 2002.

——. *Media Concentration and Democracy*. Cambridge: Cambridge University Press, 2007.

Baker, Jean H. *Affairs of Party: The Political Culture of Northern Democrats in the Mid-Nineteenth Century*. Ithaca: Cornell University Press, 1983.

——. "The Ceremonies of Politics: Nineteenth-Century Rituals of National Affirmation". In *A Master's Due: Essays in Honor of David Herbert Donald*. Edited by William J. Cooper, Jr., Michael F. Holt, and John McCardell. Baton Rouge: Louisiana State University Press, 1985.

Baker, Paula. "The Culture of Politics in the Late Nineteenth Century: Community and Political Behavior in Rural New York". *Journal of Social History*, 18(1984): 167–93.

Barber, Benjamin. *Strong Democracy: Participatory Politics for a New Age*. Berkeley, Calif.: University of California Press, 1984.

Bartels, Larry M. "Message Received: The Political Impact of Media Exposure". *American Political Science Review*, 87(1993): 267–85.

———. "Priming and Persuasion in Presidential Campaigns". In *Capturing Campaign Effects*. Edited by Henry E. Brady and Richard Johnston. Ann Arbor: University of Michigan Press, 2006.

Beeman, Richard R. "Deference, Republicanism, and the Emergence of Popular Politics in Eighteenth-Century America". *William & Mary Quarterly* 49(1992): 401–30.

Beitz, Charles R. *Political Equality: An Essay in Democratic Theory*. Princeton: Princeton University Press, 1989.

Bender, Thomas. *Community and Social Change in America*. New Brunswick, N.J.: Rutgers University Press, 1978.

Benello, C. George and Dimitrios Roussopoulos, eds. *The Case For Participatory Democracy*. New York: Grossman, 1971.

Benhabib, Seyla. "Liberal Dialogue Versus a Critical Theory of Discursive Legitimation". In *Liberalism and the Moral Life*. Edited by Nancy L. Rosenblum. Cambridge: Harvard University Press, 1989.

Benn, S.I. and R.S. Peters. *Principles of Political Thought*. New York: Free Press, 1959.

Bensel, Richard Franklin. *The American Ballot Box in the Mid-Nineteenth Century*. Cambridge: Cambridge University Press, 2004.

Benson, Lee. *The Concept of Jacksonian Democracy: New York as a Test Case*. Princeton: Princeton University Press, 1961.

Berelson, Bernard R., Paul F. Lazarsfeld, and William N. McPhee. *Voting: A Study of Opinion Formation in a Presidential Campaign*. Chicago: University of Chicago Press, 1954.

Berg, Elias. *Democracy and the Majority Principle: A Study in Twelve Contemporary Political Theories*. Göteborg, Sweden: Scandinavian University Books, 1965.

Bessette, Joseph M. *The Mild Voice of Reason*. Chicago: University of Chicago Press, 1994.

BeVier, Lillian R. "Money and Politics: A Perspective on the First Amendment and Campaign Finance Reform". *California Law Review*, 73(1985): 1045–90.

Black, Charles L., Jr. "He Cannot Choose but Hear: The Plight of the Captive Auditor". *Columbia Law Review*, 53(1953): 959–72.

Blais, André. "How Many Voters Change Their Minds in the Month Preceding an Election?" *PS*, 37(2004), 801–3.

Bogart, Leo. *Press and Public: Who Reads What, Where, When, and Why in American Newspapers*. Hillsdale, N.J.: L. Erlbaum Associates, 1989.

Bohman, James. *Public Deliberation: Pluralism, Complexity, and Democracy*. Cambridge: MIT Press, 1996.

Brader, Ted. *Campaigning for Hearts and Minds: How Emotional Appeals in Political Ads Work.* Chicago: University of Chicago Press, 2006.

Brest, Paul. "Further Beyond the Republican Revival: Toward Radical Republicanism". *Yale Law Journal.* 97(1988): 1623–32.

Briffault, Richard. "Public Funding and Democratic Elections". *University of Pennsylvania Law Review*, 148(1999): 577–90.

Broder, David. *The Party's Over: The Failure of Politics in America.* New York: Harper & Row, 1972.

Brookhiser, Richard. *Founding Father: Rediscovering George Washington.* New York: Free Press, 1996.

Brooks, Deborah Jordan and John G. Geer. "Beyond Negativity: The Effects of Incivility on the Electorate". *American Journal of Political Science*, 51(2007): 1–16.

Brown, Richard D. *The Strength of a People: The Idea of an Informed Citizenry in America, 1650–1870.* Chapel Hill: University of North Carolina Press, 1996.

Bryce, James. *The American Commonwealth.* 1893. New York: Macmillan Co., 1914.

Buchanan, Bruce. *Presidential Campaign Quality: Incentives and Reform.* Upper Saddle River, N.J.: Pearson, 2004.

Buchanan, James M. and Gordon Tullock. *The Calculus of Consent: Logical Foundations of Constitutional Democracy.* Ann Arbor: University of Michigan Press, 1962.

Burnham, Walter Dean. "The Turnout Problem". In *Elections American Style.* Edited by A. James Reichley. Washington: The Brookings Institution, 1987.

Buenker, John D. "Sovereign Individuals and Organic Networks: Political Cultures in Conflict during the Progressive Era". *American Quarterly* 40(1988): 187–204.

Caldeira, Gregory A., Aage R. Clausen, and Samuel C. Patterson. "Partisan Mobilization and Electoral Participation". *Electoral Studies*, 9(1990): 191–204.

Campbell, Angus, Philip E. Converse, Warren E. Miller, and Donald E. Stokes. *The American Voter.* Chicago: University of Chicago Press, 1960.

Campbell, James E. *The American Campaign: U.S. Presidential Campaigns and the National Vote.* College Station: Texas A&M University Press, 2000.

———. "Presidential Election Campaigns and Partisanship". In *American Political Parties: Decline or Resurgence.* Edited by Jeffrey E. Cohen, Richard Fleischer, and Paul Kantor. Washington, D.C.: CQ Press, 2001.

Caplan, Bryan. *The Myth of the Rational Voter: Why Democracies Choose Bad Policies.* Princeton: Princeton University Press, 2007.

Carwardine, Richard J. *Evangelicals and Politics in Antebellum America.* New Haven: Yale University Press, 1993.

Cassel, Carol A. "The Nonpartisan Ballot in the United States". In *Electoral Laws and Their Consequences.* Edited by Bernard Grofman and Arend Lijphart. New York: Agathon Press, 1986.

Chong, Dennis. "Creating Common Frames of Reference on Political Issues". In *Political Persuasion and Attitude Change.* Edited by Diana C. Mutz, Paul M. Sniderman, and Richard A. Brody. Ann Arbor: University of Michigan Press, 1996.

Chong, Dennis and James N. Druckman. "Framing Theory". *Annual Review of Political Science*, 10(2007): 103–26.

Christiano, Thomas. *The Rule of the Many: Fundamental Issues in Democratic Theory.* Boulder, Colo.: Westview Press, 1996.

Claassen, Ryan L. and Benjamin Highton, "Does Policy Debate Reduce Information Effects in Public Opinion? Analyzing the Evolution of Public Opinion on Health Care". *The Journal of Politics*, 68(2006): 410–20.

Cohen, Joshua. "Democracy and Liberty". In *Deliberative Democracy.* Edited by Jon Elster. Cambridge: Cambridge University Press, 1998.

———. "Reflections on Habermas on Democracy". *Ratio Juris,* 12(1999): 385–416.

———. "Deliberation and Democratic Legitimacy". In *The Good Polity: Normative Analysis of the State.* Edited by Alan Hamlin and Philip Pettit. Oxford: Basil Blackwell, 1989.

Converse, Philip E. "Information Flow and the Stability of Partisan Attitudes". *The Public Opinion Quarterly,* 26(1962), 578–99.

Cox, Gary W. *Making Votes Count: Strategic Coordination in the World's Electoral Systems.* Cambridge: Cambridge University Press, 1997.

Crenson, Matthew A., and Benjamin Ginsberg. *Downsizing Democracy: How America Sidelined Its Citizens and Privatized Its Public.* Baltimore: Johns Hopkins University Press, 2002.

Croly, Herbert. *The Promise of American Life.* 1909. North Haven, Conn.: Archon Books, 1963.

Crotty, William. *American Parties in Decline.* Boston: Little, Brown, 1984.

Dahl, Robert. *After the Revolution? Authority in a Good Society.* New Haven: Yale University Press, 1990.

Darman, Richard. "If We Were Serious". *The New York Times,* Sept., 1, 1996, 4: 9.

de Sousa Santos, Boaventura. "Participatory Budgeting in Porto Alegre: Toward a Redistributive Democracy". *Politics and Society* 26(1998): 461–510.

De Witt, Benjamin Parke. *The Progressive Movement.* 1915. Seattle: University of Washington Press, 1968.

Delli Carpini, Michael X., and Scott Keeter. *What American Know About Politics and Why It Matters.* New Haven: Yale University Press, 1996.

Dewey, John. *The Public and Its Problems.* 1927. Columbus: Ohio University Press, 1959.

Dinkin, Robert J. *Voting in Provincial America: A Study of Elections in the Thirteen Colonies, 1689–1776.* Westport, Conn.: Greenwood Press, 1977.

———. *Campaigning in America: A History of Election Practices.* Westport, Conn.: Greenwood Press, 1989.

Doppelt, Jack C. and Ellen Shearer. *Nonvoters: America's No-Shows.* Thousand Oaks, Cal.: Sage Publications, 1999.

Downs, Anthony. *An Economic Theory of Democracy.* New York: HarperCollins, 1957.

Druckman, James N. "Political Preference Formation: Competition, Deliberation, and the (Ir)relevance of Framing Effects". *American Political Science Review,* 98(2004): 671–86.

Druckman, James N. and Kjersten R. Nelson. "Framing and Deliberation: How Citizens' Conversations Limit Elite Influence". *American Journal of Political Science,* 47(2003): 729–45.

Dryzek, John S. *Discursive Democracy: Politics, Policy, and Political Science*. Cambridge: Cambridge University Press, 1990.

——. *Deliberative Democracy and Beyond: Liberals, Critics, Contestations*. Oxford: Oxford University Press, 2000.

Duverger, Maurice. *Political Parties: Their Origins and Activity in the Modern State*. New York: Science Editions, 1954.

Dworkin, Ronald. *Is Democracy Possible Here? Principles for a New Political Debate*. Princeton: Princeton University Press, 2006.

Editorial: "Refining the Debates". *The Christian Science Monitor*, Oct. 5, 2000, 10.

Editorial: "Bush and Dukakis Owe Us Answers". *Chicago Tribune*, Sept. 18, 1988, C2.

Estlund, David. "Beyond Fairness and Deliberation: The Epistemic Dimension of Democratic Authority". In *Deliberative Democracy: Essays on Reason and Politics*. Edited by James Bohman and William Rehg. Cambridge: MIT Press, 1997.

Fallows, James. "Rhetorical Questions". *The Atlantic*, Sept., 2008, 35–52.

Finkel, Steven E. "Reexamining the 'Minimal Effects' Model in Recent Presidential Campaigns". *The Journal of Politics*, 55(1993), 1–21.

Finkel, Steven E. and Howard A. Scarrow. "Party Identification and Party Enrollment: The Difference and the Consequence". *The Journal of Politics*, 47(1985): 620–42.

Fiorina, Morris P. "An Outline for a Model of Party Choice". *American Journal of Political Science*, 21(1977): 601–25.

——. *Retrospective Voting in American National Elections*. New Haven: Yale University Press, 1981.

Fishkin, James S. *The Voice of the People: Public Opinion and Democracy*. New Haven: Yale University Press, 1997.

Flanders, Chad. "Deliberative Dilemmas: A Critique of Deliberation Day from the Perspective of Election Law". *Journal of Politics*, 23(2007): 147–70.

Fleischacker, Sam. "Insignificant Communities". In *Freedom of Association*. Edited by Amy Gutmann. Princeton: Princeton University Press, 1998.

Formisano, Ronald P. *The Birth of Mass Political Parties: Michigan, 1827–1861*. Princeton: Princeton University Press, 1971.

——. *The Transformation of Political Culture: Massachusetts Parties, 1790s–1840s*. New York: Oxford University Press, 1983.

Fredman, L.E. *The Australian Ballot: The Story of an American Reform*. East Lansing, Mich.: Michigan State University Press, 1968.

Fung, Archon. *Empowered Participation: Reinventing Urban Democracy*. Princeton: Princeton University Press, 2006.

Gamson, William A. *Talking Politics*. Cambridge: Cambridge University Press, 1992.

Gardner, James A. "Shut Up and Vote: A Critique of Deliberative Democracy and the Life of Talk". *Tennessee Law Review*, 63(1996): 421–51.

——. "Madison's Hope: Virtue, Self-Interest, and the Design of Electoral Systems". *Iowa Law Review*, 86(2000): 87–172.

——. "Neutralizing the Incompetent Voter: A Comment on *Cook v. Gralike*". *Election Law Journal*, 1(2001): 49–60.

——. "Giving the Gift of Public Office". *Buffalo Law Review*, 53(2005): 859–82.

———. "What Is 'Fair' Partisan Representation, and How Can It Be Constitutionalized? The Case for a Return to Fixed Election Districts". *Marquette Law Review*, 90(2007): 555–92.

Garrett, Elizabeth. "Is the Party Over? Courts and the Political Process". *Supreme Court Review*, 2002: 95–152.

Garsten, Bryan. *Saving Persuasion: A Defense of Rhetoric and Judgment.* Cambridge, Mass.: Harvard University Press, 2006.

Gastil, John. *By Popular Demand: Revitalizing Representative Democracy through Deliberative Democracy.* Berkeley, Calif.: University of California Press, 2000.

Gastil, John and Peter Levine, eds. *The Deliberative Democracy Handbook: Strategies for Effective Civic Engagement in the Twenty-First Century.* San Francisco: John Wiley & Sons, 2005.

Gaus, Gerald F. "Reason, Justification, and Consensus: Why Democracy Can't Have It All". In *Deliberative Democracy: Essays on Reason and Politics.* Edited by James Bohman and William Rehg. Cambridge: MIT Press, 1997.

Gelman, Andrew and Gary King. "Why Are American Presidential Election Campaign Polls So Variable When Votes Are So Predictable?" *British Journal of Political Science*, 23(1993): 409–51.

Gerber, Alan S. and Donald P. Green. "The Effect of a Nonpartisan Get-Out-the-Vote Drive: An Experimental Study of Leafleting". *The Journal of Politics*, 62(2000): 846–57.

Gerber, Elizabeth R. and Rebecca B. Morton. "Primary Election Systems and Representation". *Journal of Law, Economics and Organization*, 14(1998): 304–24.

Gienapp, William E. "'Politics Seem to Enter into Everything': Political Culture in the North, 1840–1860". In *Essays on American Antebellum Politics, 1840–1860.* Edited by William E. Gienapp, Thomas B. Alexander, Michael F. Holt, Stephen E. Maizlish, and Joel H. Silbey. College Station, Tex.: Texas A&M University Press, 1982.

Goldstein, Ken and Paul Friedman. "New Evidence for New Arguments: Money and Advertising in the 1996 Senate Elections". *The Journal of Politics*, 62(2000): 1087–1108.

Goldstein, Kenneth and Travis N. Ridout. "Measuring the Effects of Televised Political Advertising in the United States". *Annual Review of Political Science*, 7(2004): 205–26.

Goodin, Robert E. *Reflective Democracy.* Oxford: Oxford University Press, 2003.

Goren, Paul. "Party Identification and Core Political Values". *American Journal of Political Science*, 49(2005): 882–97.

Gorman, Robert A. and Matthew W. Finkin. *Basic Text on Labor Law: Unionization and Collective Bargaining.* Second edition. St. Paul, Minn.: West Publishing, 2004.

Graber, Doris A. *Processing Politics: Learning from Television in the Internet Age.* Chicago: University of Chicago Press, 2001.

Green, Donald P. and Jonathan S. Krasno. "Salvation of the Spendthrift Incumbent: Reestimating the Effects of Campaign Spending in House Elections". *American Journal of Political Science*, 32(1988): 884–907.

Greenfield, Meg. "Winning Respect". *The Washington Post*, Nov. 8, 1996, A31.

Guinier, Lani. *The Tyranny of the Majority: Fundamental Fairness in Representative Democracy.* New York: The Free Press, 1994.

Gutmann, Amy, ed. *Freedom of Association.* Princeton: Princeton University Press, 1998.

———. "Freedom of Association: An Introductory Essay". In *Freedom of Association.* Edited by Amy Gutmann. Princeton: Princeton University Press, 1998.

Gutmann, Amy and Dennis Thompson. *Democracy and Disagreement.* Cambridge, Mass.: Belknap Press, 1996.

Haber, Samuel. *Efficiency and Uplift: Scientific Management in the Progressive Era, 1890–1920.* Chicago: University of Chicago Press, 1964.

Habermas, Jürgen. *Between Facts and Norms: Contributions to a Discourse Theory of Law and Democracy.* Translated, with an introduction by William Rehg. Cambridge, Mass.: MIT Press, 1996.

Hall, Van Beck. *Politics without Parties: Massachusetts, 1780–1791.* Pittsburgh: University of Pittsburgh Press, 1972.

Harris, Joseph P. *California Politics.* Fourth edition. San Francisco: Chandler, 1967.

Hart, Roderick P. *Campaign Talk: Why Elections Are Good for Us.* Princeton: Princeton University Press, 2000.

Hartz-Karp, Janette. "A Case Study in Deliberative Democracy: Dialogue with the City". *Journal of Public Deliberation,* 1(2005): 1–15.

Hasen, Richard L. "Entrenching the Duopoly: Why the Supreme Court Should Not Allow the States to Protect the Democrats and Republicans from Political Competition". *Supreme Court Review,* 1997: 331–71.

———. "Do the Parties or the People Own the Electoral Process?" *University of Pennsylvania Law Review,* 149(2001): 815–42.

Heale, M.J. *The Presidential Quest: Candidates and Images in American Political Culture, 1787–1852.* New York: Longman, 1982.

Heckman, Richard Allen. *Lincoln vs. Douglas: The Great Debates Campaign.* Washington, D.C.: Public Affairs Press, 1967.

Held, David. *Models of Democracy.* Palo Alto: Stanford University Press, 1987.

Hibbing, John R. and Elizabeth Theiss-Morse. *Stealth Democracy: Americans' Beliefs about How Government Should Work.* Cambridge: Cambridge University Press, 2002.

Hill, Steven. "How Ed Jew Got Elected". *San Francisco Chronicle,* June 24, 2007.

Hirano, Shigeo and James M. Snyder, Jr. "The Decline of Third-Party Voting in the United States". *The Journal of Politics,* 69(2007): 1–16.

Hofstadter, Richard. *The Age of Reform.* New York: Vintage Books, 1955.

———. *The Idea of a Party System: The Rise of Legitimate Opposition in the United States, 1780–1840.* Berkeley: University of California Press, 1970.

Holbrook, Thomas M. *Do Campaigns Matter?* Thousand Oaks, Cal.: Sage Publications, 1996.

Holbrook, Thomas M. and Scott D. McClurg. "The Mobilization of Core Supporters: Campaigns, Turnout, and Electoral Composition in United States Presidential Elections". *American Journal of Political Science,* 49(2005): 689–703.

Holt, Michael F. *The Rise and Fall of the American Whig Party: Jacksonian Politics and the Onset of the Civil War.* New York: Oxford University Press, 1999.

Howe, Daniel Walker. *The Political Culture of the American Whigs.* Chicago: University of Chicago Press, 1979.

Hubbell, John M. and Lynda Gledhill. "Petition Circulators Cleaning Up". *San Francisco Chronicle,* March 24, 2004, B3.

Huckfeldt, Robert, Paul Allen Beck, Russell J. Dalton, Jeffrey Levine, and William Morgan, "Ambiguity, Distorted Messages, and Nested Environmental Effects on Political Communication". *Journal of Politics,* 60(1998): 996–1030.

Huckfeldt, Robert, Paul E. Johnson, and John Sprague. *Political Disagreement: The Survival of Diverse Opinions within Communication Networks.* Cambridge: Cambridge University Press, 2004.

Huckfeldt, Robert and John Sprague. "Political Parties and Electoral Mobilization: Political Structure, Social Structure, and the Party Canvass". *American Political Science Review,* 86(1992): 70–86.

———. *Citizens, Politics, and Social Communication: Information and Influence in an Election Campaign.* Cambridge: Cambridge University Press, 1995.

Ingber, Stanley. "The Marketplace of Ideas: A Legitimizing Myth". *Duke Law Journal,* 1984: 1–91.

Issacharoff, Samuel. "The Role of Government Regulation in the Political Process: Oversight of Regulated Political Markets," *Harvard Journal of Law and Public Policy,* 24(2000): 91–100.

———. "Private Parties with Public Purposes: Political Parties, Associational Freedoms, and Partisan Competition". *Columbia Law Review,* 101(2001): 276–313.

———. "Gerrymandering and Political Cartels". *Harvard Law Review,* 116(2002): 593–648.

Issacharoff, Samuel, Pamela S. Karlan, and Richard H. Pildes. *The Law of Democracy: Legal Structure of the Political Process, revised 2d ed.* New York: Foundation Press, 2002.

Issacharoff, Samuel and Daniel R. Ortiz. "Governing through Intermediaries". *Virginia Law Review,* 85(1999): 1627–70.

Issacharoff, Samuel and Richard H. Pildes. "Politics as Markets: Partisan Lockups of the Democratic Process". *Stanford Law Review,* 50(1998): 643–718.

Iyengar, Shanto. *Is Anyone Responsible? How Television Frames Political Issues.* Chicago: University of Chicago Press, 1991.

Iyengar, Shanto and Donald R. Kinder. *News That Matters: Television and American Opinion.* Chicago: University of Chicago Press, 1987.

Iyengar, Shanto and Adam F. Simon. "New Perspectives and Evidence on Political Communication and Campaign Effects". *Annual Review of Psychology,* 51(2000): 149–69.

Jacobson, Gary C. "The Effects of Campaign Spending on Congressional Elections". *American Political Science Review,* 72(1978): 469–91.

———. "Measuring Spending Effects in U.S. House Elections". In *Capturing Campaign Effects.* Edited by Henry E. Brady and Richard Johnston. Ann Arbor: University of Michigan Press, 2006.

Jamieson, Kathleen Hall and David S. Birdsell. *Presidential Debates: The Challenge of Creating an Informed Electorate.* New York: Oxford University Press, 1988.

Jamieson, Kathleen Hall and Paul Waldman. *The Press Effect: Politicians, Journalists, and the Stories that Shape the Political World.* Oxford: Oxford University Press, 2003.

Jefferson, Thomas. *Notes on Virginia.* In *The Life and Selected Writings of Thomas Jefferson.* Edited by Adrienne Koch and William Peden. New York: Modern Library, 1972.

Jennings, M. Kent and Richard G. Niemi. *The Political Character of Adolescence: The Influence of Families and Schools.* Princeton: Princeton University Press, 1974.

———. *Generations and Politics: A Panel Study of Young Adults and Their Parents.* Princeton: Princeton University Press, 1981.

Jensen, Richard. *The Winning of the Midwest: Social and Political Conflict, 1888–1896.* Chicago: University of Chicago Press, 1971.

Jones, Bryan D. *Reconceiving Decision-Making in Democratic Politics: Attention, Choice, and Public Policy.* Chicago: University of Chicago Press, 1994.

Judd, Dennis R. *The Politics of American Cities: Private Power and Public Policy.* Boston: Little, Brown, 1979.

Kahan, Dan M. "The Cognitively Illiberal State". *Stanford Law Review,* 60(2007): 115–54.

Kahan, Dan M. and Donald Braman. "Cultural Cognition and Public Policy". *Yale Law and Policy Review,* 24(2006): 149–72.

Kateb, George. "The Value of Association". In *Freedom of Association.* Edited by Amy Gutmann. Princeton: Princeton University Press, 1998.

Katz, Elihu and Paul F. Lazarsfeld. *Personal Influence: The Part Played by People in the Flow of Mass Communications.* New York: Free Press, 1955.

Keith, Bruce E., David B. Magleby, Candice J. Nelson, Elizabeth Orr, Mark C. Westlye, and Raymond E. Wolfinger. *The Myth of the Independent Voter.* Berkeley: University of California Press, 1992.

Keller, Morton. *Affairs of State: Public Life in Late Nineteenth Century America.* Cambridge: Belknap Press, 1977.

Kelly, Michael. "Clinton May Carry the Campaign into Office". *New York Times,* Nov. 30, 1992, A1.

Kendall, Willmoore and George W. Carey. "The 'Intensity' Problem and Democratic Theory". *American Political Science Review,* 62(1968): 5–24.

Ketcham, Ralph. *Presidents Above Party: The First American Presidency, 1789–1829.* Chapel Hill: University of North Carolina Press, 1984.

Keyssar, Alexander. *The Right to Vote: The Contested History of Democracy in the United States.* New York: Basic Books, 2001.

Kinder, Donald R. "Communication and Opinion". *Annual Review of Political Science,* 1(1998): 167–97.

Kinsley, Michael. "Electio ad Absurdum". *The Washington Post,* Oct. 31, 2004, B7.

Kirkpatrick, Jean J. *Dismantling the Parties: Reflections on Party Reform and Party Decomposition.* Washington, D.C.: American Enterprise Institute, 1978.

Kishlansky, Mark A. *Parliamentary Selection: Social and Political Choice in Early Modern England.* Cambridge: Cambridge University Press, 1986.

Kleppner, Paul. *The Third Electoral System, 1853–1892: Parties, Voters, and Political Cultures.* Chapel Hill: University of North Carolina Press, 1979.

Koch, Adrienne. *The Philosophy of Thomas Jefferson.* Gloucester, Mass.: Peter Smith, 1943.

Kornbluh, Mark Lawrence. *Why America Stopped Voting: The Decline of Participatory Democracy and the Emergence of Modern American Politics.* New York: New York University Press, 2000.

Knops, Andrew. "Delivering Deliberation's Emancipatory Potential". *Political Theory,* 34(2006): 594–623.

Lacy, Dean and Barry C. Burden. "The Vote-Stealing and Turnout Effects of Ross Perot in the 1992 U.S. Presidential Elections". *American Journal of Political Science,* 43(1999): 233–55.

Ladd, Everett Carll. "1996 Vote: The 'No Majority' Realignment Continues". *Political Science Quarterly,* 112(1997): 1–28.

Lane, Robert E. "The Joyless Polity: Contributions of Democratic Processes to Ill-Being". In *Citizen Competence and Democratic Institutions.* Edited by Stephen L. Elkin and Karol Edward Soltan. University Park: Pennsylvania State University Press, 1999.

Larson, Edward J. *A Magnificent Catastrophe: The Tumultuous Election of 1800, America's First Presidential Campaign.* New York: Free Press, 2007.

Lau, Richard R. and David P. Redlawsk. *How Voters Decide: Information Processing during Election Campaigns.* Cambridge: Cambridge University Press, 2006.

Lazarsfeld, Paul F., Bernard Berelson, and Hazel Gaudet. *The People's Choice: How the Voter Makes Up His Mind in a Presidential Campaign.* 3rd ed. New York: Columbia University Press, 1968.

Leib, Ethan. *Deliberative Democracy in America.* College Park: Pennsylvania State University Press, 2004.

Leonard, Gerald. *The Invention of Party Politics: Federalism, Popular Sovereignty, and Constitutional Development in Jacksonian Illinois,* Chapel Hill: University of North Carolina Press, 2002.

Levine, Lawrence W. *Highbrow/Lowbrow: The Emergence of Cultural Hierarchy in America.* Cambridge: Harvard University Press, 1988.

Levine, Peter. *The New Progressive Era: Toward a Fair and Deliberative Democracy.* Lanham, Md.: Rowman & Littlefield, 2000.

Lichtman, Douglas. "How the Law Responds to Self-Help". *Journal of Law, Economics and Policy,* Vol. 1(2005): 215–57.

Liptak, Adam, Neil A. Lewis, and Benjamin Weiser. "After Sept. 11, a Legal Battle On the Limits of Civil Liberty". *New York Times,* Aug. 4, 2002, 1:1.

Livy. *The Early History of Rome.* Translated by Aubrey de Selincourt. New York: Penguin, 1960.

Locke, John. *The Second Treatise of Government.* 1690. Edited, with an introduction, by Thomas P. Peardon. Indianapolis: Bobbs-Merrill, 1952.

Macpherson, C.B. *The Life and Times of Liberal Democracy.* New York: Oxford University Press, 1977.

Madison, James. *Notes of the Debates in the Federal Convention of 1787.* Edited by Adrienne Koch. New York: Norton, 1981.

Madison, James, Alexander Hamilton, and John Jay. *The Federalist Papers*. 1787–1788. Edited, with an introduction by Clinton Rossiter. New York: Mentor, 1961.

Maisel, L. Sandy, Darrell M. West, and Brett M. Clifton. *Evaluating Campaign Quality: Can the Electoral Process Be Improved?* Cambridge: Cambridge University Press, 2007.

Malbin, Michael, J. "A Public Funding System in Jeopardy: Lessons from the Presidential Nomination Contest of 2004". *Election Law Journal*, 5(2006): 2–22.

Manin, Bernard. *The Principles of Representative Government*. Cambridge: Cambridge University Press, 1997.

Mansbridge, Jane. *Beyond Adversary Democracy*. New York: Basic Books, 1983.

Marcus, George E. *The Sentimental Citizen: Emotion in Democratic Politics*. University Park, Pennsylvania: Pennsylvania State University Press, 2002.

Marcus, George E., W. Russell Neuman, and Michael Mackuen. *Affective Intelligence and Political Judgment*. Chicago: University of Chicago Press, 2000.

Marelius, John and Ed Mendel. "Governor's Backers, Foes Scramble to Make Ballot". *San Diego Union-Tribune*, March 28, 2005, A-1.

Markus, Gregory B. "The Impact of Personal and National Economic Conditions on the Presidential Vote: A Pooled Cross-Sectional Analysis". *American Journal of Political Science*, 32(1988), 137–54.

Marshall, William P. "False Campaign Speech and the First Amendment". *University of Pennsylvania Law Review*, 153(2005): 285–324.

McCarthy, Colman. "A 'Minor' Problem With the Debates". *The Washington Post*, Oct., 1, 1996, D20.

McCormick, Richard P. *The Second American Party System: Party Formation in the Jacksonian Era*. Chapel Hill: University of North Carolina Press, 1966.

McGerr, Michael E. *The Decline of Popular Politics: The American North, 1865–1928*. New York: Oxford University Press, 1986.

McPhee, William N., Jack Ferguson, and Robert B. Smith. "A Theory of Informal Social Influence". In *Formal Theories of Mass Behavior*. Edited by William N. McPhee. Glencoe, Ill.: Free Press, 1963.

Meiklejohn, Alexander. *Free Speech and its Relation to Self-Government*. New York: Harper Brothers, 1948.

Mendelberg, Tali. "The Deliberative Citizen: Theory and Evidence". In *Research in Micropolitics, Vol. 6: Political Decision-Making, Deliberation and Participation*. Edited by Michael X. Delli Carpini, Leonie Huddy, and Robert Y. Shapiro. New York: Elsevier Science, 2002.

Meyers, Marvin. *The Jacksonian Persuasion: Politics and Belief*. Palo Alto: Stanford University Press, 1960.

Milburn, Michael A. *Persuasion and Politics: The Social Psychology of Public Opinion*. Pacific Grove, Calif.: Brooks/Cole Publishing Co., 1991.

Mill, John Stuart. *Considerations on Representative Government*. In John Stuart Mill. *On Liberty and Other Essays*. New York: Oxford University Press, 1998.

Miller, Joanne M. and Jon A. Krosnick. "News Media Impact on the Ingredients of Presidential Evaluations: A Program of Research on the Priming Hypothesis".

In *Political Persuasion and Attitude Change*. Edited by Diana C. Mutz, Paul M. Sniderman, and Richard A. Brody. Ann Arbor: University of Michigan Press, 1996.

Miller, Matt. "Is Persuasion Dead?" *The New York Times*, June 4, 2005.

Miller, Warren E. and J. Merrill Shanks. *The New American Voter*. Cambridge.: Harvard University Press, 1996.

Montesquieu, Baron Secondat de. *The Spirit of the Laws*. 1748. Edited by Franz Neumann. Translated by Thomas Nugent. New York: Hafner Press, 1949.

Morton, Rebecca and Charles Cameron. "Elections and the Theory of Campaign Contributions: A Survey and Critical Analysis". *Economics and Politics*, 4(1992): 79–108.

Murphy, Dean E. "New Runoff System in San Francisco Has the Rival Candidates Cooperating". *The New York Times*, Sept. 30, 2004.

Mutz, Diana C. *Hearing the Other Side: Deliberative* versus *Participatory Democracy*. Cambridge: Cambridge University Press, 2006.

Mutz, Diana C., Paul M. Sniderman, and Richard A. Brody. *Political Persuasion and Attitude Change*. Ann Arbor: University of Michigan Press, 1996.

Nelson, William N. *On Justifying Democracy*. London: Routledge & Kegan Paul, 1980.

Neuman, W. Russell, Marion R. Just, and Ann N. Crigler. *Common Knowledge: News and the Construction of Political Meaning*. Chicago: University of Chicago Press, 1992.

Nino, Carlos Santiago. *The Constitution of Deliberative Democracy*. New Haven: Yale University Press, 1996.

Ortiz, Daniel R. "The Democratic Paradox of Campaign Finance Reform". *Stanford Law Review*, 50(1998): 893–914.

Page, Benjamin I. *Who Deliberates? Mass Media in Modern Democracy*. Chicago: University of Chicago Press, 1996.

Page, Benjamin I. and Robert Y. Shapiro. *The Rational Public: Fifty Years of Trends in Americans' Policy Preferences*. Chicago: University of Chicago Press, 1992.

Pateman, Carole. *Participation and Democratic Theory*. Cambridge: Cambridge University Press, 1970.

Pennock, J. Roland and John W. Chapman eds. *Nomos XVI: Participation in Politics*. New York: Lieber-Atherton, 1975.

Persily, Nathaniel. "Toward a Functional Defense of Political Party Autonomy". *New York University Law Review*, 76(2001): 750–824.

Pessen, Edward. *Jacksonian America: Society, Personality, and Politics*. Homewood, Ill.: The Dorsey Press, 1969.

Pildes, Richard H. "The Theory of Political Competition". *Virginia Law Review*, 85(1999): 1605–26.

———. "Democracy and Disorder". In *The Vote: Bush, Gore and the Supreme Court*. Edited by Cass Sunstein and Richard A. Epstein. Chicago: University of Chicago Press, 2001.

———. "Foreword: The Constitution of Democratic Politics". *Harvard Law Review*, 118(2004): 28–154.

———. "The Constitution and Political Competition". *Nova Law Review* 30(2006): 253–78.

Plutarch. "Lycurgus". In *Greek Lives.* Introduction by Philip A. Stadter. Translated by Robin Waterfield. New York: Oxford University Press, 1998.

Polakoff, Keith Ian. *The Politics of Inertia: The Election of 1876 and the End of Reconstruction.* Baton Rouge: Louisiana State University Press, 1973.

Pole, J.R. *Political Representation in England and the Origins of the American Republic.* New York: St. Martin's Press, 1966.

Pomper, Gerald. *The Election of 1984: Reports and Interpretations.* Chatham, N.J.: Chatham House, 1985.

Popkin, Samuel L. *The Reasoning Voter: Communication and Persuasion in Presidential Campaigns.* Chicago: University of Chicago Press, 1991.

Posner, Richard A. *Law, Pragmatism, and Democracy.* Cambridge, Mass.: Harvard University Press, 2003.

Powell, G. Bingham. *Elections as Instruments of Democracy: Majoritarian and Proportional Visions.* New Haven: Yale University Press, 2000.

Prior, Markus and Arthur Lupia. "Money, Time, and Political Knowledge: Distinguishing Quick Recall and Political Learning Skills". *American Journal of Political Science,* 52(2008): 169–83.

Putnam, Robert D. *Bowling Alone: The Collapse and Revival of American Community.* New York: Simon & Schuster, 2000.

Ranney, Austin. *The Doctrine of Responsible Party Government: Its Origin and Present State.* Urbana, Ill.: University of Illinois Press, 1954.

Rawls, John. *Political Liberalism.* New York: Columbia University Press, 1996.

——. *The Idea of Public Reason Revisited.* In *The Law of Peoples.* By John Rawls. Cambridge, Mass.: Harvard University Press, 1999.

Remini, Robert V. *The Jacksonian Era.* Wheeling, Ill.: Harlan Davidson, 1989.

Reynolds, John F. *Testing Democracy: Electoral Behavior and Progressive Reform in New Jersey, 1880-1920.* Chapel Hill: University of North Carolina Press, 1988.

Rich, Frank. "The Next Infomercials". *The New York Times,* Sept. 14, 1996, 1:19.

Richardson, Henry S. *Democratic Autonomy: Public Reasoning about the Ends of Policy.* Oxford: Oxford University Press, 2002.

Riker, William H. *Liberalism against Populism: A Confrontation between the Theory of Democracy and the Theory of Social Choice.* W.H. Freeman and Company, 1982.

Risen, James and Eric Lichtblau. "Bush Lets U.S. Spy on Callers without Courts". *New York Times,* Dec. 15, 2005, A1.

Rosenblum, Nancy L. *Membership and Morals: The Personal Uses of Pluralism in America.* Princeton: Princeton University Press, 1998.

——. "Political Parties as Membership Groups". *Columbia Law Review,* 100(2000): 813–44.

Rosenstone, S.J. *Forecasting Presidential Elections.* New Haven: Yale University Press, 1983.

Salladay, Robert. "Game of the Name Is Profit". *Los Angeles Times,* Apr. 20, 2005, B-1.

Samples, John. *The Fallacy of Campaign Finance Reform.* Chicago: University of Chicago Press, 2006.

Sandel, Michael J. *Democracy's Discontent: America in Search of a Public Philosophy.* Cambridge, Mass.: Belknap Press, 1996.

——. *Liberalism and the Limits of Justice*. Cambridge: Cambridge University Press, 1998.

Sanders, Lynn M. "Against Deliberation". *Political Theory*, 25(1997): 347–76.

Saward, Michael. "The Representative Claim". *Contemporary Political Theory*, 5(2006): 297–318.

Schattschneider, E.E. *Party Government*. New York: Holt, Rinehart and Winston, 1942.

——. *The Semi-Sovereign People: A Realist's View of Democracy*. New York: Harcourt Brace, 1975.

Schlesinger, Arthur M., Jr. *The Age of Jackson*. Boston: Little, Brown, 1946.

Schudson, Michael. *The Good Citizen: A History of American Civic Life*. Cambridge, Mass.: Harvard University Press, 1998.

——. "Politics as Cultural Practice". *Political Communication*, 18(2001): 421–31.

Schroeder, Alan. *Presidential Debates: Forty Years of High-Risk TV*. New York: Columbia University Press, 2001.

Schumpeter, Joseph. *Capitalism, Socialism, and Democracy*. New York: Harper, 1950.

Sears, David O. "Symbolic Politics: A Socio-Psychological Theory". In *Explorations in Political Psychology*. Edited by Shanto Iyengar and William J. McGuire. Durham, N.C.: Duke University Press, 1993.

Sexton, John. "That Was No Debate". *Los Angeles Times*, Oct. 8, 2004, B11.

Shanker, Thom and Jacques Steinberg. "Bush Voices 'Disgust' at Abuse of Iraqi Prisoners". *New York Times*, May 1, 2004, A1.

Shapiro, Ian. "Optimal Deliberation?" In *Debating Deliberative Democracy*. James S Fishkin and Peter Laslett, eds. Malden, Mass.: Blackwell Publishing, 2003.

——. *The State of Democratic Theory*. Princeton: Princeton University Press, 2003.

Shiffrin, Seana Valentine. "What Is Really Wrong with Compelled Association?" *Northwestern University Law Review*, 99(2005): 839–88.

Sigelman, Lee and Mark Kugler. "Why Is Research on the Effects of Negative Campaigning So Inconclusive? Understanding Citizens' Perceptions of Negativity". *Journal of Politics*, 65(2003): 142–60.

Silbey, Joel H. *The Partisan Imperative: The Dynamics of Politics before the Civil War*. New York: Oxford University Press, 1985.

——. *The American Political Nation, 1838–1893*. Stanford: Stanford University Press, 1991.

Skelly-Wright, J. "Politics and the Constitution: Is Money Speech?" *Yale Law Journal*, 85(1976): 1001–21.

Skelton, George. "Gov.'s Performance in Role of 'Reformer' Seems a Little Strained". *Los Angeles Times*, March 14, 2005, B-3.

Smith, Bradley A. *Unfree Speech: The Folly of Campaign Finance Reform*. Princeton: Princeton University Press, 2003.

Smith, Eric R.A.N. *The Unchanging American Voter*. Berkeley: University of California Press, 1989.

Smith, Mark A. *The Right Talk: How Conservatives Transformed the Great Society into the Economic Society*. Princeton: Princeton University Press, 2007.

Sorauf, Frank J. *Party Politics in America.* Second edition. Boston: Little, Brown, 1972.

Stanley, Harold W., and Richard G. Niemi. *Vital Statistics on American Politics, 2001–2002.* Washington, D.C.: CQ Press, 2001.

Steenbergen, Marco R. and Milton Lodge. "Process Matters: Cognitive Models of Candidate Evaluation". In *Electoral Democracy.* Edited by Michael B. MacKuen and George Rabinowitz. Ann Arbor: University of Michigan Press, 2003.

Stratmann, Thomas. "Contribution Limits and the Effectiveness of Campaign Spending". *Public Choice,* 129(2006): 461–74.

Strauss, David A. "Persuasion, Autonomy, and Freedom of Expression". *Columbia Law Review,* 91(1991): 334–72.

———. "What is the Goal of Campaign Finance Reform?" *University of Chicago Legal Forum,* 1995: 141–62.

Sullivan, Kathleen. "Political Money and Freedom of Speech". *University of California, Davis Law Review,* 30(1997): 663–90.

Sunstein, Cass R. *Democracy and the Problem of Free Speech.* New York: Free Press, 1993.

———. "Deliberative Trouble? Why Groups Go to Extremes". *Yale Law Journal,* 110(2000): 71–119.

———. *Republic.com.* Princeton: Princeton University Press, 2001.

———. *Why Societies Need Dissent.* Cambridge: Harvard University Press, 2003.

Sunstein, Cass R. and Adrian Vermeule. "Conspiracy Theories". University of Chicago Law School Public Law & Legal Theory Research Paper Series. Paper No. 199 Preliminary Draft, January 15, 2008.

Taber, Charles S. and Milton Lodge. "Motivated Skepticism in the Evaluation of Political Beliefs". *American Journal of Political Science,* 50(2006): 755–69.

Taylor, Bob Pepperman. *Citizenship and Democratic Doubt: The Legacy of Progressive Thought.* Lawrence, Kan.: University Press of Kansas, 2004.

Thompson, Dennis F. *Just Elections: Creating a Fair Electoral Process in the United States.* Chicago: University of Chicago Press, 2002.

———. "Election Time: Normative Implications of Temporal Properties of the Electoral Process in the United States". *American Political Science Review,* 98(2004): 51–64.

———. "Two Concepts of Corruption: Making Campaigns Safe for Democracy". *George Washington Law Review,* 73(2005): 1036–69.

Thornton, J. Mills, III. *Politics and Power in a Slave Society, 1800–1860.* Baton Rouge: Louisiana State University Press, 1978.

Tocqueville, Alexis de. *Democracy in America.* Two volumes. Edited by Phillips Bradley. New York: Vintage Books, 1945.

Trost, Melanie R. and Douglas T. Kenrick. "Ego Involvement in the Minority Influence Paradigm: The Double-Edged Sword of Minority Advocacy". In *Minority Influence.* Edited by Serge Moscovici, Angelica Mucchi-Faina, and Anne Maass. Chicago: Nelson-Hall, 1994.

Troy, Gil. *See How They Ran: The Changing Role of the Presidential Candidate.* Revised ed. Cambridge, Mass.: Harvard University Press, 1996.

Unger, Roberto Mangabeira. *False Necessity: Anti-Necessitarian Social Theory in the Service of Radical Democracy.* Cambridge: Cambridge University Press, 1987.

Van Natta, Don, Jr. "Questioning Terror Suspects in a Dark and Surreal World". *New York Times*, March 9, 2003, 1:1.

Warren, Jennifer. "Election 2002: Election Turnout Hits a New Low". *Los Angeles Times*, Mar. 8, 2002, 2:1.

Watson, Harry L. *Jacksonian Politics and Community Conflict: The Emergence of the Second Party System in Cumberland County, North Carolina*. Baton Rouge: Louisiana State University Press, 1981.

———. *Liberty and Power: The Politics of Jacksonian America*. New York: Farrar, Straus and Giroux, 2006.

Wattenberg, Martin P. *The Decline of American Political Parties, 1952–1996*. Cambridge, Mass.: Harvard University Press, 1990.

Weisberg, Herbert F. and Steven H. Greene. "The Political Psychology of Party Identification". In *Electoral Democracy*. Edited by Michael B. MacKuen and George Rabinowitz. Ann Arbor: University of Michigan Press, 2003.

White, William Allen. *The Old Order Changeth: A View of American Democracy*. New York: Macmilan, 1910.

Wiebe, Robert H. *The Search for Order 1877–1920*. New York: Hill and Wang, 1967.

———. *Self-Rule: Of American Democracy*. Chicago: University of Chicago Press, 1995.

Wilentz, Sean. *The Rise of American Democracy: Jefferson to Lincoln*. New York: W.W. Norton & Co., 2005.

Will, George F. "The Uselessness of Debates". *The Washington Post*, Sept. 11, 1988, C7.

Williams, Melissa S. *Voice, Trust and Memory: Marginalized Groups and the Failings of Liberal Representation*. Princeton: Princeton University Press, 1998.

Winger, Richard. "The Supreme Court and the Burial of Ballot Access: A Critical Review of *Jenness v. Fortson*". *Election Law Journal*, 1(2002): 235–52.

———. "Ballot Access: A Formidable Barrier to Fair Participation". www.ballot-access.org/winger/fbfp.html, May 17, 2005.

———. "How Many Parties Ought to Be on the Ballot?: An Analysis of *Nader v. Keith*". *Election Law Journal*, 5(2006): 170–200.

Winkler, Adam. "Other People's Money: Corporations, Agency Costs, and Campaign Finance Law". *Georgetown Law Journal*, 92(2004): 871–940.

Wood, Gordon S. *The Radicalism of the American Revolution*. New York: Vintage Books 1992.

———. *The Creation of the American Republic, 1776–1787*. Chapel Hill: University of North Carolina Press, 1998.

Young, Iris Marion. *Justice and the Politics of Difference*. Princeton: Princeton University Press, 1990.

———. *Inclusion and Democracy*. New York: Oxford University Press, 2000.

Zaller, John. *The Nature and Origins of Mass Opinion*. Cambridge: Cambridge University Press, 1992.

———. "The Myth of Massive Media Impact Revived: New Support for a Discredited Idea". In *Political Persuasion and Attitude Change*. Edited by Diana C. Mutz, Paul M. Sniderman, and Richard A. Brody. Ann Arbor: University of Michigan Press, 1996.

Zarefsky, David. *Lincoln, Douglas and Slavery: In the Crucible of Public Debate*. Chicago: University of Chicago Press, 1990.

Zick, Timothy. "Speech and Spatial Tactics". *Texas Law Review*, 84(2006): 581–651.

Zuckerman, Michael. *Peaceable Kingdoms: New England Towns in the Eighteenth Century*. New York: Vintage Books, 1970.

Index